# Proxmox VE 5.0 Administration Guide

A catalogue record for this book is available from the Hong Kong Public Libraries.

Published in Hong Kong by Samurai Media Limited.

Email: info@samuraimedia.org

ISBN 978-988-8407-19-4

Background Cover Image by https://www.flickr.com/people/webtreatsetc/

# Contents

# Chapter 1

# Introduction

Proxmox VE is a platform to run virtual machines and containers. It is based on Debian Linux, and completely open source. For maximum flexibility, we implemented two virtualization technologies - Kernel-based Virtual Machine (KVM) and container-based virtualization (LXC).

One main design goal was to make administration as easy as possible. You can use Proxmox VE on a single node, or assemble a cluster of many nodes. All management tasks can be done using our web-based management interface, and even a novice user can setup and install Proxmox VE within minutes.

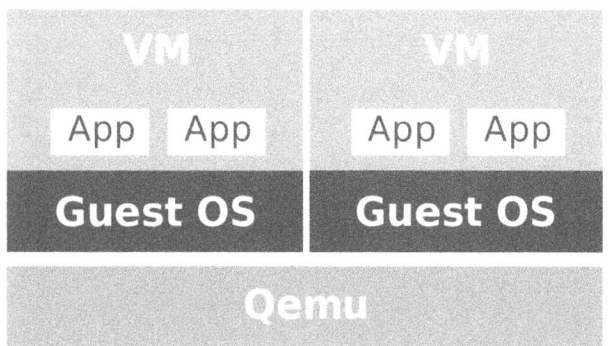

## 1.1 Central Management

While many people start with a single node, Proxmox VE can scale out to a large set of clustered nodes. The cluster stack is fully integrated and ships with the default installation.

### Unique Multi-Master Design

The integrated web-based management interface gives you a clean overview of all your KVM guests and Linux containers and even of your whole cluster. You can easily manage your VMs and containers, storage or cluster from the GUI. There is no need to install a separate, complex, and pricey management server.

### Proxmox Cluster File System (pmxcfs)

Proxmox VE uses the unique Proxmox Cluster file system (pmxcfs), a database-driven file system for storing configuration files. This enables you to store the configuration of thousands of virtual machines. By using corosync, these files are replicated in real time on all cluster nodes. The file system stores all data inside a persistent database on disk, nonetheless, a copy of the data resides in RAM which provides a maximum storage size is 30MB - more than enough for thousands of VMs.

Proxmox VE is the only virtualization platform using this unique cluster file system.

### Web-based Management Interface

Proxmox VE is simple to use. Management tasks can be done via the included web based management interface - there is no need to install a separate management tool or any additional management node with huge databases. The multi-master tool allows you to manage your whole cluster from any node of your cluster. The central web-based management - based on the JavaScript Framework (ExtJS) - empowers you to control all functionalities from the GUI and overview history and syslogs of each single node. This includes running backup or restore jobs, live-migration or HA triggered activities.

### Command Line

For advanced users who are used to the comfort of the Unix shell or Windows Powershell, Proxmox VE provides a command line interface to manage all the components of your virtual environment. This command line interface has intelligent tab completion and full documentation in the form of UNIX man pages.

### REST API

Proxmox VE uses a RESTful API. We choose JSON as primary data format, and the whole API is formally defined using JSON Schema. This enables fast and easy integration for third party management tools like custom hosting environments.

### Role-based Administration

You can define granular access for all objects (like VMs, storages, nodes, etc.) by using the role based user- and permission management. This allows you to define privileges and helps you to control access to objects. This concept is also known as access control lists: Each permission specifies a subject (a user or group) and a role (set of privileges) on a specific path.

### Authentication Realms

Proxmox VE supports multiple authentication sources like Microsoft Active Directory, LDAP, Linux PAM standard authentication or the built-in Proxmox VE authentication server.

## 1.2 Flexible Storage

The Proxmox VE storage model is very flexible. Virtual machine images can either be stored on one or several local storages or on shared storage like NFS and on SAN. There are no limits, you may configure as many storage definitions as you like. You can use all storage technologies available for Debian Linux.

One major benefit of storing VMs on shared storage is the ability to live-migrate running machines without any downtime, as all nodes in the cluster have direct access to VM disk images.

We currently support the following Network storage types:

- LVM Group (network backing with iSCSI targets)

- iSCSI target

- NFS Share

- Ceph RBD

- Directly use iSCSI LUNs

- GlusterFS

Local storage types supported are:

- LVM Group (local backing devices like block devices, FC devices, DRBD, etc.)

- Directory (storage on existing filesystem)

- ZFS

## 1.3 Integrated Backup and Restore

The integrated backup tool (`vzdump`) creates consistent snapshots of running Containers and KVM guests. It basically creates an archive of the VM or CT data which includes the VM/CT configuration files.

KVM live backup works for all storage types including VM images on NFS, iSCSI LUN, Ceph RBD or Sheepdog. The new backup format is optimized for storing VM backups fast and effective (sparse files, out of order data, minimized I/O).

## 1.4 High Availability Cluster

A multi-node Proxmox VE HA Cluster enables the definition of highly available virtual servers. The Proxmox VE HA Cluster is based on proven Linux HA technologies, providing stable and reliable HA services.

## 1.5    Flexible Networking

Proxmox VE uses a bridged networking model. All VMs can share one bridge as if virtual network cables from each guest were all plugged into the same switch. For connecting VMs to the outside world, bridges are attached to physical network cards assigned a TCP/IP configuration.

For further flexibility, VLANs (IEEE 802.1q) and network bonding/aggregation are possible. In this way it is possible to build complex, flexible virtual networks for the Proxmox VE hosts, leveraging the full power of the Linux network stack.

## 1.6    Integrated Firewall

The integrated firewall allows you to filter network packets on any VM or Container interface. Common sets of firewall rules can be grouped into "security groups".

## 1.7    Why Open Source

Proxmox VE uses a Linux kernel and is based on the Debian GNU/Linux Distribution. The source code of Proxmox VE is released under the GNU Affero General Public License, version 3. This means that you are free to inspect the source code at any time or contribute to the project yourself.

At Proxmox we are committed to use open source software whenever possible. Using open source software guarantees full access to all functionalities - as well as high security and reliability. We think that everybody should have the right to access the source code of a software to run it, build on it, or submit changes back to the project. Everybody is encouraged to contribute while Proxmox ensures the product always meets professional quality criteria.

Open source software also helps to keep your costs low and makes your core infrastructure independent from a single vendor.

## 1.8    Your benefit with Proxmox VE

• Open source software

• No vendor lock-in

• Linux kernel

• Fast installation and easy-to-use

• Web-based management interface

• REST API

• Huge active community

• Low administration costs and simple deployment

## 1.9   Getting Help

### 1.9.1   Proxmox VE Wiki

The primary source of information is the Proxmox VE Wiki. It combines the reference documentation with user contributed content.

### 1.9.2   Community Support Forum

Proxmox VE itself is fully open source, so we always encourage our users to discuss and share their knowledge using the Proxmox VE Community Forum. The forum is fully moderated by the Proxmox support team, and has a quite large user base around the whole world. Needless to say that such a large forum is a great place to get information.

### 1.9.3   Mailing Lists

This is a fast way to communicate via email with the Proxmox VE community

• Mailing list for users: PVE User List

The primary communication channel for developers is:

• Mailing list for developer: PVE development discussion

### 1.9.4   Commercial Support

Proxmox Server Solutions Gmbh also offers commercial Proxmox VE Subscription Service Plans. System Administrators with a standard subscription plan can access a dedicated support portal with guaranteed reponse time, where Proxmox VE developers help them should an issue appear. Please contact the Proxmox sales team for more information or volume discounts.

### 1.9.5   Bug Tracker

We also run a public a public bug tracker at https://bugzilla.proxmox.com. If you ever detect a bug, you can file an bug entry there. This makes it easy to track the bug status, and you will get notified as soon as the bug is fixed.

## 1.10   Project History

The project started in 2007, followed by a first stable version in 2008. At the time we used OpenVZ for containers, and KVM for virtual machines. The clustering features were limited, and the user interface was simple (server generated web page).

But we quickly developed new features using the Corosync cluster stack, and the introduction of the new Proxmox cluster file system (pmxcfs) was a big step forward, because it completely hides the cluster complexity from the user. Managing a cluster of 16 nodes is as simple as managing a single node.

We also introduced a new REST API, with a complete declarative specification written in JSON-Schema. This enabled other people to integrate Proxmox VE into their infrastructure, and made it easy to provide additional services.

Also, the new REST API made it possible to replace the original user interface with a modern HTML5 application using JavaScript. We also replaced the old Java based VNC console code with noVNC. So you only need a web browser to manage your VMs.

The support for various storage types is another big task. Notably, Proxmox VE was the first distribution to ship ZFS on Linux by default in 2014. Another milestone was the ability to run and manage Ceph storage on the hypervisor nodes. Such setups are extremely cost effective.

When we started we were among the first companies providing commercial support for KVM. The KVM project itself continuously evolved, and is now a widely used hypervisor. New features arrive with each release. We developed the KVM live backup feature, which makes it possible to create snapshot backups on any storage type.

The most notable change with version 4.0 was the move from OpenVZ to LXC. Containers are now deeply integrated, and they can use the same storage and network features as virtual machines.

# 1.11   Improving the Proxmox VE Documentation

Depending on which issue you want to improve, you can use a variety of communication mediums to reach the developers.

If you notice an error in the current documentation, use the Proxmox bug tracker and propose an alternate text/wording.

If you want to propose new content, it depends on what you want to document:

- if the content is specific to your setup, a wiki article is the best option. For instance if you want to document specific options for guest systems, like which combination of Qemu drivers work best with a less popular OS, this is a perfect fit for a wiki article.

- if you think the content is generic enough to be of interest for all users, then you should try to get it into the reference documentation. The reference documentation is written in the easy to use *asciidoc* document format. Editing the official documentation requires to clone the git repository at `git://git.proxmox.com/git/pve-docs.git` and then follow the REAME.adoc document.

Improving the documentation is just as easy as editing a Wikipedia article and is an interesting foray in the development of a large opensource project.

---

**Note**
If you are interested in working on the Proxmox VE codebase, the Developer Documentation wiki article will show you where to start.

---

# Chapter 2

# Installing Proxmox VE

Proxmox VE is based on Debian and comes with an installation CD-ROM which includes a complete Debian ("stretch" for Proxmox VE 5.x) system as well as all necessary Proxmox VE packages. The installer just asks you a few questions, then partitions the local disk(s), installs all required packages, and configures the system including a basic network setup. You can get a fully functional system within a few minutes. This is the preferred and recommended installation method.

Alternatively, Proxmox VE can be installed on top of an existing Debian system. This option is only recommended for advanced users since detail knowledge about Proxmox VE is necessary.

## 2.1  System Requirements

For production servers, high quality server equipment is needed. Keep in mind, if you run 10 Virtual Servers on one machine and you then experience a hardware failure, 10 services are lost. Proxmox VE supports clustering, this means that multiple Proxmox VE installations can be centrally managed thanks to the included cluster functionality.

Proxmox VE can use local storage (DAS), SAN, NAS and also distributed storage (Ceph RBD). For details see chapter storage Chapter 8.

### 2.1.1  Minimum Requirements, for Evaluation

- CPU: 64bit (Intel EMT64 or AMD64)

- Intel VT/AMD-V capable CPU/Mainboard for KVM Full Virtualization support

- RAM: 1 GB RAM, plus additional RAM used for guests

- Hard drive

- One NIC

### 2.1.2  Recommended System Requirements

- CPU: 64bit (Intel EMT64 or AMD64), Multi core CPU recommended

- Intel VT/AMD-V capable CPU/Mainboard for KVM Full Virtualization support

- RAM: 8 GB RAM, plus additional RAM used for guests

- Hardware RAID with batteries protected write cache ("BBU") or flash based protection

- Fast hard drives, best results with 15k rpm SAS, Raid10

- At least two NICs, depending on the used storage technology you need more

### 2.1.3  Simple Performance Overview

On an installed Proxmox VE system, you can run the included `pveperf` script to obtain an overview of the CPU and hard disk performance.

---

**Note**

this is just a very quick and general benchmark. More detailed tests are recommended, especially regarding the I/O performance of your system.

---

### 2.1.4  Supported web browsers for accessing the web interface

To use the web interface you need a modern browser, this includes:

- Firefox, a release from the current year, or the latest Extended Support Release

- Chrome, a release from the current year

- the Microsoft currently supported versions of Internet Explorer (as of 2016, this means IE 11 or IE Edge)

- the Apple currently supported versions of Safari (as of 2016, this means Safari 9)

If Proxmox VE detects you're connecting from a mobile device, you will be redirected to a lightweight touch-based UI.

## 2.2  Using the Proxmox VE Installation CD-ROM

Includes the following:

- Complete operating system (Debian Linux, 64-bit)

- Partitioning of the hard drive(s) containing the operating system with ext4, ext3, xfs or ZFS

- Proxmox VE kernel with LXC and KVM support

- Complete toolset for administering virtual machines, containers and all necessary resources

- Web based management interface for using the toolset

---

**Note**

By default, the complete server is used and all existing data is removed.

---

Please insert the installation CD-ROM, then boot from that drive. Immediately afterwards you can choose the following menu options:

**Install Proxmox VE**

Start normal installation.

**Install Proxmox VE (Debug mode)**

Start installation in debug mode. It opens a shell console at several installation steps, so that you can debug things if something goes wrong. Please press CTRL-D to exit those debug consoles and continue installation. This option is mostly for developers and not meant for general use.

**Rescue Boot**

This option allows you to boot an existing installation. It searches all attached hard disks and, if it finds an existing installation, boots directly into that disk using the existing Linux kernel. This can be useful if there are problems with the boot block (grub), or the BIOS is unable to read the boot block from the disk.

**Test Memory**

Runs memtest86+. This is useful to check if your memory is functional and error free.

You normally select **Install Proxmox VE** to start the installation. After that you get prompted to select the target hard disk(s). The Options button lets you select the target file system, which defaults to ext4. The installer uses LVM if you select ext3, ext4 or xfs as file system, and offers additional option to restrict LVM space (see below)

If you have more than one disk, you can also use ZFS as file system. ZFS supports several software RAID levels, so this is specially useful if you do not have a hardware RAID controller. The Options button lets you select the ZFS RAID level, and you can choose disks there.

The next pages just ask for basic configuration options like time zone and keyboard layout. You also need to specify your email address and superuser (root) password (must have at least 5 characters).

The last step is the network configuration. Please note that you can use either IPv4 or IPv6 here, but not both. If you want to configure a dual stack node, you can easily do that after installation.

If you press Next now, installation starts to format disks, and copies packages to the target. Please wait until that is finished, then reboot the server.

Further configuration is done via the Proxmox web interface. Just point your browser to the IP address given during installation (https://youripaddress:8006).

---

**Note**

Default login is "root" (realm *PAM*) and the root password is defined during the installation process.

---

### 2.2.1  Advanced LVM Configuration Options

The installer creates a Volume Group (VG) called `pve`, and additional Logical Volumes (LVs) called `root`, `data` and `swap`. The size of those volumes can be controlled with:

**`hdsize`**

Defines the total HD size to be used. This way you can save free space on the HD for further partitioning (i.e. for an additional PV and VG on the same hard disk that can be used for LVM storage).

**`swapsize`**

Defines the size of the `swap` volume. The default is the size of the installed memory, minimum 4 GB and maximum 8 GB. The resulting value cannot be greater than `hdsize/8`.

**`maxroot`**

Defines the maximum size of the `root` volume, which stores the operation system. The maximum limit of the `root` volume size is `hdsize/4`.

**`maxvz`**

Defines the maximum size of the `data` volume. The actual size of the `data` volume is:

`datasize = hdsize - rootsize - swapsize - minfree`

Where `datasize` cannot be bigger than `maxvz`.

**`minfree`**

Defines the amount of free space left in LVM volume group `pve`. With more than 128GB storage available the default is 16GB, else `hdsize/8` will be used.

---

**Note**

LVM requires free space in the VG for snapshot creation (not required for lvmthin snapshots).

---

### 2.2.2  ZFS Performance Tips

ZFS uses a lot of memory, so it is best to add additional RAM if you want to use ZFS. A good calculation is 4GB plus 1GB RAM for each TB RAW disk space.

ZFS also provides the feature to use a fast SSD drive as write cache. The write cache is called the ZFS Intent Log (ZIL). You can add that after installation using the following command:

```
zpool add <pool-name> log </dev/path_to_fast_ssd>
```

## 2.3  Install Proxmox VE on Debian

Proxmox VE ships as a set of Debian packages, so you can install it on top of a normal Debian installation. After configuring the repositories, you need to run:

```
apt-get update
apt-get install proxmox-ve
```

Installing on top of an existing Debian installation looks easy, but it presumes that you have correctly installed the base system, and you know how you want to configure and use the local storage. Network configuration is also completely up to you.

In general, this is not trivial, especially when you use LVM or ZFS.

You can find a detailed step by step howto on the wiki.

## 2.4 Install from USB Stick

The Proxmox VE installation media is now a hybrid ISO image, working in two ways:

- An ISO image file ready to burn on CD

- A raw sector (IMG) image file ready to directly copy to flash media (USB Stick)

Using USB sticks is faster and more environmental friendly and therefore the recommended way to install Proxmox VE.

### 2.4.1 Prepare a USB flash drive as install medium

In order to boot the installation media, copy the ISO image to a USB media.

First download the ISO image from https://www.proxmox.com/en/downloads/category/iso-images-pve

You need at least a 1 GB USB media.

---

**Note**
Using UNetbootin or Rufus does not work.

---

 **Important**
Make sure that the USB media is not mounted and does not contain any important data.

---

### 2.4.2 Instructions for GNU/Linux

You can simply use `dd` on UNIX like systems. First download the ISO image, then plug in the USB stick. You need to find out what device name gets assigned to the USB stick (see below). Then run:

```
dd if=proxmox-ve_*.iso of=/dev/XYZ bs=1M
```

---

**Note**
Be sure to replace /dev/XYZ with the correct device name.

---

 **Caution**
Be very careful, and do not overwrite the hard disk!

---

**Find Correct USB Device Name**

You can compare the last lines of *dmesg* command before and after the insertion, or use the *lsblk* command. Open a terminal and run:

```
lsblk
```

Then plug in your USB media and run the command again:

```
lsblk
```

A new device will appear, and this is the USB device you want to use.

### 2.4.3  Instructions for OSX

Open the terminal (query Terminal in Spotlight).

Convert the .iso file to .img using the convert option of hdiutil for example.

```
hdiutil convert -format UDRW -o proxmox-ve_*.dmg proxmox-ve_*.iso
```

---

**Tip**
OS X tends to put the .dmg ending on the output file automatically.

---

To get the current list of devices run the command again:

```
diskutil list
```

Now insert your USB flash media and run this command again to determine the device node assigned to your flash media (e.g. /dev/diskX).

```
diskutil list
```

```
diskutil unmountDisk /dev/diskX
```

---

**Note**
replace X with the disk number from the last command.

---

```
sudo dd if=proxmox-ve_*.dmg of=/dev/rdiskN bs=1m
```

### 2.4.4  Instructions for Windows

Download Etcher from https://etcher.io , select the ISO and your USB Drive.

If this doesn't work, alternatively use the OSForsenics USB installer from http://www.osforensics.com/portability.html

### 2.4.5  Boot your server from USB media

Connect your USB media to your server and make sure that the server boots from USB (see server BIOS). Then follow the installation wizard.

# Chapter 3

# Host System Administration

Proxmox VE is based on the famous Debian Linux distribution. That means that you have access to the whole world of Debian packages, and the base system is well documented. The Debian Administrator's Handbook is available online, and provides a comprehensive introduction to the Debian operating system (see [Hertzog13]).

A standard Proxmox VE installation uses the default repositories from Debian, so you get bug fixes and security updates through that channel. In addition, we provide our own package repository to roll out all Proxmox VE related packages. This includes updates to some Debian packages when necessary.

We also deliver a specially optimized Linux kernel, where we enable all required virtualization and container features. That kernel includes drivers for ZFS, and several hardware drivers. For example, we ship Intel network card drivers to support their newest hardware.

The following sections will concentrate on virtualization related topics. They either explains things which are different on Proxmox VE, or tasks which are commonly used on Proxmox VE. For other topics, please refer to the standard Debian documentation.

## 3.1 Package Repositories

All Debian based systems use APT as package management tool. The list of repositories is defined in /etc/apt/sources.list and .list files found inside /etc/apt/sources.d/. Updates can be installed directly using apt-get, or via the GUI.

Apt sources.list files list one package repository per line, with the most preferred source listed first. Empty lines are ignored, and a # character anywhere on a line marks the remainder of that line as a comment. The information available from the configured sources is acquired by apt-get update.

**File /etc/apt/sources.list**

```
deb http://ftp.debian.org/debian stretch main contrib

# security updates
deb http://security.debian.org stretch/updates main contrib
```

In addition, Proxmox VE provides three different package repositories.

### 3.1.1 Proxmox VE Enterprise Repository

This is the default, stable and recommended repository, available for all Proxmox VE subscription users. It contains the most stable packages, and is suitable for production use. The `pve-enterprise` repository is enabled by default:

**File /etc/apt/sources.list.d/pve-enterprise.list**

```
deb https://enterprise.proxmox.com/debian/pve stretch pve-enterprise
```

As soon as updates are available, the `root@pam` user is notified via email about the available new packages. On the GUI, the change-log of each package can be viewed (if available), showing all details of the update. So you will never miss important security fixes.

Please note that and you need a valid subscription key to access this repository. We offer different support levels, and you can find further details at http://www.proxmox.com/en/proxmox-ve/pricing.

---

**Note**

You can disable this repository by commenting out the above line using a # (at the start of the line). This prevents error messages if you do not have a subscription key. Please configure the `pve-no-subscription` repository in that case.

---

### 3.1.2 Proxmox VE No-Subscription Repository

As the name suggests, you do not need a subscription key to access this repository. It can be used for testing and non-production use. Its not recommended to run on production servers, as these packages are not always heavily tested and validated.

We recommend to configure this repository in `/etc/apt/sources.list`.

**File /etc/apt/sources.list**

```
deb http://ftp.debian.org/debian stretch main contrib

# PVE pve-no-subscription repository provided by proxmox.com,
# NOT recommended for production use
deb http://download.proxmox.com/debian/pve stretch pve-no-subscription

# security updates
deb http://security.debian.org stretch/updates main contrib
```

### 3.1.3 Proxmox VE Test Repository

Finally, there is a repository called `pvetest`. This one contains the latest packages and is heavily used by developers to test new features. As usual, you can configure this using `/etc/apt/sources.list` by adding the following line:

**sources.list entry for pvetest**

```
deb http://download.proxmox.com/debian/pve stretch pvetest
```

 **Warning**

the `pvetest` repository should (as the name implies) only be used for testing new features or bug fixes.

### 3.1.4 SecureApt

We use GnuPG to sign the `Release` files inside those repositories, and APT uses that signatures to verify that all packages are from a trusted source.

The key used for verification is already installed if you install from our installation CD. If you install by other means, you can manually download the key with:

```
# wget http://download.proxmox.com/debian/proxmox-ve-release-5.x.gpg ↩
    -O /etc/apt/trusted.gpg.d/proxmox-ve-release-5.x.gpg
```

Please verify the checksum afterwards:

```
# sha512sum /etc/apt/trusted.gpg.d/proxmox-ve-release-5.x.gpg
ffb95f0f4be68d2e753c8875ea2f8465864a58431d5361e88789568673551501ae574283a4e0492f1
    /etc/apt/trusted.gpg.d/proxmox-ve-release-5.x.gpg
```

or

```
# md5sum /etc/apt/trusted.gpg.d/proxmox-ve-release-5.x.gpg
511d36d0f1350c01c42a3dc9f3c27939  /etc/apt/trusted.gpg.d/proxmox-ve-release ↩
    -5.x.gpg
```

## 3.2 System Software Updates

We provide regular package updates on all repositories. You can install those update using the GUI, or you can directly run the CLI command `apt-get`:

```
apt-get update
apt-get dist-upgrade
```

**Note**

The `apt` package management system is extremely flexible and provides countless of feature - see `man apt-get` or [Hertzog13] for additional information.

You should do such updates at regular intervals, or when we release versions with security related fixes. Major system upgrades are announced at the Proxmox VE Community Forum. Those announcement also contain detailed upgrade instructions.

**Tip**

We recommend to run regular upgrades, because it is important to get the latest security updates.

# 3.3  Network Configuration

Proxmox VE uses a bridged networking model. Each host can have up to 4094 bridges. Bridges are like physical network switches implemented in software. All VMs can share a single bridge, as if virtual network cables from each guest were all plugged into the same switch. But you can also create multiple bridges to separate network domains.

For connecting VMs to the outside world, bridges are attached to physical network cards. For further flexibility, you can configure VLANs (IEEE 802.1q) and network bonding, also known as "link aggregation". That way it is possible to build complex and flexible virtual networks.

Debian traditionally uses the `ifup` and `ifdown` commands to configure the network. The file `/etc/network/interfaces` contains the whole network setup. Please refer to to manual page (`man interfaces`) for a complete format description.

---

**Note**

Proxmox VE does not write changes directly to `/etc/network/interfaces`. Instead, we write into a temporary file called `/etc/network/interfaces.new`, and commit those changes when you reboot the node.

---

It is worth mentioning that you can directly edit the configuration file. All Proxmox VE tools tries hard to keep such direct user modifications. Using the GUI is still preferable, because it protect you from errors.

## 3.3.1  Naming Conventions

We currently use the following naming conventions for device names:

- New Ethernet devices: en*, systemd network interface names.

- Legacy Ethernet devices: eth[N], where $0 \leq N$ (`eth0`, `eth1`, ...) They are available when Proxmox VE has been updated by an earlier version.

- Bridge names: vmbr[N], where $0 \leq N \leq 4094$ (`vmbr0` - `vmbr4094`)

- Bonds: bond[N], where $0 \leq N$ (`bond0`, `bond1`, ...)

- VLANs: Simply add the VLAN number to the device name, separated by a period (`eno1.50`, `bond1.30`)

This makes it easier to debug networks problems, because the device names implies the device type.

### Systemd Network Interface Names

Systemd uses the two character prefix *en* for Ethernet network devices. The next characters depends on the device driver and the fact which schema matches first.

- o<index>[n<phys_port_name>|d<dev_port>] — devices on board

- s<slot>[f<function>][n<phys_port_name>|d<dev_port>] — device by hotplug id

- [P<domain>]p<bus>s<slot>[f<function>][n<phys_port_name>|d<dev_port>] — devices by bus id

- x<MAC> — device by MAC address

The most common patterns are:

- eno1 — is the first on board NIC

- enp3s0f1 — is the NIC on pcibus 3 slot 0 and use the NIC function 1.

For more information see Predictable Network Interface Names.

### 3.3.2 Default Configuration using a Bridge

The installation program creates a single bridge named `vmbr0`, which is connected to the first Ethernet card `eno0`. The corresponding configuration in `/etc/network/interfaces` looks like this:

```
auto lo
iface lo inet loopback

iface eno1 inet manual

auto vmbr0
iface vmbr0 inet static
        address 192.168.10.2
        netmask 255.255.255.0
        gateway 192.168.10.1
        bridge_ports eno1
        bridge_stp off
        bridge_fd 0
```

Virtual machines behave as if they were directly connected to the physical network. The network, in turn, sees each virtual machine as having its own MAC, even though there is only one network cable connecting all of these VMs to the network.

### 3.3.3 Routed Configuration

Most hosting providers do not support the above setup. For security reasons, they disable networking as soon as they detect multiple MAC addresses on a single interface.

---

**Tip**
Some providers allows you to register additional MACs on there management interface. This avoids the problem, but is clumsy to configure because you need to register a MAC for each of your VMs.

---

You can avoid the problem by "routing" all traffic via a single interface. This makes sure that all network packets use the same MAC address.

A common scenario is that you have a public IP (assume `192.168.10.2` for this example), and an additional IP block for your VMs (`10.10.10.1/255.255.255.0`). We recommend the following setup for such situations:

```
auto lo
iface lo inet loopback

auto eno1
iface eno1 inet static
        address  192.168.10.2
        netmask  255.255.255.0
        gateway  192.168.10.1
        post-up echo 1 > /proc/sys/net/ipv4/conf/eno1/proxy_arp


auto vmbr0
iface vmbr0 inet static
        address  10.10.10.1
        netmask  255.255.255.0
        bridge_ports none
        bridge_stp off
        bridge_fd 0
```

### 3.3.4  Masquerading (NAT) with `iptables`

In some cases you may want to use private IPs behind your Proxmox host's true IP, and masquerade the traffic using NAT:

```
auto lo
iface lo inet loopback

auto eno0
#real IP adress
iface eno1 inet static
        address  192.168.10.2
        netmask  255.255.255.0
        gateway  192.168.10.1

auto vmbr0
#private sub network
iface vmbr0 inet static
        address  10.10.10.1
        netmask  255.255.255.0
        bridge_ports none
        bridge_stp off
        bridge_fd 0

        post-up echo 1 > /proc/sys/net/ipv4/ip_forward
        post-up   iptables -t nat -A POSTROUTING -s '10.10.10.0/24' -o eno1 ←
            -j MASQUERADE
        post-down iptables -t nat -D POSTROUTING -s '10.10.10.0/24' -o eno1 ←
            -j MASQUERADE
```

### 3.3.5 Linux Bond

Bonding (also called NIC teaming or Link Aggregation) is a technique for binding multiple NIC's to a single network device. It is possible to achieve different goals, like make the network fault-tolerant, increase the performance or both together.

High-speed hardware like Fibre Channel and the associated switching hardware can be quite expensive. By doing link aggregation, two NICs can appear as one logical interface, resulting in double speed. This is a native Linux kernel feature that is supported by most switches. If your nodes have multiple Ethernet ports, you can distribute your points of failure by running network cables to different switches and the bonded connection will failover to one cable or the other in case of network trouble.

Aggregated links can improve live-migration delays and improve the speed of replication of data between Proxmox VE Cluster nodes.

There are 7 modes for bonding:

- **Round-robin (balance-rr):** Transmit network packets in sequential order from the first available network interface (NIC) slave through the last. This mode provides load balancing and fault tolerance.

- **Active-backup (active-backup):** Only one NIC slave in the bond is active. A different slave becomes active if, and only if, the active slave fails. The single logical bonded interface's MAC address is externally visible on only one NIC (port) to avoid distortion in the network switch. This mode provides fault tolerance.

- **XOR (balance-xor):** Transmit network packets based on [(source MAC address XOR'd with destination MAC address) modulo NIC slave count]. This selects the same NIC slave for each destination MAC address. This mode provides load balancing and fault tolerance.

- **Broadcast (broadcast):** Transmit network packets on all slave network interfaces. This mode provides fault tolerance.

- **IEEE 802.3ad Dynamic link aggregation (802.3ad)(LACP):** Creates aggregation groups that share the same speed and duplex settings. Utilizes all slave network interfaces in the active aggregator group according to the 802.3ad specification.

- **Adaptive transmit load balancing (balance-tlb):** Linux bonding driver mode that does not require any special network-switch support. The outgoing network packet traffic is distributed according to the current load (computed relative to the speed) on each network interface slave. Incoming traffic is received by one currently designated slave network interface. If this receiving slave fails, another slave takes over the MAC address of the failed receiving slave.

- **Adaptive load balancing (balance-alb):** Includes balance-tlb plus receive load balancing (rlb) for IPV4 traffic, and does not require any special network switch support. The receive load balancing is achieved by ARP negotiation. The bonding driver intercepts the ARP Replies sent by the local system on their way out and overwrites the source hardware address with the unique hardware address of one of the NIC slaves in the single logical bonded interface such that different network-peers use different MAC addresses for their network packet traffic.

For the most setups the active-backup are the best choice or if your switch support LACP "IEEE 802.3ad" this mode should be preferred.

The following bond configuration can be used as distributed/shared storage network. The benefit would be that you get more speed and the network will be fault-tolerant.

**Example: Use bond with fixed IP address**

```
auto lo
iface lo inet loopback

iface eno1 inet manual

iface eno2 inet manual

auto bond0
iface bond0 inet static
      slaves eno1 eno2
      address  192.168.1.2
      netmask  255.255.255.0
      bond_miimon 100
      bond_mode 802.3ad
      bond_xmit_hash_policy layer2+3

auto vmbr0
iface vmbr0 inet static
        address  10.10.10.2
        netmask  255.255.255.0
        gateway  10.10.10.1
        bridge_ports eno1
        bridge_stp off
        bridge_fd 0
```

Another possibility it to use the bond directly as bridge port. This can be used to make the guest network fault-tolerant.

**Example: Use a bond as bridge port**

```
auto lo
iface lo inet loopback

iface eno1 inet manual

iface eno2 inet manual

auto bond0
iface bond0 inet maunal
      slaves eno1 eno2
      bond_miimon 100
      bond_mode 802.3ad
      bond_xmit_hash_policy layer2+3

auto vmbr0
iface vmbr0 inet static
        address  10.10.10.2
        netmask  255.255.255.0
        gateway  10.10.10.1
        bridge_ports bond0
```

```
bridge_stp off
bridge_fd 0
```

## 3.4 Time Synchronization

The Proxmox VE cluster stack itself relies heavily on the fact that all the nodes have precisely synchronized time. Some other components, like Ceph, also refuse to work properly if the local time on nodes is not in sync.

Time synchronization between nodes can be achieved with the "Network Time Protocol" (NTP). Proxmox VE uses `systemd-timesyncd` as NTP client by default, preconfigured to use a set of public servers. This setup works out of the box in most cases.

### 3.4.1 Using Custom NTP Servers

In some cases, it might be desired to not use the default NTP servers. For example, if your Proxmox VE nodes do not have access to the public internet (e.g., because of restrictive firewall rules), you need to setup local NTP servers and tell `systemd-timesyncd` to use them:

**File /etc/systemd/timesyncd.conf**

```
[Time]
Servers=ntp1.example.com ntp2.example.com ntp3.example.com ntp4.example.com
```

After restarting the synchronization service (`systemctl restart systemd-timesyncd`) you should verify that your newly configured NTP servers are used by checking the journal (`journalctl --since -1h -u systemd-timesyncd`):

```
...
Oct 07 14:58:36 node1 systemd[1]: Stopping Network Time Synchronization...
Oct 07 14:58:36 node1 systemd[1]: Starting Network Time Synchronization...
Oct 07 14:58:36 node1 systemd[1]: Started Network Time Synchronization.
Oct 07 14:58:36 node1 systemd-timesyncd[13514]: Using NTP server  ↩
    10.0.0.1:123 (ntp1.example.com).
Oct 07 14:58:36 nora systemd-timesyncd[13514]: interval/delta/delay/jitter/ ↩
    drift 64s/-0.002s/0.020s/0.000s/-31ppm
...
```

## 3.5 External Metric Server

Starting with Proxmox VE 4.0, you can define external metric servers, which will be sent various stats about your hosts, virtual machines and storages.

Currently supported are:

• graphite (see http://graphiteapp.org )

• influxdb (see https://www.influxdata.com/time-series-platform/influxdb/ )

The server definitions are saved in /etc/pve/status.cfg

### 3.5.1   Graphite server configuration

The definition of a server is:

```
graphite:
    server your-server
    port your-port
    path your-path
```

where your-port defaults to **2003** and your-path defaults to **proxmox**

Proxmox VE sends the data over udp, so the graphite server has to be configured for this

### 3.5.2   Influxdb plugin configuration

The definition is:

```
influxdb:
    server your-server
    port your-port
```

Proxmox VE sends the data over udp, so the influxdb server has to be configured for this

Here is an example configuration for influxdb (on your influxdb server):

```
[[udp]]
  enabled = true
  bind-address = "0.0.0.0:8089"
  database = "proxmox"
  batch-size = 1000
  batch-timeout = "1s"
```

With this configuration, your server listens on all IP adresses on port 8089, and writes the data in the **proxmox** database

## 3.6   Disk Health Monitoring

Although a robust and redundant storage is recommended, it can be very helpful to monitor the health of your local disks.

Starting with Proxmox VE 4.3, the package smartmontools [1] is installed and required. This is a set of tools to monitor and control the S.M.A.R.T. system for local hard disks.

You can get the status of a disk by issuing the following command:

```
# smartctl -a /dev/sdX
```

where /dev/sdX is the path to one of your local disks.

If the output says:

---

[1] smartmontools homepage https://www.smartmontools.org

```
SMART support is: Disabled
```

you can enable it with the command:

```
# smartctl -s on /dev/sdX
```

For more information on how to use smartctl, please see `man smartctl`.

By default, smartmontools daemon smartd is active and enabled, and scans the disks under /dev/sdX and /dev/hdX every 30 minutes for errors and warnings, and sends an e-mail to root if it detects a problem.

For more information about how to configure smartd, please see `man smartd` and `man smartd.conf`.

If you use your hard disks with a hardware raid controller, there are most likely tools to monitor the disks in the raid array and the array itself. For more information about this, please refer to the vendor of your raid controller.

## 3.7   Logical Volume Manager (LVM)

Most people install Proxmox VE directly on a local disk. The Proxmox VE installation CD offers several options for local disk management, and the current default setup uses LVM. The installer let you select a single disk for such setup, and uses that disk as physical volume for the **V**olume **G**roup (VG) `pve`. The following output is from a test installation using a small 8GB disk:

```
# pvs
  PV          VG    Fmt   Attr PSize PFree
  /dev/sda3   pve   lvm2  a--  7.87g 876.00m

# vgs
  VG    #PV #LV #SN Attr   VSize VFree
  pve     1   3   0 wz--n- 7.87g 876.00m
```

The installer allocates three **L**ogical **V**olumes (LV) inside this VG:

```
# lvs
  LV   VG    Attr       LSize   Pool Origin Data%  Meta%
  data pve   twi-a-tz--  4.38g               0.00   0.63
  root pve   -wi-ao----  1.75g
  swap pve   -wi-ao---- 896.00m
```

**root**
Formatted as `ext4`, and contains the operation system.

**swap**
Swap partition

**data**
This volume uses LVM-thin, and is used to store VM images. LVM-thin is preferable for this task, because it offers efficient support for snapshots and clones.

For Proxmox VE versions up to 4.1, the installer creates a standard logical volume called "data", which is mounted at /var/lib/vz.

Starting from version 4.2, the logical volume "data" is a LVM-thin pool, used to store block based guest images, and /var/lib/vz is simply a directory on the root file system.

### 3.7.1  Hardware

We highly recommend to use a hardware RAID controller (with BBU) for such setups. This increases performance, provides redundancy, and make disk replacements easier (hot-pluggable).

LVM itself does not need any special hardware, and memory requirements are very low.

### 3.7.2  Bootloader

We install two boot loaders by default. The first partition contains the standard GRUB boot loader. The second partition is an **E**FI **S**ystem **P**artition (ESP), which makes it possible to boot on EFI systems.

### 3.7.3  Creating a Volume Group

Let's assume we have an empty disk /dev/sdb, onto which we want to create a volume group named "vmdata".

---

 **Caution**
Please note that the following commands will destroy all existing data on /dev/sdb.

---

First create a partition.

```
# sgdisk -N 1 /dev/sdb
```

Create a **P**hysical **V**olume (PV) without confirmation and 250K metadatasize.

```
# pvcreate --metadatasize 250k -y -ff /dev/sdb1
```

Create a volume group named "vmdata" on /dev/sdb1

```
# vgcreate vmdata /dev/sdb1
```

### 3.7.4  Creating an extra LV for /var/lib/vz

This can be easily done by creating a new thin LV.

```
# lvcreate -n <Name> -V <Size[M,G,T]> <VG>/<LVThin_pool>
```

A real world example:

```
# lvcreate -n vz -V 10G pve/data
```

Now a filesystem must be created on the LV.

```
# mkfs.ext4 /dev/pve/vz
```

At last this has to be mounted.

 **Warning**
be sure that /var/lib/vz is empty. On a default installation it's not.

To make it always accessible add the following line in /etc/fstab.

```
# echo '/dev/pve/vz /var/lib/vz ext4 defaults 0 2' >> /etc/fstab
```

### 3.7.5 Resizing the thin pool

Resize the LV and the metadata pool can be achieved with the following command.

```
# lvresize --size +<size[\M,G,T]> --poolmetadatasize +<size[\M,G]> < ↵
   VG>/<LVThin_pool>
```

**Note**
When extending the data pool, the metadata pool must also be extended.

### 3.7.6 Create a LVM-thin pool

A thin pool has to be created on top of a volume group. How to create a volume group see Section LVM.

```
# lvcreate -L 80G -T -n vmstore vmdata
```

## 3.8 ZFS on Linux

ZFS is a combined file system and logical volume manager designed by Sun Microsystems. Starting with Proxmox VE 3.4, the native Linux kernel port of the ZFS file system is introduced as optional file system and also as an additional selection for the root file system. There is no need for manually compile ZFS modules - all packages are included.

By using ZFS, its possible to achieve maximum enterprise features with low budget hardware, but also high performance systems by leveraging SSD caching or even SSD only setups. ZFS can replace cost intense hardware raid cards by moderate CPU and memory load combined with easy management.

GENERAL ZFS ADVANTAGES

• Easy configuration and management with Proxmox VE GUI and CLI.

• Reliable

- Protection against data corruption

- Data compression on file system level

- Snapshots

- Copy-on-write clone

- Various raid levels: RAID0, RAID1, RAID10, RAIDZ-1, RAIDZ-2 and RAIDZ-3

- Can use SSD for cache

- Self healing

- Continuous integrity checking

- Designed for high storage capacities

- Protection against data corruption

- Asynchronous replication over network

- Open Source

- Encryption

- . . .

### 3.8.1 Hardware

ZFS depends heavily on memory, so you need at least 8GB to start. In practice, use as much you can get for your hardware/budget. To prevent data corruption, we recommend the use of high quality ECC RAM.

If you use a dedicated cache and/or log disk, you should use an enterprise class SSD (e.g. Intel SSD DC S3700 Series). This can increase the overall performance significantly.

---

 **Important**
Do not use ZFS on top of hardware controller which has its own cache management. ZFS needs to directly communicate with disks. An HBA adapter is the way to go, or something like LSI controller flashed in "IT" mode.

---

If you are experimenting with an installation of Proxmox VE inside a VM (Nested Virtualization), don't use `virtio` for disks of that VM, since they are not supported by ZFS. Use IDE or SCSI instead (works also with `virtio` SCSI controller type).

### 3.8.2 Installation as Root File System

When you install using the Proxmox VE installer, you can choose ZFS for the root file system. You need to select the RAID type at installation time:

| RAID0 | Also called "striping". The capacity of such volume is the sum of the capacities of all disks. But RAID0 does not add any redundancy, so the failure of a single drive makes the volume unusable. |
| --- | --- |
| RAID1 | Also called "mirroring". Data is written identically to all disks. This mode requires at least 2 disks with the same size. The resulting capacity is that of a single disk. |
| RAID10 | A combination of RAID0 and RAID1. Requires at least 4 disks. |
| RAIDZ-1 | A variation on RAID-5, single parity. Requires at least 3 disks. |
| RAIDZ-2 | A variation on RAID-5, double parity. Requires at least 4 disks. |
| RAIDZ-3 | A variation on RAID-5, triple parity. Requires at least 5 disks. |

The installer automatically partitions the disks, creates a ZFS pool called `rpool`, and installs the root file system on the ZFS subvolume `rpool/ROOT/pve-1`.

Another subvolume called `rpool/data` is created to store VM images. In order to use that with the Proxmox VE tools, the installer creates the following configuration entry in `/etc/pve/storage.cfg`:

```
zfspool: local-zfs
        pool rpool/data
        sparse
        content images,rootdir
```

After installation, you can view your ZFS pool status using the `zpool` command:

```
# zpool status
  pool: rpool
 state: ONLINE
  scan: none requested
config:

        NAME        STATE     READ WRITE CKSUM
        rpool       ONLINE       0     0     0
          mirror-0  ONLINE       0     0     0
            sda2    ONLINE       0     0     0
            sdb2    ONLINE       0     0     0
          mirror-1  ONLINE       0     0     0
            sdc     ONLINE       0     0     0
            sdd     ONLINE       0     0     0

errors: No known data errors
```

The `zfs` command is used configure and manage your ZFS file systems. The following command lists all file systems after installation:

```
# zfs list
NAME               USED  AVAIL  REFER  MOUNTPOINT
rpool             4.94G  7.68T    96K  /rpool
rpool/ROOT         702M  7.68T    96K  /rpool/ROOT
```

```
rpool/ROOT/pve-1    702M   7.68T    702M   /
rpool/data           96K   7.68T     96K   /rpool/data
rpool/swap          4.25G  7.69T     64K   -
```

### 3.8.3  Bootloader

The default ZFS disk partitioning scheme does not use the first 2048 sectors. This gives enough room to install a GRUB boot partition. The Proxmox VE installer automatically allocates that space, and installs the GRUB boot loader there. If you use a redundant RAID setup, it installs the boot loader on all disk required for booting. So you can boot even if some disks fail.

---

**Note**
It is not possible to use ZFS as root file system with UEFI boot.

---

### 3.8.4  ZFS Administration

This section gives you some usage examples for common tasks. ZFS itself is really powerful and provides many options. The main commands to manage ZFS are `zfs` and `zpool`. Both commands come with great manual pages, which can be read with:

```
# man zpool
# man zfs
```

**Create a new zpool**

To create a new pool, at least one disk is needed. The `ashift` should have the same sector-size (2 power of `ashift`) or larger as the underlying disk.

```
zpool create -f -o ashift=12 <pool> <device>
```

To activate compression

```
zfs set compression=lz4 <pool>
```

**Create a new pool with RAID-0**

Minimum 1 Disk

```
zpool create -f -o ashift=12 <pool> <device1> <device2>
```

**Create a new pool with RAID-1**

Minimum 2 Disks

```
zpool create -f -o ashift=12 <pool> mirror <device1> <device2>
```

### Create a new pool with RAID-10

Minimum 4 Disks

```
zpool create -f -o ashift=12 <pool> mirror <device1> <device2>  ↩
   mirror <device3> <device4>
```

### Create a new pool with RAIDZ-1

Minimum 3 Disks

```
zpool create -f -o ashift=12 <pool> raidz1 <device1> <device2> < ↩
   device3>
```

### Create a new pool with RAIDZ-2

Minimum 4 Disks

```
zpool create -f -o ashift=12 <pool> raidz2 <device1> <device2> < ↩
   device3> <device4>
```

### Create a new pool with cache (L2ARC)

It is possible to use a dedicated cache drive partition to increase the performance (use SSD).

As `<device>` it is possible to use more devices, like it's shown in "Create a new pool with RAID*".

```
zpool create -f -o ashift=12 <pool> <device> cache <cache_device>
```

### Create a new pool with log (ZIL)

It is possible to use a dedicated cache drive partition to increase the performance(SSD).

As `<device>` it is possible to use more devices, like it's shown in "Create a new pool with RAID*".

```
zpool create -f -o ashift=12 <pool> <device> log <log_device>
```

### Add cache and log to an existing pool

If you have an pool without cache and log. First partition the SSD in 2 partition with `parted` or `gdisk`

---

 **Important**
Always use GPT partition tables.

---

The maximum size of a log device should be about half the size of physical memory, so this is usually quite small. The rest of the SSD can be used as cache.

```
zpool add -f <pool> log <device-part1> cache <device-part2>
```

**Changing a failed device**

```
zpool replace -f <pool> <old device> <new-device>
```

### 3.8.5  Activate E-Mail Notification

ZFS comes with an event daemon, which monitors events generated by the ZFS kernel module. The daemon can also send emails on ZFS events like pool errors. Newer ZFS packages ships the daemon in a sparate package, and you can install it using `apt-get`:

```
# apt-get install zfs-zed
```

To activate the daemon it is necessary to edit `/etc/zfs/zed.d/zed.rc` with your favourite editor, and uncomment the `ZED_EMAIL_ADDR` setting:

```
ZED_EMAIL_ADDR="root"
```

Please note Proxmox VE forwards mails to `root` to the email address configured for the root user.

---

   **Important**

The only setting that is required is `ZED_EMAIL_ADDR`. All other settings are optional.

---

### 3.8.6  Limit ZFS Memory Usage

It is good to use at most 50 percent (which is the default) of the system memory for ZFS ARC to prevent performance shortage of the host. Use your preferred editor to change the configuration in `/etc/modprobe.d/zfs.conf` and insert:

```
options zfs zfs_arc_max=8589934592
```

This example setting limits the usage to 8GB.

---

   **Important**

If your root file system is ZFS you must update your initramfs every time this value changes:

```
update-initramfs -u
```

---

**SWAP on ZFS**

SWAP on ZFS on Linux may generate some troubles, like blocking the server or generating a high IO load, often seen when starting a Backup to an external Storage.

We strongly recommend to use enough memory, so that you normally do not run into low memory situations. Additionally, you can lower the "swappiness" value. A good value for servers is 10:

```
sysctl -w vm.swappiness=10
```

To make the swappiness persistent, open `/etc/sysctl.conf` with an editor of your choice and add the following line:

```
vm.swappiness = 10
```

Table 3.1: Linux kernel `swappiness` parameter values

| Value | Strategy |
|---|---|
| `vm.swappiness = 0` | The kernel will swap only to avoid an *out of memory* condition |
| `vm.swappiness = 1` | Minimum amount of swapping without disabling it entirely. |
| `vm.swappiness = 10` | This value is sometimes recommended to improve performance when sufficient memory exists in a system. |
| `vm.swappiness = 60` | The default value. |
| `vm.swappiness = 100` | The kernel will swap aggressively. |

# Chapter 4

# Hyper-converged Infrastructure

Proxmox VE is a virtualization platform that tightly integrates compute, storage and networking resources, manages highly available clusters, backup/restore as well as disaster recovery. All components are software-defined and compatible with one another.

Therefore it is possible to administrate them like a single system via the centralized web management interface. These capabilities make Proxmox VE an ideal choice to deploy and manage an open source hyper-converged infrastructure.

## 4.1   Benefits of a Hyper-Converged Infrastructure (HCI) with Proxmox VE

A hyper-converged infrastructure is especially useful for deployments in which a high infrastructure demand meets a low administration budget, for distributed setups such as remote and branch office environments or for virtual private and public clouds.

HCI provides the following advantages:

- Scalability: seamless expansion of compute, network and storage devices (i.e. scale up servers and storage quickly and independently from each other).

- Low cost: Proxmox VE is open source and integrates all components you need such as compute, storage, networking, backup, and management center. It can replace an expensive compute/storage infrastructure.

- Data protection and efficiency: services such as backup and disaster recovery are integrated.

- Simplicity: easy configuration and centralized administration.

- Open Source: No vendor lock-in.

## 4.2 Manage Ceph Services on Proxmox VE Nodes

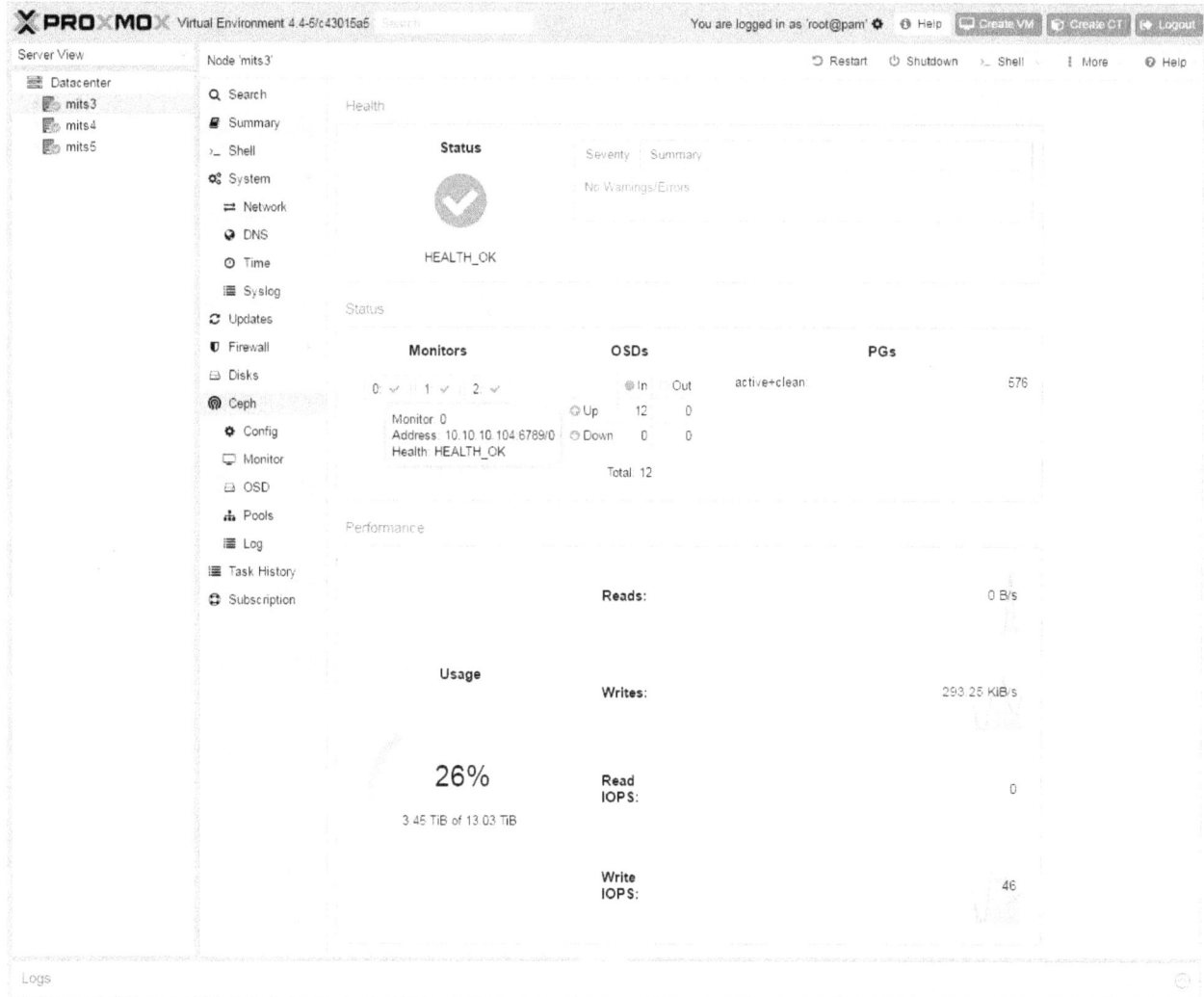

Proxmox VE unifies your compute and storage systems, i.e. you can use the same physical nodes within a cluster for both computing (processing VMs and containers) and replicated storage. The traditional silos of compute and storage resources can be wrapped up into a single hyper-converged appliance. Separate storage networks (SANs) and connections via network (NAS) disappear. With the integration of Ceph, an open source software-defined storage platform, Proxmox VE has the ability to run and manage Ceph storage directly on the hypervisor nodes.

Ceph is a distributed object store and file system designed to provide excellent performance, reliability and scalability. For smaller deployments, it is possible to install a Ceph server for RADOS Block Devices (RBD) directly on your Proxmox VE cluster nodes, see Ceph RADOS Block Devices (RBD) Section 8.13. Recent hardware has plenty of CPU power and RAM, so running storage services and VMs on the same node is possible.

To simplify management, we provide *pveceph* - a tool to install and manage Ceph services on Proxmox VE nodes.

### 4.2.1 Precondition

To build a Proxmox Ceph Cluster there should be at least three (preferably) identical servers for the setup.

A 10Gb network, exclusively used for Ceph, is recommmended. A meshed network setup is also an option if there are no 10Gb switches available, see wiki .

Check also the recommendations from Ceph's website.

## 4.2.2   Installation of Ceph Packages

On each node run the installation script as follows:

```
pveceph install
```

This sets up an `apt` package repository in `/etc/apt/sources.list.d/ceph.list` and installs the required software.

## 4.2.3   Creating initial Ceph configuration

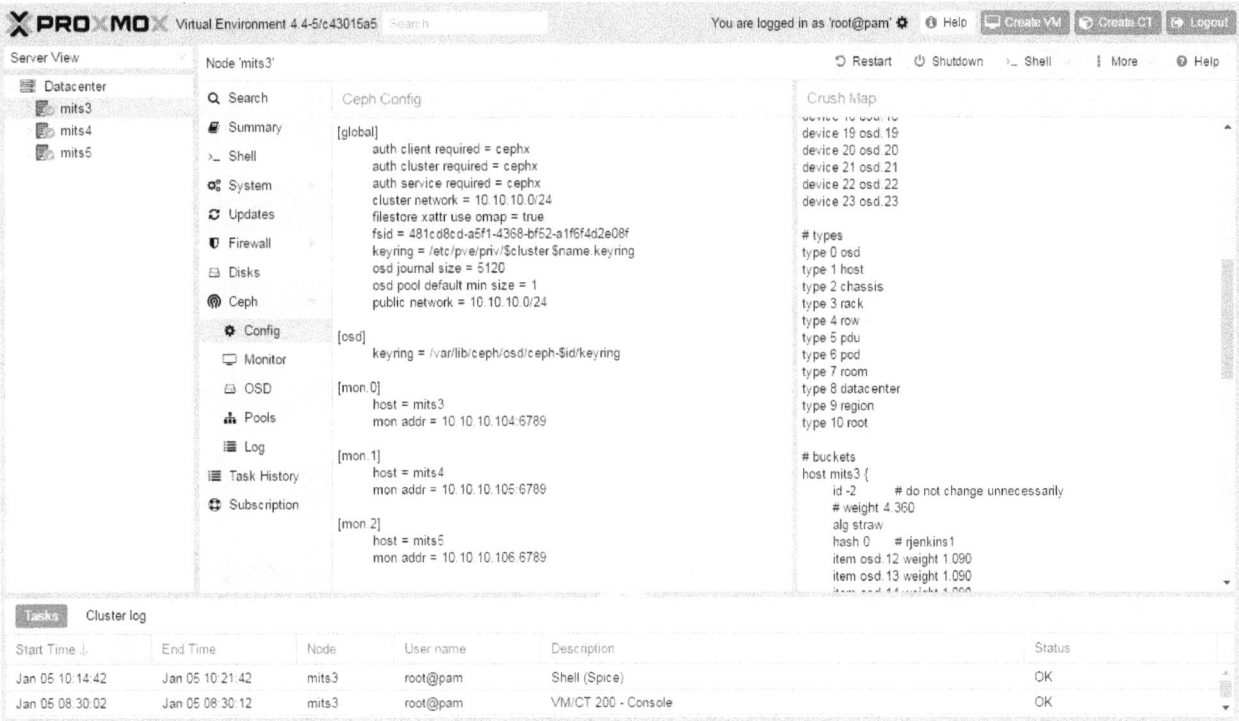

After installation of packages, you need to create an initial Ceph configuration on just one node, based on your network (`10.10.10.0/24` in the following example) dedicated for Ceph:

```
pveceph init --network 10.10.10.0/24
```

This creates an initial config at `/etc/pve/ceph.conf`. That file is automatically distributed to all Proxmox VE nodes by using pmxcfs Chapter 7. The command also creates a symbolic link from `/etc/ceph/ceph.conf` pointing to that file. So you can simply run Ceph commands without the need to specify a configuration file.

### 4.2.4 Creating Ceph Monitors

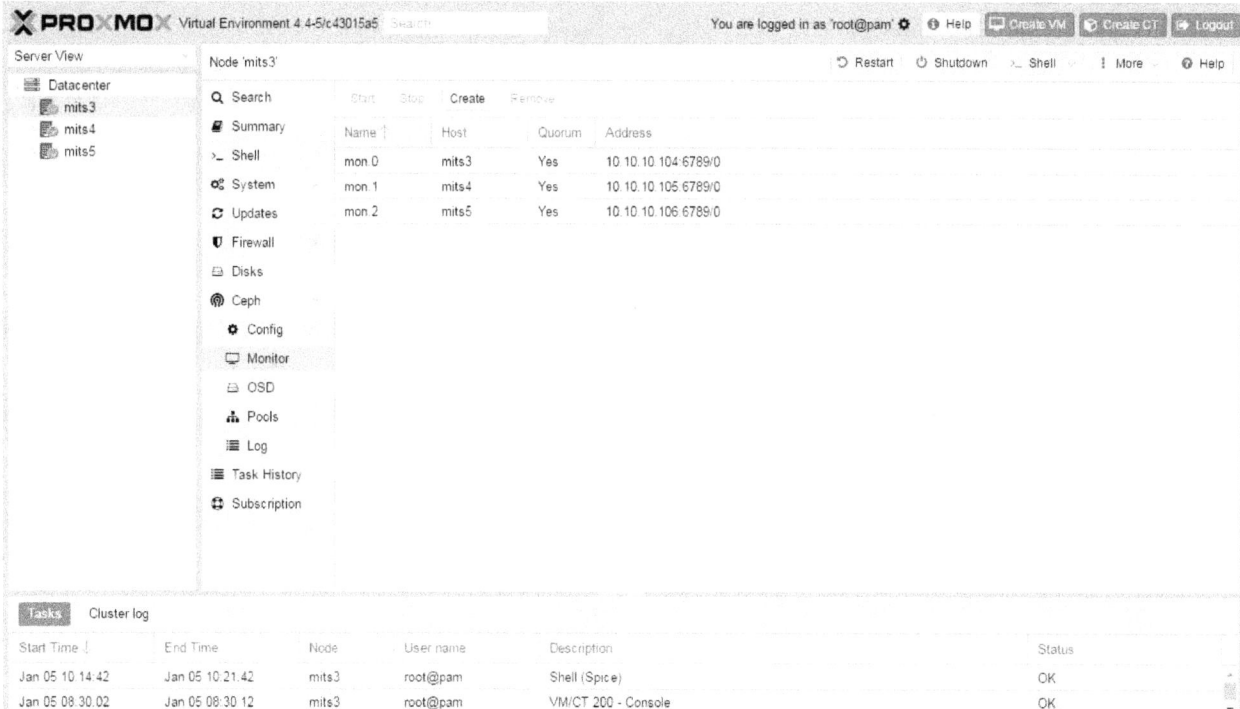

On each node where a monitor is requested (three monitors are recommended) create it by using the "Ceph" item in the GUI or run.

```
pveceph createmon
```

### 4.2.5 Creating Ceph OSDs

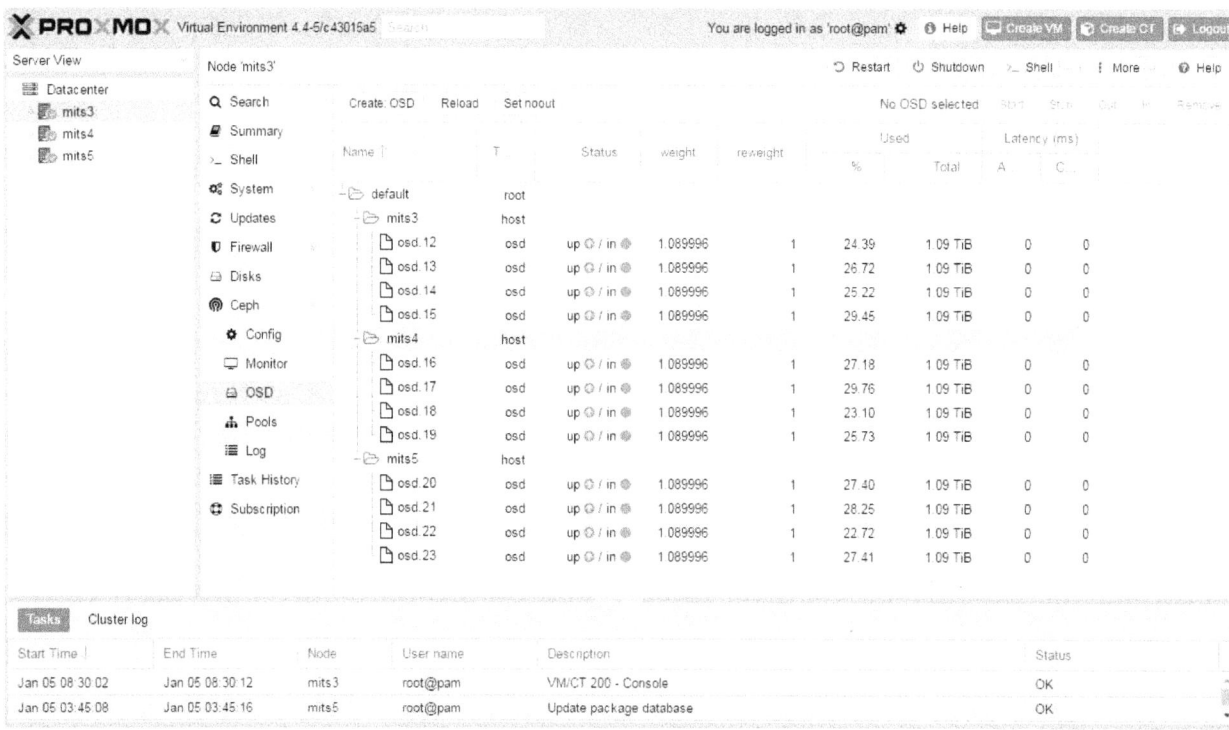

via GUI or via CLI as follows:

```
pveceph createosd /dev/sd[X]
```

If you want to use a dedicated SSD journal disk:

---

**Note**

In order to use a dedicated journal disk (SSD), the disk needs to have a GPT partition table. You can create this with `gdisk /dev/sd(x)`. If there is no GPT, you cannot select the disk as journal. Currently the journal size is fixed to 5 GB.

---

```
pveceph createosd /dev/sd[X] -journal_dev /dev/sd[X]
```

Example: Use /dev/sdf as data disk (4TB) and /dev/sdb is the dedicated SSD journal disk.

```
pveceph createosd /dev/sdf -journal_dev /dev/sdb
```

This partitions the disk (data and journal partition), creates filesystems and starts the OSD, afterwards it is running and fully functional. Please create at least 12 OSDs, distributed among your nodes (4 OSDs on each node).

It should be noted that this command refuses to initialize disk when it detects existing data. So if you want to overwrite a disk you should remove existing data first. You can do that using:

```
ceph-disk zap /dev/sd[X]
```

You can create OSDs containing both journal and data partitions or you can place the journal on a dedicated SSD. Using a SSD journal disk is highly recommended if you expect good performance.

## 4.2.6 Ceph Pools

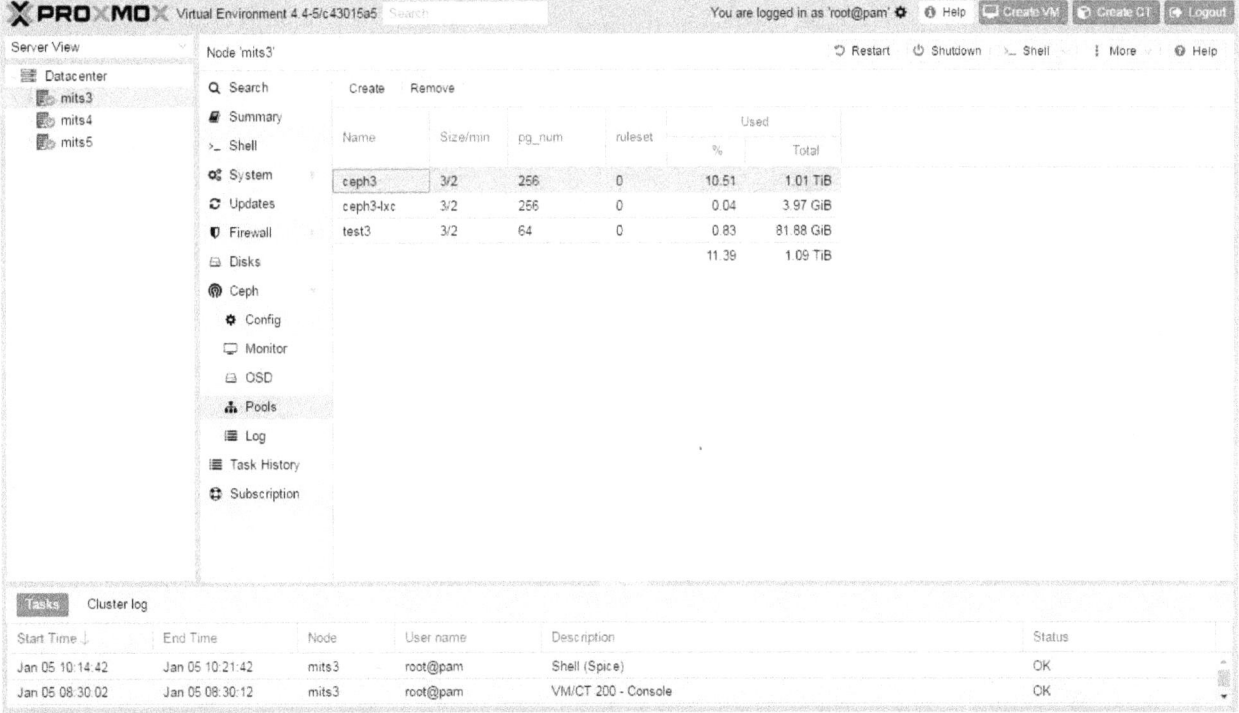

The standard installation creates per default the pool *rbd*, additional pools can be created via GUI.

### 4.2.7  Ceph Client

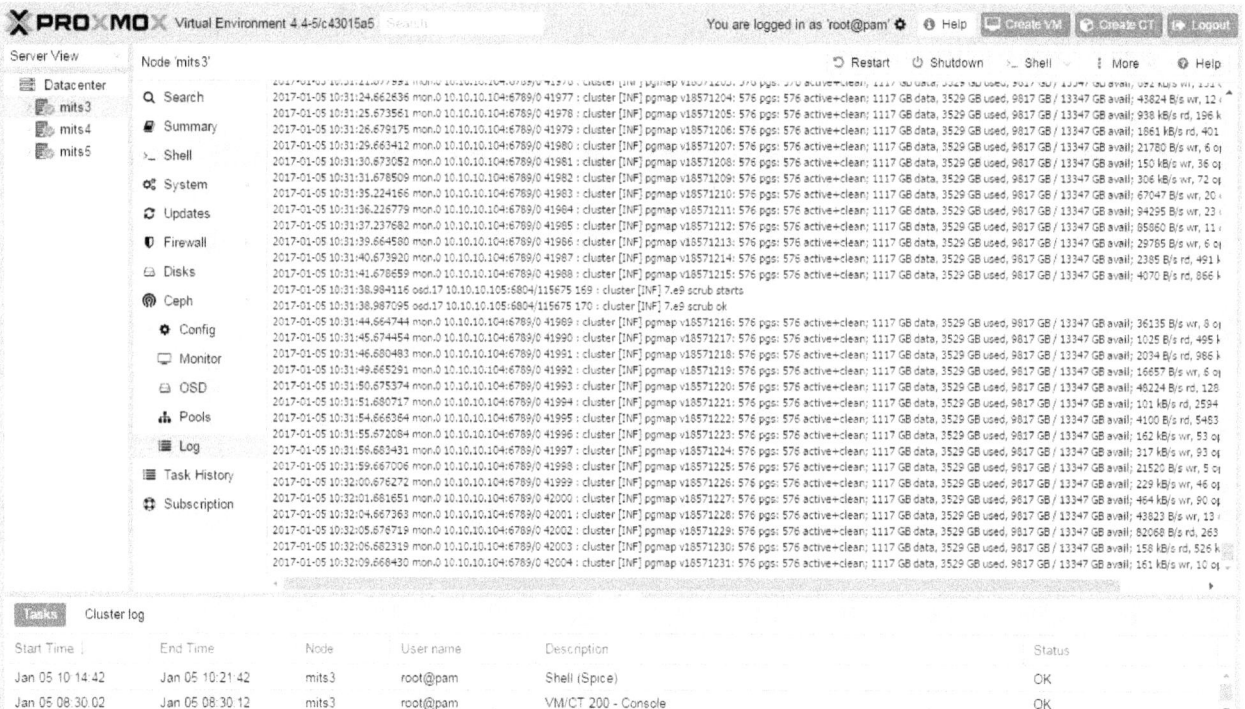

You can then configure Proxmox VE to use such pools to store VM or Container images. Simply use the GUI too add a new RBD storage (see section Ceph RADOS Block Devices (RBD) Section 8.13).

You also need to copy the keyring to a predefined location.

---

**Note**

The file name needs to be `<storage_id>` + `` `.keyring ``-`<storage_id>` is the expression after *rbd:* in `/etc/pve/storage.cfg` which is `my-ceph-storage` in the following example:

---

```
mkdir /etc/pve/priv/ceph
cp /etc/ceph/ceph.client.admin.keyring /etc/pve/priv/ceph/my-ceph-storage. ↩
    keyring
```

# Chapter 5

# Graphical User Interface

Proxmox VE is simple. There is no need to install a separate management tool, and everything can be done through your web browser (Latest Firefox or Google Chrome is preferred). A built-in HTML5 console is used to access the guest console. As an alternative, SPICE can be used.

Because we use the Proxmox cluster file system (pmxcfs), you can connect to any node to manage the entire cluster. Each node can manage the entire cluster. There is no need for a dedicated manager node.

You can use the web-based administration interface with any modern browser. When Proxmox VE detects that you are connecting from a mobile device, you are redirected to a simpler, touch-based user interface.

The web interface can be reached via https://youripaddress:8006 (default login is: *root*, and the password is specified during the installation process).

## 5.1 Features

• Seamless integration and management of Proxmox VE clusters

• AJAX technologies for dynamic updates of resources

• Secure access to all Virtual Machines and Containers via SSL encryption (https)

• Fast search-driven interface, capable of handling hundreds and probably thousands of VMs

• Secure HTML5 console or SPICE

• Role based permission management for all objects (VMs, storages, nodes, etc.)

• Support for multiple authentication sources (e.g. local, MS ADS, LDAP, ... )

• Two-Factor Authentication (OATH, Yubikey)

• Based on ExtJS 6.x JavaScript framework

## 5.2 Login

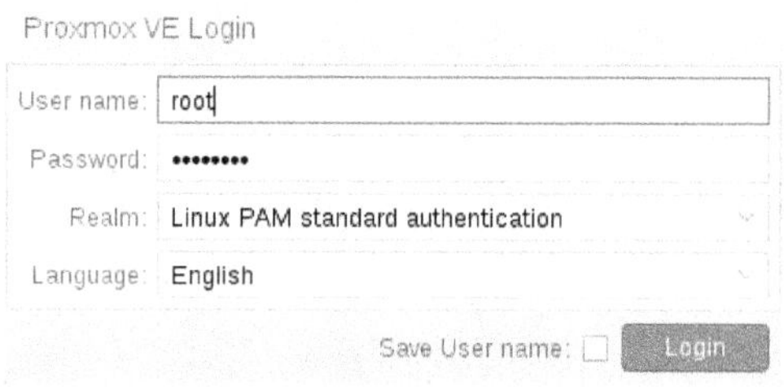


When you connect to the server, you will first see the longin window. Proxmox VE supports various authentication backends (*Realm*), and you can select the langauage here. The GUI is translated to more than 20 languages.

---

**Note**

You can save the user name on the client side by selection the checkbox at the bottom. This saves some typing when you login next time.

---

## 5.3 GUI Overview

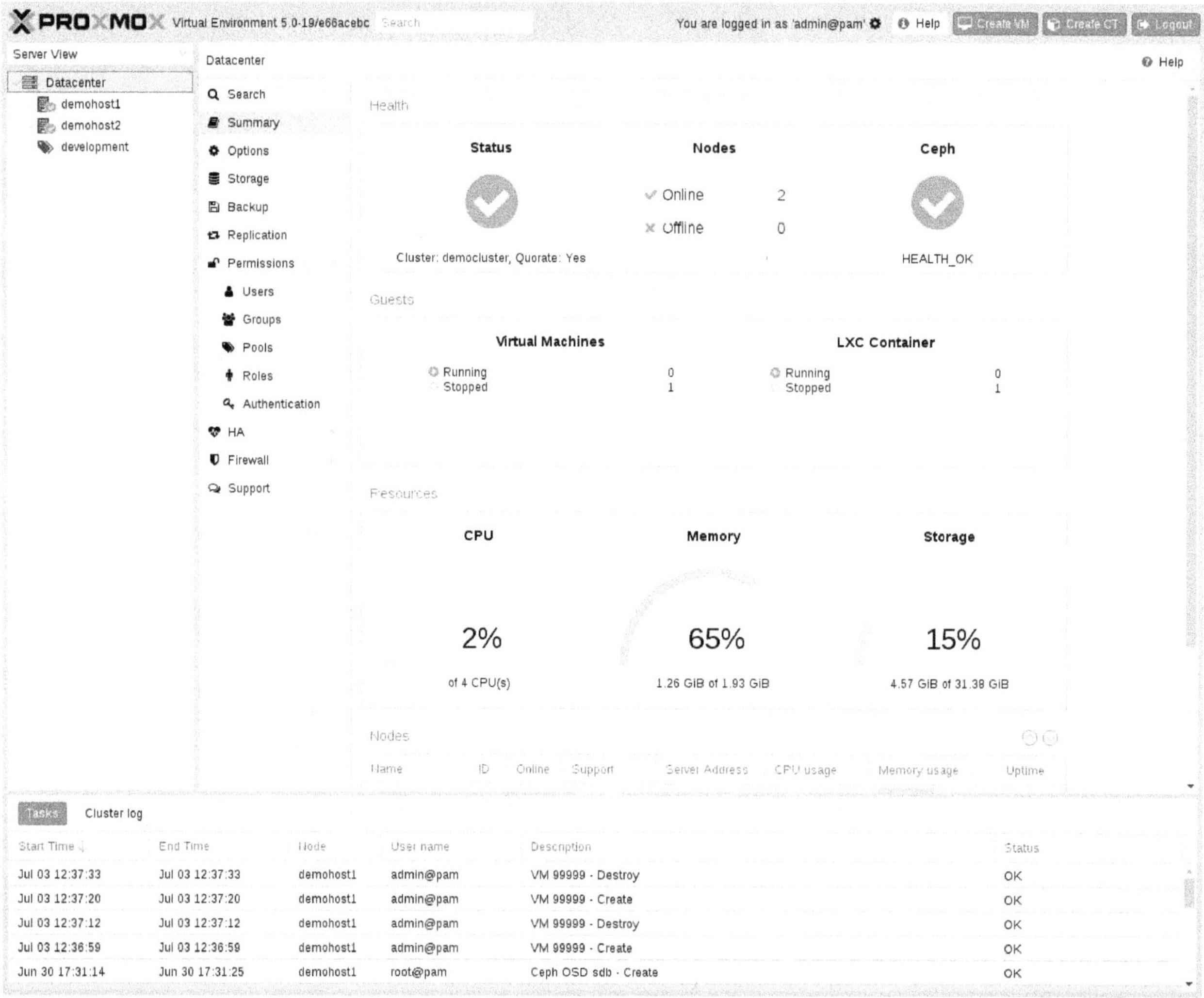

The Proxmox VE user interface consists of four regions.

Header             On top. Shows status information and contains buttons for most important actions.

Resource Tree    At the left side. A navigation tree where you can select specific objects.

Content Panel    Center region. Selected objects displays configuration options and status here.

Log Panel        At the bottom. Displays log entries for recent tasks. You can double-click on those
                 log entries to get more details, or to abort a running task.

---

**Note**

You can shrink and expand the size of the resource tree and log panel, or completely hide the log panel.
This can be helpful when you work on small displays and want more space to view other content.

---

### 5.3.1  Header

On the top left side, the first thing you see is the Proxmox logo. Next to it is the current running version of
Proxmox VE. In the search bar nearside you can search for specific objects (VMs, containers, nodes, ...).
This is sometimes faster than selecting an object in the resource tree.

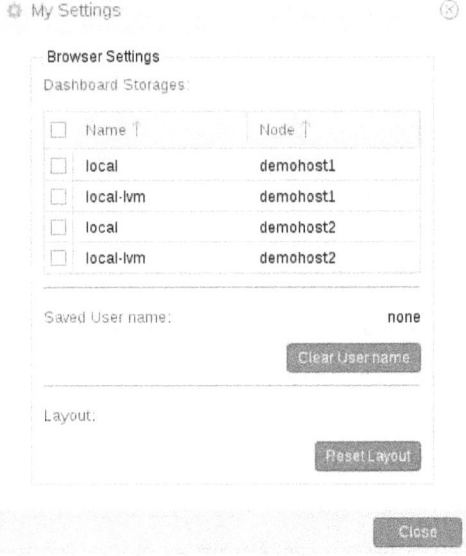

To the right of the search bar we see the identity (login name). The gear symbol is a button opening the
*My Settings* dialog. There you can customize some client side user interface setting (reset the saved login
name, reset saved layout).

The rightmost part of the header contains four buttons:

Help             Opens a new browser window showing the reference documenation.

Create VM        Opens the virtual machine creation wizard.

Create CT        Open the container creation wizard.

Logout            Logout, and show the login dialog again.

## 5.3.2  Resource Tree

This is the main navigation tree. On top of the tree you can select some predefined views, which changes the structure of the tree below. The default view is **Server View**, and it shows the following object types:

Datacenter        Contains cluster wide setting (relevant for all nodes).

Node              Represents the hosts inside a cluster, where the guests runs.

Guest             VMs, Containers and Templates.

Storage           Data Storage.

Pool              It is possible to group guests using a pool to simplify management.

The following view types are available:

Server View       Shows all kind of objects, grouped by nodes.

Folder View       Shows all kind of objects, grouped by object type.

Storage View      Only show storage objects, grouped by nodes.

Pool View         Show VMs and Containers, grouped by pool.

## 5.3.3  Log Panel

The main purpose of the log panel is to show you what is currently going on in your cluster. Actions like creating an new VM are executed in background, and we call such background job a *task*.

Any output from such task is saved into a separate log file. You can view that log by simply double-click a task log entry. It is also possible to abort a running task there.

Please note that we display most recent tasks from all cluster nodes here. So you can see when somebody else is working on another cluster node in real-time.

---

**Note**
We remove older and finished task from the log panel to keep that list short. But you can still find those tasks in the *Task History* within the node panel.

---

Some short running actions simply sends logs to all cluster members. You can see those messages in the *Cluster log* panel.

---

## 5.4   Content Panels

When you select something in the resource tree, the correnponding object displays configuration and status information in the content panel. The following sections gives a brief overview of the functionality. Please refer to the individual chapters inside the reference documentatin to get more detailed information.

### 5.4.1   Datacenter

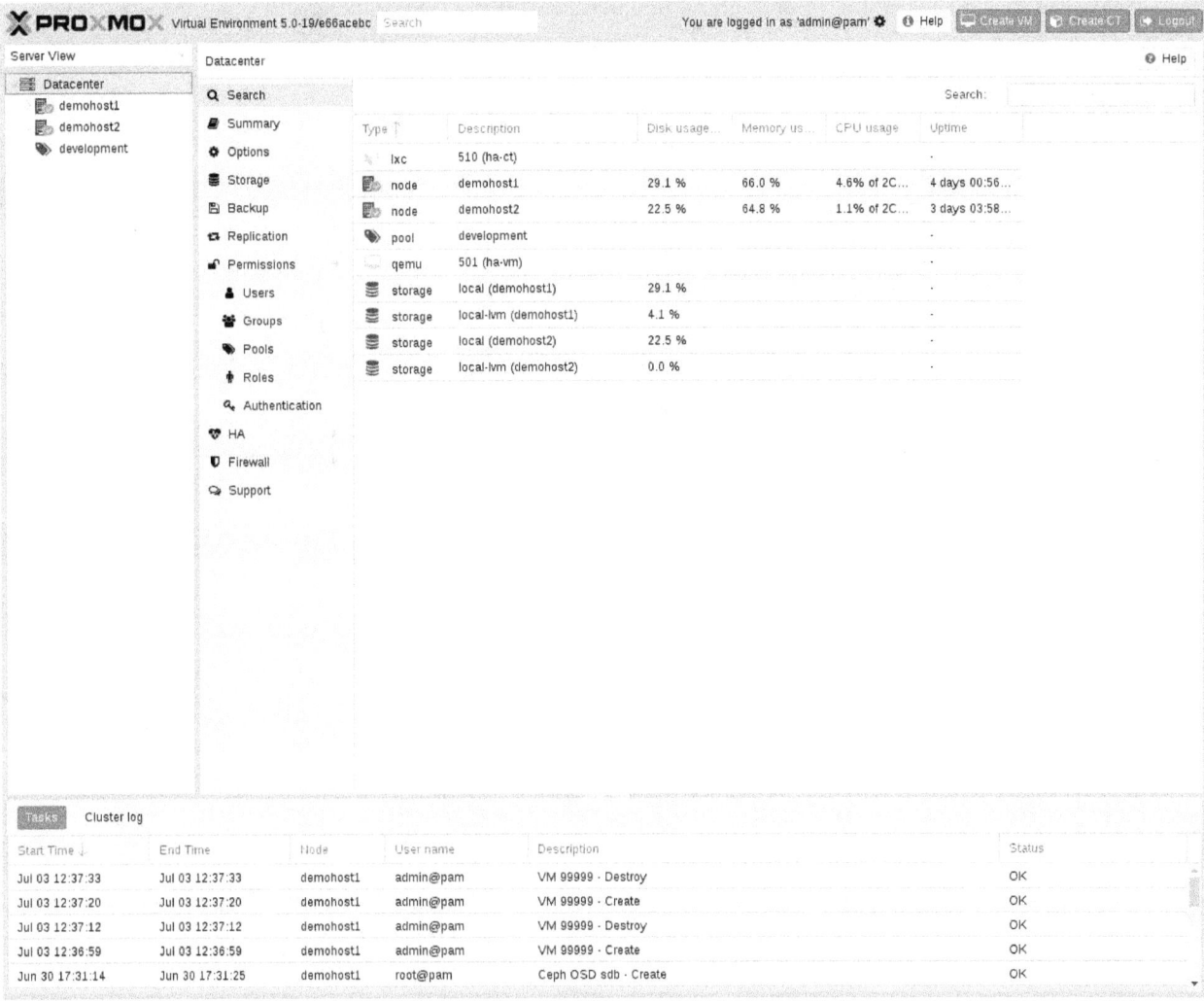

On the datacenter level you can access cluster wide settings and information.

- **Search:** it is possible to search anything in cluster ,this can be a node, VM, Container, Storage or a pool.

- **Summary:** gives a brief overview over the cluster health.

- **Options:** can show and set defaults, which apply cluster wide.

- **Storage:** is the place where a storage will add/managed/removed.

- **Backup:** has the capability to schedule Backups. This is cluster wide, so you do not care about where the VM/Container are on your cluster at schedule time.

- **Permissions:** will manage user and group permission, LDAP, MS-AD and Two-Factor authentication can be setup here.

- **HA:** will manage the Proxmox VE High-Availability

- **Firewall:** on this level the Proxmox Firewall works cluster wide and makes templates which are cluster wide available.

- **Support:** here you get all information about your support subscription.

If you like to have more information about this see the corresponding chapter.

## 5.4.2 Nodes

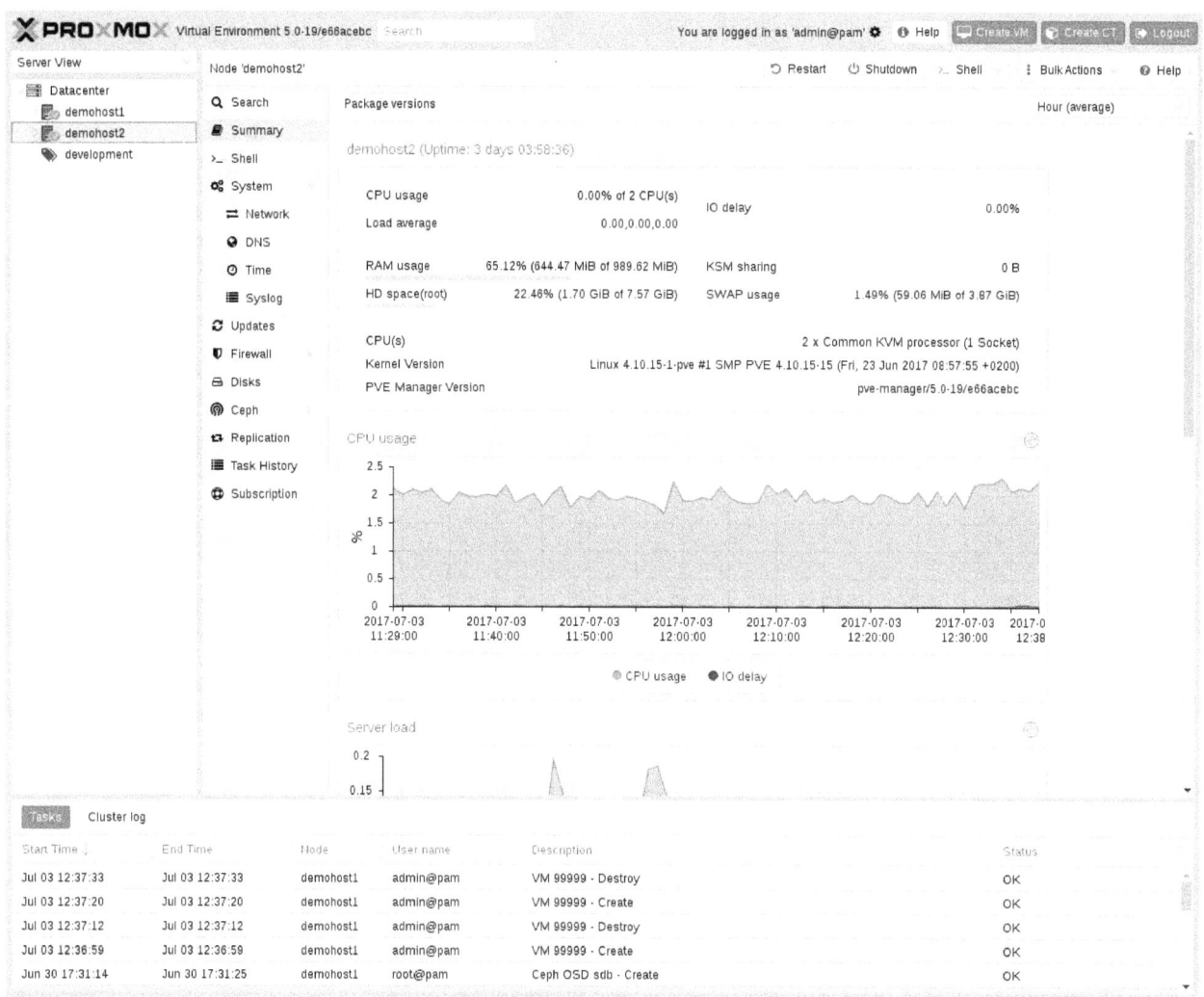

All belongs of a node can be managed at this level.

- **Search:** it is possible to search anything on the node, this can be a VM, Container, Storage or a pool.

- **Summary:** gives a brief overview over the resource usage.

- **Shell:** log you in the shell of the node.

- **System:** is for configuring the network, dns and time, and also shows your syslog.

- **Updates:** will upgrade the system and informs you about new packets.

- **Firewall:** on this level is only for this node.

- **Disk:** gives you an brief overview about you physical hard drives and how they are used.

- **Ceph:** is only used if you have installed a Ceph sever on you host. Then you can manage your Ceph cluster and see the status of it here.

- **Task History:** here all past task are shown.

- **Subscription:** here you can upload you subscription key and get a system overview in case of a support case.

### 5.4.3  Guests

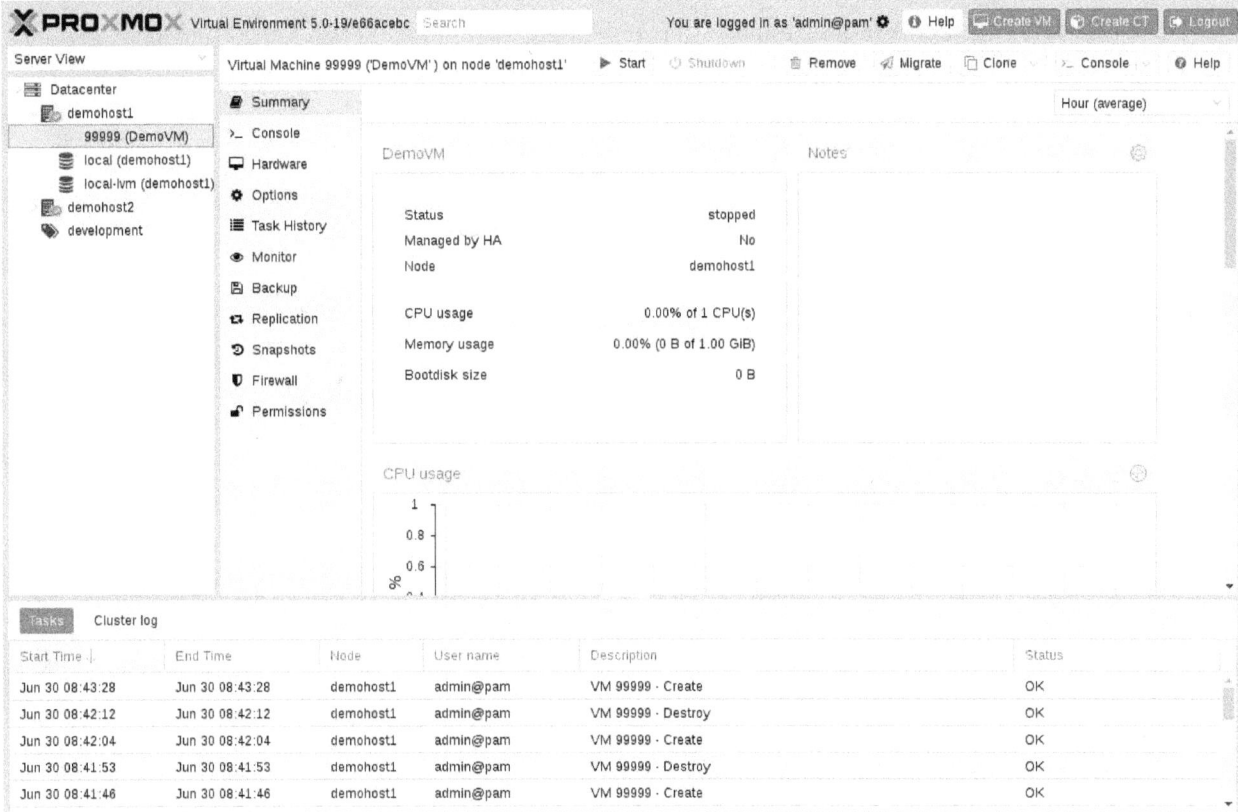

There are two differed kinds of VM types and both types can be converted to a template. One of them are Kernel-based Virtual Machine (KVM) and the other one are Linux Containers (LXC). General the navigation are the same only some option are different.

In the main management center the VM navigation begin if a VM is selected in the left tree.

The top header contains important VM operation commands like *Start*, *Shutdown*, *Rest*, *Remove*, *Migrate*, *Console* and *Help*. Two of them have hidden buttons like *Shutdown* has *Stop* and *Console* contains the different consolen typs *SPICE* or *noVNC*.

On the right side the content switch white the focus of the option.

On the left side. All available options are listed one below the other.

- **Summary:** gives a brief overview over the VM activity.

- **Console:** an interactive console to your VM.

- **(KVM)Hardware:** shows and set the Hardware of the KVM VM.

- **(LXC)Resources:** defines the LXC Hardware opportunities.

- **(LXC)Network:** the LXC Network settings.

- **(LXC)DNS:** the LXC DNS settings.

- **Options:** all VM options can be set here, this distinguishes between KVM and LXC.

- **Task History:** here all previous task from this VM will be shown.

- **(KVM) Monitor:** is the interactive communication interface to the KVM process.

- **Backup:** shows the available backups from this VM and also create a backupset.

- **Snapshots:** manage VM snapshots.

- **Firewall:** manage the firewall on VM level.

- **Permissions:** manage the user permission for this VM.

## 5.4.4 Storage

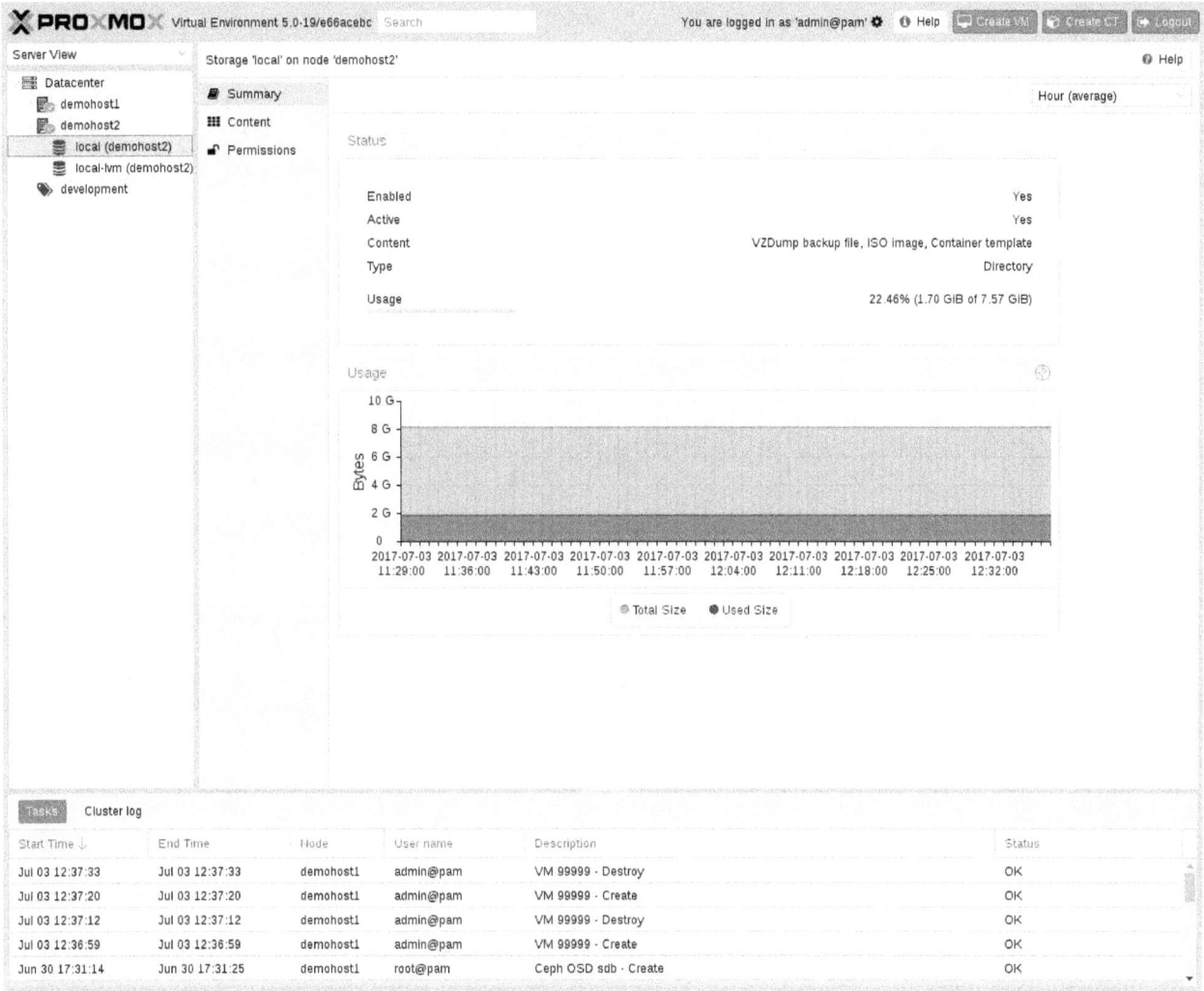

In this view we have a two partition split view. On the left side we have the storage options and on the right side the content of the selected option will shown.

- **Summary:** show you important information about your storage like *Usage*, *Type*, *Content*, *Active* and *Enabled*.

- **Content:** Here all contend will listed grouped by content.

- **Permissions:** manage the user permission for this storage.

## 5.4.5 Pools

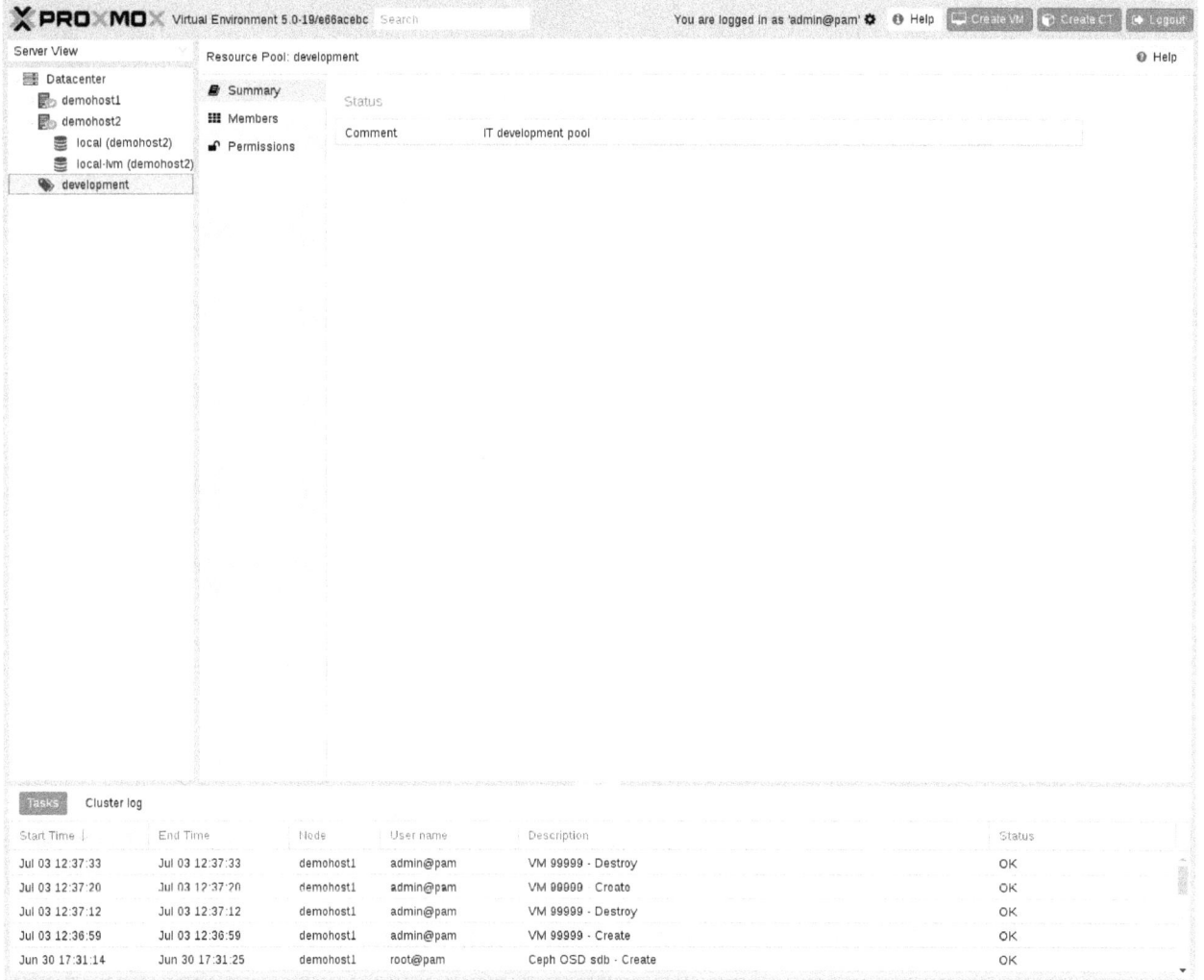

In this view we have a two partition split view. On the left side we have the logical pool options and on the right side the content of the selected option will shown.

- **Summary:** show the description of the pool.

- **Members:** Here all members of this pool will listed and can be managed.

- **Permissions:** manage the user permission for this pool.

# Chapter 6

# Cluster Manager

The Proxmox VE cluster manager `pvecm` is a tool to create a group of physical servers. Such a group is called a **cluster**. We use the Corosync Cluster Engine for reliable group communication, and such clusters can consist of up to 32 physical nodes (probably more, dependent on network latency).

`pvecm` can be used to create a new cluster, join nodes to a cluster, leave the cluster, get status information and do various other cluster related tasks. The **Proxmox Cluster File System** ("pmxcfs") is used to transparently distribute the cluster configuration to all cluster nodes.

Grouping nodes into a cluster has the following advantages:

- Centralized, web based management

- Multi-master clusters: each node can do all management task

- `pmxcfs`: database-driven file system for storing configuration files, replicated in real-time on all nodes using `corosync`.

- Easy migration of virtual machines and containers between physical hosts

- Fast deployment

- Cluster-wide services like firewall and HA

## 6.1  Requirements

- All nodes must be in the same network as `corosync` uses IP Multicast to communicate between nodes (also see Corosync Cluster Engine). Corosync uses UDP ports 5404 and 5405 for cluster communication.

---

**Note**
Some switches do not support IP multicast by default and must be manually enabled first.

---

- Date and time have to be synchronized.

- SSH tunnel on TCP port 22 between nodes is used.

- If you are interested in High Availability, you need to have at least three nodes for reliable quorum. All nodes should have the same version.

- We recommend a dedicated NIC for the cluster traffic, especially if you use shared storage.

**Note**
It is not possible to mix Proxmox VE 3.x and earlier with Proxmox VE 4.0 cluster nodes.

## 6.2 Preparing Nodes

First, install Proxmox VE on all nodes. Make sure that each node is installed with the final hostname and IP configuration. Changing the hostname and IP is not possible after cluster creation.

Currently the cluster creation has to be done on the console, so you need to login via `ssh`.

## 6.3 Create the Cluster

Login via `ssh` to the first Proxmox VE node. Use a unique name for your cluster. This name cannot be changed later.

```
hp1# pvecm create YOUR-CLUSTER-NAME
```

 **Caution**
The cluster name is used to compute the default multicast address. Please use unique cluster names if you run more than one cluster inside your network.

To check the state of your cluster use:

```
hp1# pvecm status
```

## 6.4 Adding Nodes to the Cluster

Login via `ssh` to the node you want to add.

```
hp2# pvecm add IP-ADDRESS-CLUSTER
```

For `IP-ADDRESS-CLUSTER` use the IP from an existing cluster node.

 **Caution**
A new node cannot hold any VMs, because you would get conflicts about identical VM IDs. Also, all existing configuration in `/etc/pve` is overwritten when you join a new node to the cluster. To workaround, use `vzdump` to backup and restore to a different VMID after adding the node to the cluster.

To check the state of cluster:

```
# pvecm status
```

**Cluster status after adding 4 nodes**

```
hp2# pvecm status
Quorum information
~~~~~~~~~~~~~~~~~~
Date:                Mon Apr 20 12:30:13 2015
Quorum provider:     corosync_votequorum
Nodes:               4
Node ID:             0x00000001
Ring ID:             1928
Quorate:             Yes

Votequorum information
~~~~~~~~~~~~~~~~~~~~~~~
Expected votes:    4
Highest expected:  4
Total votes:       4
Quorum:            2
Flags:             Quorate

Membership information
~~~~~~~~~~~~~~~~~~~~~~~
    Nodeid      Votes Name
0x00000001        1 192.168.15.91
0x00000002        1 192.168.15.92 (local)
0x00000003        1 192.168.15.93
0x00000004        1 192.168.15.94
```

If you only want the list of all nodes use:

```
# pvecm nodes
```

**List nodes in a cluster**

```
hp2# pvecm nodes

Membership information
~~~~~~~~~~~~~~~~~~~~~~~
    Nodeid      Votes Name
         1        1 hp1
         2        1 hp2 (local)
         3        1 hp3
         4        1 hp4
```

## 6.4.1 Adding Nodes With Separated Cluster Network

When adding a node to a cluster with a separated cluster network you need to use the *ringX_addr* parameters to set the nodes address on those networks:

```
pvecm add IP-ADDRESS-CLUSTER -ring0_addr IP-ADDRESS-RING0
```

If you want to use the Redundant Ring Protocol you will also want to pass the *ring1_addr* parameter.

## 6.5   Remove a Cluster Node

 **Caution**

Read carefully the procedure before proceeding, as it could not be what you want or need.

Move all virtual machines from the node. Make sure you have no local data or backups you want to keep, or save them accordingly. In the following example we will remove the node hp4 from the cluster.

Log in to a **different** cluster node (not hp4), and issue a `pvecm nodes` command to identify the node ID to remove:

```
hp1# pvecm nodes

Membership information
~~~~~~~~~~~~~~~~~~~~~~~
    Nodeid      Votes Name
         1          1 hp1 (local)
         2          1 hp2
         3          1 hp3
         4          1 hp4
```

At this point you must power off hp4 and make sure that it will not power on again (in the network) as it is.

 **Important**

As said above, it is critical to power off the node **before** removal, and make sure that it will **never** power on again (in the existing cluster network) as it is. If you power on the node as it is, your cluster will be screwed up and it could be difficult to restore a clean cluster state.

After powering off the node hp4, we can safely remove it from the cluster.

```
hp1# pvecm delnode hp4
```

If the operation succeeds no output is returned, just check the node list again with `pvecm nodes` or `pvecm status`. You should see something like:

```
hp1# pvecm status

Quorum information
~~~~~~~~~~~~~~~~~~
Date:               Mon Apr 20 12:44:28 2015
Quorum provider:    corosync_votequorum
Nodes:              3
Node ID:            0x00000001
Ring ID:            1992
Quorate:            Yes

Votequorum information
~~~~~~~~~~~~~~~~~~~~~~~
Expected votes:     3
```

```
Highest expected: 3
Total votes:      3
Quorum:           3
Flags:            Quorate

Membership information
~~~~~~~~~~~~~~~~~~~~~~~
    Nodeid      Votes Name
0x00000001          1 192.168.15.90 (local)
0x00000002          1 192.168.15.91
0x00000003          1 192.168.15.92
```

If, for whatever reason, you want that this server joins the same cluster again, you have to

- reinstall Proxmox VE on it from scratch

- then join it, as explained in the previous section.

### 6.5.1   Separate A Node Without Reinstalling

---

 **Caution**
This is **not** the recommended method, proceed with caution. Use the above mentioned method if you're unsure.

---

You can also separate a node from a cluster without reinstalling it from scratch. But after removing the node from the cluster it will still have access to the shared storages! This must be resolved before you start removing the node from the cluster. A Proxmox VE cluster cannot share the exact same storage with another cluster, as storage locking doesn't work over cluster boundary. Further, it may also lead to VMID conflicts.

Its suggested that you create a new storage where only the node which you want to separate has access. This can be an new export on your NFS or a new Ceph pool, to name a few examples. Its just important that the exact same storage does not gets accessed by multiple clusters. After setting this storage up move all data from the node and its VMs to it. Then you are ready to separate the node from the cluster.

---

 **Warning**
Ensure all shared resources are cleanly separated! You will run into conflicts and problems else.

---

First stop the corosync and the pve-cluster services on the node:

```
systemctl stop pve-cluster
systemctl stop corosync
```

Start the cluster filesystem again in local mode:

```
pmxcfs -l
```

Delete the corosync configuration files:

---

```
rm /etc/pve/corosync.conf
rm /etc/corosync/*
```

You can now start the filesystem again as normal service:

```
killall pmxcfs
systemctl start pve-cluster
```

The node is now separated from the cluster. You can deleted it from a remaining node of the cluster with:

```
pvecm delnode oldnode
```

If the command failed, because the remaining node in the cluster lost quorum when the now separate node exited, you may set the expected votes to 1 as a workaround:

```
pvecm expected 1
```

And the repeat the *pvecm delnode* command.

Now switch back to the separated node, here delete all remaining files left from the old cluster. This ensures that the node can be added to another cluster again without problems.

```
rm /var/lib/corosync/*
```

As the configuration files from the other nodes are still in the cluster filesystem you may want to clean those up too. Remove simply the whole directory recursive from */etc/pve/nodes/NODENAME*, but check three times that you used the correct one before deleting it.

---

**Caution**
The nodes SSH keys are still in the *authorized_key* file, this means the nodes can still connect to each other with public key authentication. This should be fixed by removing the respective keys from the */etc/pve/priv/authorized_keys* file.

---

## 6.6  Quorum

Proxmox VE use a quorum-based technique to provide a consistent state among all cluster nodes.

> A quorum is the minimum number of votes that a distributed transaction has to obtain in order to be allowed to perform an operation in a distributed system.
>
> — from Wikipedia *Quorum (distributed computing)*

In case of network partitioning, state changes requires that a majority of nodes are online. The cluster switches to read-only mode if it loses quorum.

---

**Note**
Proxmox VE assigns a single vote to each node by default.

---

## 6.7  Cluster Network

The cluster network is the core of a cluster. All messages sent over it have to be delivered reliable to all nodes in their respective order. In Proxmox VE this part is done by corosync, an implementation of a high performance low overhead high availability development toolkit. It serves our decentralized configuration file system (pmxcfs).

### 6.7.1  Network Requirements

This needs a reliable network with latencies under 2 milliseconds (LAN performance) to work properly. While corosync can also use unicast for communication between nodes its **highly recommended** to have a multicast capable network. The network should not be used heavily by other members, ideally corosync runs on its own network. **never** share it with network where storage communicates too.

Before setting up a cluster it is good practice to check if the network is fit for that purpose.

- Ensure that all nodes are in the same subnet. This must only be true for the network interfaces used for cluster communication (corosync).

- Ensure all nodes can reach each other over those interfaces, using `ping` is enough for a basic test.

- Ensure that multicast works in general and a high package rates. This can be done with the `omping` tool. The final "%loss" number should be < 1%.

  ```
  omping -c 10000 -i 0.001 -F -q NODE1-IP NODE2-IP ...
  ```

- Ensure that multicast communication works over an extended period of time. This uncovers problems where IGMP snooping is activated on the network but no multicast querier is active. This test has a duration of around 10 minutes.

  ```
  omping -c 600 -i 1 -q NODE1-IP NODE2-IP ...
  ```

Your network is not ready for clustering if any of these test fails. Recheck your network configuration. Especially switches are notorious for having multicast disabled by default or IGMP snooping enabled with no IGMP querier active.

In smaller cluster its also an option to use unicast if you really cannot get multicast to work.

### 6.7.2  Separate Cluster Network

When creating a cluster without any parameters the cluster network is generally shared with the Web UI and the VMs and its traffic. Depending on your setup even storage traffic may get sent over the same network. Its recommended to change that, as corosync is a time critical real time application.

#### Setting Up A New Network

First you have to setup a new network interface. It should be on a physical separate network. Ensure that your network fulfills the cluster network requirements.

**Separate On Cluster Creation**

This is possible through the *ring0_addr* and *bindnet0_addr* parameter of the *pvecm create* command used for creating a new cluster.

If you have setup a additional NIC with a static address on 10.10.10.1/25 and want to send and receive all cluster communication over this interface you would execute:

```
pvecm create test --ring0_addr 10.10.10.1 --bindnet0_addr 10.10.10.0
```

To check if everything is working properly execute:

```
systemctl status corosync
```

**Separate After Cluster Creation**

You can do this also if you have already created a cluster and want to switch its communication to another network, without rebuilding the whole cluster. This change may lead to short durations of quorum loss in the cluster, as nodes have to restart corosync and come up one after the other on the new network.

Check how to edit the corosync.conf file first. The open it and you should see a file similar to:

```
logging {
  debug: off
  to_syslog: yes
}

nodelist {

  node {
    name: due
    nodeid: 2
    quorum_votes: 1
    ring0_addr: due
  }

  node {
    name: tre
    nodeid: 3
    quorum_votes: 1
    ring0_addr: tre
  }

  node {
    name: uno
    nodeid: 1
    quorum_votes: 1
    ring0_addr: uno
  }

}

quorum {
```

```
    provider: corosync_votequorum
}

totem {
  cluster_name: thomas-testcluster
  config_version: 3
  ip_version: ipv4
  secauth: on
  version: 2
  interface {
    bindnetaddr: 192.168.30.50
    ringnumber: 0
  }

}
```

The first you want to do is add the *name* properties in the node entries if you do not see them already. Those **must** match the node name.

Then replace the address from the *ring0_addr* properties with the new addresses. You may use plain IP addresses or also hostnames here. If you use hostnames ensure that they are resolvable from all nodes.

In my example I want to switch my cluster communication to the 10.10.10.1/25 network. So I replace all *ring0_addr* respectively. I also set the bindetaddr in the totem section of the config to an address of the new network. It can be any address from the subnet configured on the new network interface.

After you increased the *config_version* property the new configuration file should look like:

```
logging {
  debug: off
  to_syslog: yes
}

nodelist {

  node {
    name: due
    nodeid: 2
    quorum_votes: 1
    ring0_addr: 10.10.10.2
  }

  node {
    name: tre
    nodeid: 3
    quorum_votes: 1
    ring0_addr: 10.10.10.3
  }

  node {
    name: uno
    nodeid: 1
    quorum_votes: 1
    ring0_addr: 10.10.10.1
```

```
  }

}

quorum {
  provider: corosync_votequorum
}

totem {
  cluster_name: thomas-testcluster
  config_version: 4
  ip_version: ipv4
  secauth: on
  version: 2
  interface {
    bindnetaddr: 10.10.10.1
    ringnumber: 0
  }

}
```

Now after a final check whether all changed information is correct we save it and see again the edit corosync.conf file section to learn how to bring it in effect.

As our change cannot be enforced live from corosync we have to do an restart.

On a single node execute:

```
systemctl restart corosync
```

Now check if everything is fine:

```
systemctl status corosync
```

If corosync runs again correct restart corosync also on all other nodes. They will then join the cluster membership one by one on the new network.

### 6.7.3  Redundant Ring Protocol

To avoid a single point of failure you should implement counter measurements. This can be on the hardware and operating system level through network bonding.

Corosync itself offers also a possibility to add redundancy through the so called *Redundant Ring Protocol*. This protocol allows running a second totem ring on another network, this network should be physically separated from the other rings network to actually increase availability.

### 6.7.4  RRP On Cluster Creation

The *pvecm create* command provides the additional parameters *bindnetX_addr*, *ringX_addr* and *rrp_mode*, can be used for RRP configuration.

---

**Note**

See the glossary if you do not know what each parameter means.

---

So if you have two networks, one on the 10.10.10.1/24 and the other on the 10.10.20.1/24 subnet you would execute:

```
pvecm create CLUSTERNAME -bindnet0_addr 10.10.10.1 -ring0_addr 10.10.10.1 \
-bindnet1_addr 10.10.20.1 -ring1_addr 10.10.20.1
```

### 6.7.5  RRP On Existing Clusters

You will take similar steps as described in separating the cluster network to enable RRP on an already running cluster. The single difference is, that you will add ring1 and use it instead of ring0.

First add a new interface subsection in the totem section, set its ringnumber property to 1. Set the interfaces bindnetaddr property to an address of the subnet you have configured for your new ring. Further set the rrp_mode to passive, this is the only stable mode.

Then add to each node entry in the nodelist section its new ring1_addr property with the nodes additional ring address.

So if you have two networks, one on the 10.10.10.1/24 and the other on the 10.10.20.1/24 subnet, the final configuration file should look like:

```
totem {
  cluster_name: tweak
  config_version: 9
  ip_version: ipv4
  rrp_mode: passive
  secauth: on
  version: 2
  interface {
    bindnetaddr: 10.10.10.1
    ringnumber: 0
  }
  interface {
    bindnetaddr: 10.10.20.1
    ringnumber: 1
  }
}

nodelist {
  node {
    name: pvecm1
    nodeid: 1
    quorum_votes: 1
    ring0_addr: 10.10.10.1
    ring1_addr: 10.10.20.1
  }

  node {
    name: pvecm2
```

```
    nodeid: 2
    quorum_votes: 1
    ring0_addr: 10.10.10.2
    ring1_addr: 10.10.20.2
  }

  [...] # other cluster nodes here
}

[...] # other remaining config sections here
```

Bring it in effect like described in the edit the corosync.conf file section.

This is a change which cannot take live in effect and needs at least a restart of corosync. Recommended is a restart of the whole cluster.

If you cannot reboot the whole cluster ensure no High Availability services are configured and the stop the corosync service on all nodes. After corosync is stopped on all nodes start it one after the other again.

## 6.8   Corosync Configuration

The /ect/pve/corosync.conf file plays a central role in Proxmox VE cluster. It controls the cluster member ship and its network. For reading more about it check the corosync.conf man page:

```
man corosync.conf
```

For node membership you should always use the pvecm tool provided by Proxmox VE. You may have to edit the configuration file manually for other changes. Here are a few best practice tips for doing this.

### 6.8.1   Edit corosync.conf

Editing the corosync.conf file can be not always straight forward. There are two on each cluster, one in /etc/pve/corosync.conf and the other in /etc/corosync/corosync.conf. Editing the one in our cluster file system will propagate the changes to the local one, but not vice versa.

The configuration will get updated automatically as soon as the file changes. This means changes which can be integrated in a running corosync will take instantly effect. So you should always make a copy and edit that instead, to avoid triggering some unwanted changes by an in between safe.

```
cp /etc/pve/corosync.conf /etc/pve/corosync.conf.new
```

Then open the Config file with your favorite editor, nano and vim.tiny are preinstalled on Proxmox VE for example.

---

**Note**

Always increment the *config_version* number on configuration changes, omitting this can lead to problems.

---

After making the necessary changes create another copy of the current working configuration file. This serves as a backup if the new configuration fails to apply or makes problems in other ways.

---

```
cp /etc/pve/corosync.conf /etc/pve/corosync.conf.bak
```

Then move the new configuration file over the old one:

```
mv /etc/pve/corosync.conf.new /etc/pve/corosync.conf
```

You may check with the commands

```
systemctl status corosync
journalctl -b -u corosync
```

If the change could applied automatically. If not you may have to restart the corosync service via:

```
systemctl restart corosync
```

On errors check the troubleshooting section below.

### 6.8.2 Troubleshooting

#### Issue: *quorum.expected_votes must be configured*

When corosync starts to fail and you get the following message in the system log:

```
[...]
corosync[1647]:   [QUORUM] Quorum provider: corosync_votequorum failed to  ←
   initialize.
corosync[1647]:   [SERV  ] Service engine 'corosync_quorum' failed to load  ←
   for reason
    'configuration error: nodelist or quorum.expected_votes must be  ←
       configured!'
[...]
```

It means that the hostname you set for corosync *ringX_addr* in the configuration could not be resolved.

#### Write Configuration When Not Quorate

If you need to change */etc/pve/corosync.conf* on an node with no quorum, and you know what you do, use:

```
pvecm expected 1
```

This sets the expected vote count to 1 and makes the cluster quorate. You can now fix your configuration, or revert it back to the last working backup.

This is not enough if corosync cannot start anymore. Here its best to edit the local copy of the corosync configuration in */etc/corosync/corosync.conf* so that corosync can start again. Ensure that on all nodes this configuration has the same content to avoid split brains. If you are not sure what went wrong it's best to ask the Proxmox Community to help you.

### 6.8.3  Corosync Configuration Glossary

**ringX_addr**

> This names the different ring addresses for the corosync totem rings used for the cluster communication.

**bindnetaddr**

> Defines to which interface the ring should bind to. It may be any address of the subnet configured on the interface we want to use. In general its the recommended to just use an address a node uses on this interface.

**rrp_mode**

> Specifies the mode of the redundant ring protocol and may be passive, active or none. Note that use of active is highly experimental and not official supported. Passive is the preferred mode, it may double the cluster communication throughput and increases availability.

## 6.9  Cluster Cold Start

It is obvious that a cluster is not quorate when all nodes are offline. This is a common case after a power failure.

---

**Note**

It is always a good idea to use an uninterruptible power supply ("UPS", also called "battery backup") to avoid this state, especially if you want HA.

---

On node startup, service `pve-manager` is started and waits for quorum. Once quorate, it starts all guests which have the `onboot` flag set.

When you turn on nodes, or when power comes back after power failure, it is likely that some nodes boots faster than others. Please keep in mind that guest startup is delayed until you reach quorum.

## 6.10  Guest Migration

Migrating virtual guests to other nodes is a useful feature in a cluster. There are settings to control the behavior of such migrations. This can be done via the configuration file `datacenter.cfg` or for a specific migration via API or command line parameters.

It makes a difference if a Guest is online or offline, or if it has local resources (like a local disk).

For Details about Virtual Machine Migration see the QEMU/KVM Migration Chapter Section 10.3

For Details about Container Migration see the Container Migration Chapter Section 11.9

### 6.10.1  Migration Type

The migration type defines if the migration data should be sent over a encrypted (`secure`) channel or an unencrypted (`insecure`) one. Setting the migration type to insecure means that the RAM content of a virtual guest gets also transfered unencrypted, which can lead to information disclosure of critical data from inside the guest (for example passwords or encryption keys).

Therefore, we strongly recommend using the secure channel if you do not have full control over the network and can not guarantee that no one is eavesdropping to it.

---

**Note**
Storage migration does not follow this setting. Currently, it always sends the storage content over a secure channel.

---

Encryption requires a lot of computing power, so this setting is often changed to "unsafe" to achieve better performance. The impact on modern systems is lower because they implement AES encryption in hardware. The performance impact is particularly evident in fast networks where you can transfer 10 Gbps or more.

### 6.10.2  Migration Network

By default, Proxmox VE uses the network in which cluster communication takes place to send the migration traffic. This is not optimal because sensitive cluster traffic can be disrupted and this network may not have the best bandwidth available on the node.

Setting the migration network parameter allows the use of a dedicated network for the entire migration traffic. In addition to the memory, this also affects the storage traffic for offline migrations.

The migration network is set as a network in the CIDR notation. This has the advantage that you do not have to set individual IP addresses for each node. Proxmox VE can determine the real address on the destination node from the network specified in the CIDR form. To enable this, the network must be specified so that each node has one, but only one IP in the respective network.

**Example**

We assume that we have a three-node setup with three separate networks. One for public communication with the Internet, one for cluster communication and a very fast one, which we want to use as a dedicated network for migration.

A network configuration for such a setup might look as follows:

```
iface eno1 inet manual

# public network
auto vmbr0
iface vmbr0 inet static
    address 192.X.Y.57
    netmask 255.255.250.0
    gateway 192.X.Y.1
    bridge_ports eno1
    bridge_stp off
    bridge_fd 0
```

```
# cluster network
auto eno2
iface eno2 inet static
    address   10.1.1.1
    netmask   255.255.255.0

# fast network
auto eno3
iface eno3 inet static
    address   10.1.2.1
    netmask   255.255.255.0
```

Here, we will use the network 10.1.2.0/24 as a migration network. For a single migration, you can do this using the migration_network parameter of the command line tool:

```
# qm migrate 106 tre --online --migration_network 10.1.2.0/24
```

To configure this as the default network for all migrations in the cluster, set the migration property of the /etc/pve/datacenter.cfg file:

```
# use dedicated migration network
migration: secure,network=10.1.2.0/24
```

---

**Note**

The migration type must always be set when the migration network gets set in /etc/pve/datacen
ter.cfg.

---

# Chapter 7

# Proxmox Cluster File System (pmxcfs)

The Proxmox Cluster file system ("pmxcfs") is a database-driven file system for storing configuration files, replicated in real time to all cluster nodes using `corosync`. We use this to store all PVE related configuration files.

Although the file system stores all data inside a persistent database on disk, a copy of the data resides in RAM. That imposes restriction on the maximum size, which is currently 30MB. This is still enough to store the configuration of several thousand virtual machines.

This system provides the following advantages:

- seamless replication of all configuration to all nodes in real time

- provides strong consistency checks to avoid duplicate VM IDs

- read-only when a node loses quorum

- automatic updates of the corosync cluster configuration to all nodes

- includes a distributed locking mechanism

## 7.1 POSIX Compatibility

The file system is based on FUSE, so the behavior is POSIX like. But some feature are simply not implemented, because we do not need them:

- you can just generate normal files and directories, but no symbolic links, . . .

- you can't rename non-empty directories (because this makes it easier to guarantee that VMIDs are unique).

- you can't change file permissions (permissions are based on path)

- `O_EXCL` creates were not atomic (like old NFS)

- `O_TRUNC` creates are not atomic (FUSE restriction)

## 7.2   File Access Rights

All files and directories are owned by user `root` and have group `www-data`. Only root has write permissions, but group `www-data` can read most files. Files below the following paths:

```
/etc/pve/priv/
/etc/pve/nodes/${NAME}/priv/
```

are only accessible by root.

## 7.3   Technology

We use the Corosync Cluster Engine for cluster communication, and SQlite for the database file. The file system is implemented in user space using FUSE.

## 7.4   File System Layout

The file system is mounted at:

```
/etc/pve
```

### 7.4.1   Files

| | |
|---|---|
| `corosync.conf` | Corosync cluster configuration file (previous to Proxmox VE 4.x this file was called cluster.conf) |
| `storage.cfg` | Proxmox VE storage configuration |
| `datacenter.cfg` | Proxmox VE datacenter wide configuration (keyboard layout, proxy, . . . ) |
| `user.cfg` | Proxmox VE access control configuration (users/groups/. . . ) |
| `domains.cfg` | Proxmox VE authentication domains |
| `status.cfg` | Proxmox VE external metrics server configuration |
| `authkey.pub` | Public key used by ticket system |
| `pve-root-ca.pem` | Public certificate of cluster CA |
| `priv/shadow.cfg` | Shadow password file |
| `priv/authkey.key` | Private key used by ticket system |
| `priv/pve-root-ca.key` | Private key of cluster CA |
| `nodes/<NAME>/pve-ssl.pem` | Public SSL certificate for web server (signed by cluster CA) |
| `nodes/<NAME>/pve-ssl.key` | Private SSL key for `pve-ssl.pem` |
| `nodes/<NAME>/pveproxy-ssl.pem` | Public SSL certificate (chain) for web server (optional override for `pve-ssl.pem`) |
| `nodes/<NAME>/pveproxy-ssl.key` | Private SSL key for `pveproxy-ssl.pem` (optional) |

| nodes/<NAME>/qemu-server/<VMID>. conf | VM configuration data for KVM VMs |
| nodes/<NAME>/lxc/<VMID>.conf | VM configuration data for LXC containers |
| firewall/cluster.fw | Firewall configuration applied to all nodes |
| firewall/<NAME>.fw | Firewall configuration for individual nodes |
| firewall/<VMID>.fw | Firewall configuration for VMs and Containers |

### 7.4.2 Symbolic links

| local | nodes/<LOCAL_HOST_NAME> |
| qemu-server | nodes/<LOCAL_HOST_NAME>/qemu-server/ |
| lxc | nodes/<LOCAL_HOST_NAME>/lxc/ |

### 7.4.3 Special status files for debugging (JSON)

| .version | File versions (to detect file modifications) |
| .members | Info about cluster members |
| .vmlist | List of all VMs |
| .clusterlog | Cluster log (last 50 entries) |
| .rrd | RRD data (most recent entries) |

### 7.4.4 Enable/Disable debugging

You can enable verbose syslog messages with:

```
echo "1" >/etc/pve/.debug
```

And disable verbose syslog messages with:

```
echo "0" >/etc/pve/.debug
```

## 7.5 Recovery

If you have major problems with your Proxmox VE host, e.g. hardware issues, it could be helpful to just copy the pmxcfs database file /var/lib/pve-cluster/config.db and move it to a new Proxmox VE host. On the new host (with nothing running), you need to stop the pve-cluster service and replace the config.db file (needed permissions 0600). Second, adapt /etc/hostname and /etc/hosts according to the lost Proxmox VE host, then reboot and check. (And don't forget your VM/CT data)

### 7.5.1 Remove Cluster configuration

The recommended way is to reinstall the node after you removed it from your cluster. This makes sure that all secret cluster/ssh keys and any shared configuration data is destroyed.

In some cases, you might prefer to put a node back to local mode without reinstall, which is described in Separate A Node Without Reinstalling

### 7.5.2 Recovering/Moving Guests from Failed Nodes

For the guest configuration files in `nodes/<NAME>/qemu-server/` (VMs) and `nodes/<NAME>/lxc/` (containers), Proxmox VE sees the containing node `<NAME>` as owner of the respective guest. This concept enables the usage of local locks instead of expensive cluster-wide locks for preventing concurrent guest configuration changes.

As a consequence, if the owning node of a guest fails (e.g., because of a power outage, fencing event, ..), a regular migration is not possible (even if all the disks are located on shared storage) because such a local lock on the (dead) owning node is unobtainable. This is not a problem for HA-managed guests, as Proxmox VE's High Availability stack includes the necessary (cluster-wide) locking and watchdog functionality to ensure correct and automatic recovery of guests from fenced nodes.

If a non-HA-managed guest has only shared disks (and no other local resources which are only available on the failed node are configured), a manual recovery is possible by simply moving the guest configuration file from the failed node's directory in `/etc/pve/` to an alive node's directory (which changes the logical owner or location of the guest).

For example, recovering the VM with ID `100` from a dead `node1` to another node `node2` works with the following command executed when logged in as root on any member node of the cluster:

```
mv /etc/pve/nodes/node1/qemu-server/100.conf /etc/pve/nodes/node2/
```

**Warning**
Before manually recovering a guest like this, make absolutely sure that the failed source node is really powered off/fenced. Otherwise Proxmox VE's locking principles are violated by the `mv` command, which can have unexpected consequences.

**Warning**
Guest with local disks (or other local resources which are only available on the dead node) are not recoverable like this. Either wait for the failed node to rejoin the cluster or restore such guests from backups.

# Chapter 8

# Proxmox VE Storage

The Proxmox VE storage model is very flexible. Virtual machine images can either be stored on one or several local storages, or on shared storage like NFS or iSCSI (NAS, SAN). There are no limits, and you may configure as many storage pools as you like. You can use all storage technologies available for Debian Linux.

One major benefit of storing VMs on shared storage is the ability to live-migrate running machines without any downtime, as all nodes in the cluster have direct access to VM disk images. There is no need to copy VM image data, so live migration is very fast in that case.

The storage library (package `libpve-storage-perl`) uses a flexible plugin system to provide a common interface to all storage types. This can be easily adopted to include further storage types in future.

## 8.1  Storage Types

There are basically two different classes of storage types:

**Block level storage**
> Allows to store large *raw* images. It is usually not possible to store other files (ISO, backups, ..) on such storage types. Most modern block level storage implementations support snapshots and clones. RADOS, Sheepdog and GlusterFS are distributed systems, replicating storage data to different nodes.

**File level storage**
> They allow access to a full featured (POSIX) file system. They are more flexible, and allows you to store any content type. ZFS is probably the most advanced system, and it has full support for snapshots and clones.

Table 8.1: Available storage types

| Description | PVE type | Level | Shared | Snapshots | Stable |
|-------------|----------|-------|--------|-----------|--------|
| ZFS (local) | `zfspool` | file | no | yes | yes |
| Directory | `dir` | file | no | no[1] | yes |
| NFS | `nfs` | file | yes | no[1] | yes |
| GlusterFS | `glusterfs` | file | yes | no[1] | yes |
| LVM | `lvm` | block | no[2] | no | yes |

Table 8.1: (continued)

| Description | PVE type | Level | Shared | Snapshots | Stable |
|---|---|---|---|---|---|
| LVM-thin | lvmthin | block | no | yes | yes |
| iSCSI/kernel | iscsi | block | yes | no | yes |
| iSCSI/libiscsi | iscsidir ect | block | yes | no | yes |
| Ceph/RBD | rbd | block | yes | yes | yes |
| Sheepdog | sheepdog | block | yes | yes | beta |
| ZFS over iSCSI | zfs | block | yes | yes | yes |

[1]: On file based storages, snapshots are possible with the *qcow2* format.

[2]: It is possible to use LVM on top of an iSCSI storage. That way you get a `shared` LVM storage.

### 8.1.1 Thin Provisioning

A number of storages, and the Qemu image format `qcow2`, support *thin provisioning*. With thin provisioning activated, only the blocks that the guest system actually use will be written to the storage.

Say for instance you create a VM with a 32GB hard disk, and after installing the guest system OS, the root file system of the VM contains 3 GB of data. In that case only 3GB are written to the storage, even if the guest VM sees a 32GB hard drive. In this way thin provisioning allows you to create disk images which are larger than the currently available storage blocks. You can create large disk images for your VMs, and when the need arises, add more disks to your storage without resizing the VMs' file systems.

All storage types which have the "Snapshots" feature also support thin provisioning.

**Caution**
If a storage runs full, all guests using volumes on that storage receive IO errors. This can cause file system inconsistencies and may corrupt your data. So it is advisable to avoid over-provisioning of your storage resources, or carefully observe free space to avoid such conditions.

## 8.2 Storage Configuration

All Proxmox VE related storage configuration is stored within a single text file at `/etc/pve/storage.cfg`. As this file is within `/etc/pve/`, it gets automatically distributed to all cluster nodes. So all nodes share the same storage configuration.

Sharing storage configuration make perfect sense for shared storage, because the same "shared" storage is accessible from all nodes. But is also useful for local storage types. In this case such local storage is available on all nodes, but it is physically different and can have totally different content.

## 8.2.1   Storage Pools

Each storage pool has a `<type>`, and is uniquely identified by its `<STORAGE_ID>`. A pool configuration looks like this:

```
<type>: <STORAGE_ID>
        <property> <value>
        <property> <value>
        . . .
```

The `<type>:   <STORAGE_ID>` line starts the pool definition, which is then followed by a list of properties. Most properties have values, but some of them come with reasonable default. In that case you can omit the value.

To be more specific, take a look at the default storage configuration after installation. It contains one special local storage pool named `local`, which refers to the directory `/var/lib/vz` and is always available. The Proxmox VE installer creates additional storage entries depending on the storage type chosen at installation time.

**Default storage configuration (/etc/pve/storage.cfg)**

```
dir: local
        path /var/lib/vz
        content iso,vztmpl,backup

# default image store on LVM based installation
lvmthin: local-lvm
        thinpool data
        vgname pve
        content rootdir,images

# default image store on ZFS based installation
zfspool: local-zfs
        pool rpool/data
        sparse
        content images,rootdir
```

## 8.2.2   Common Storage Properties

A few storage properties are common among different storage types.

**nodes**
   List of cluster node names where this storage is usable/accessible.  One can use this property to restrict storage access to a limited set of nodes.

**content**
   A storage can support several content types, for example virtual disk images, cdrom iso images, container templates or container root directories. Not all storage types support all content types. One can set this property to select for what this storage is used for.

**images**
    KVM-Qemu VM images.

**rootdir**
    Allow to store container data.

**vztmpl**
    Container templates.

**backup**
    Backup files (`vzdump`).

**iso**
    ISO images

**shared**
    Mark storage as shared.

**disable**
    You can use this flag to disable the storage completely.

**maxfiles**
    Maximum number of backup files per VM. Use `0` for unlimited.

**format**
    Default image format (`raw | qcow2 | vmdk`)

> **Warning**
> It is not advisable to use the same storage pool on different Proxmox VE clusters. Some storage operation need exclusive access to the storage, so proper locking is required. While this is implemented within a cluster, it does not work between different clusters.

## 8.3 Volumes

We use a special notation to address storage data. When you allocate data from a storage pool, it returns such a volume identifier. A volume is identified by the `<STORAGE_ID>`, followed by a storage type dependent volume name, separated by colon. A valid `<VOLUME_ID>` looks like:

```
local:230/example-image.raw
```

```
local:iso/debian-501-amd64-netinst.iso
```

```
local:vztmpl/debian-5.0-joomla_1.5.9-1_i386.tar.gz
```

```
iscsi-storage:0.0.2.scsi-14 ↩
    f504e46494c4500494b5042546d2d646744372d31616d61
```

To get the file system path for a `<VOLUME_ID>` use:

```
pvesm path <VOLUME_ID>
```

### 8.3.1  Volume Ownership

There exists an ownership relation for `image` type volumes. Each such volume is owned by a VM or Container. For example volume `local:230/example-image.raw` is owned by VM 230. Most storage backends encodes this ownership information into the volume name.

When you remove a VM or Container, the system also removes all associated volumes which are owned by that VM or Container.

# 8.4  Using the Command Line Interface

It is recommended to familiarize yourself with the concept behind storage pools and volume identifiers, but in real life, you are not forced to do any of those low level operations on the command line. Normally, allocation and removal of volumes is done by the VM and Container management tools.

Nevertheless, there is a command line tool called `pvesm` ("Proxmox VE Storage Manager"), which is able to perform common storage management tasks.

### 8.4.1  Examples

Add storage pools

```
pvesm add <TYPE> <STORAGE_ID> <OPTIONS>
pvesm add dir <STORAGE_ID> --path <PATH>
pvesm add nfs <STORAGE_ID> --path <PATH> --server <SERVER> --export  ↩
    <EXPORT>
pvesm add lvm <STORAGE_ID> --vgname <VGNAME>
pvesm add iscsi <STORAGE_ID> --portal <HOST[:PORT]> --target <TARGET ↩
    >
```

Disable storage pools

```
pvesm set <STORAGE_ID> --disable 1
```

Enable storage pools

```
pvesm set <STORAGE_ID> --disable 0
```

Change/set storage options

```
pvesm set <STORAGE_ID> <OPTIONS>
pvesm set <STORAGE_ID> --shared 1
pvesm set local --format qcow2
pvesm set <STORAGE_ID> --content iso
```

Remove storage pools. This does not delete any data, and does not disconnect or unmount anything. It just removes the storage configuration.

```
pvesm remove <STORAGE_ID>
```

Allocate volumes

```
pvesm alloc <STORAGE_ID> <VMID> <name> <size> [--format <raw|qcow2>]
```

Allocate a 4G volume in local storage. The name is auto-generated if you pass an empty string as `<name>`

```
pvesm alloc local <VMID> '' 4G
```

Free volumes

```
pvesm free <VOLUME_ID>
```

 **Warning**
This really destroys all volume data.

List storage status

```
pvesm status
```

List storage contents

```
pvesm list <STORAGE_ID> [--vmid <VMID>]
```

List volumes allocated by VMID

```
pvesm list <STORAGE_ID> --vmid <VMID>
```

List iso images

```
pvesm list <STORAGE_ID> --iso
```

List container templates

```
pvesm list <STORAGE_ID> --vztmpl
```

Show file system path for a volume

```
pvesm path <VOLUME_ID>
```

## 8.5 Directory Backend

Storage pool type: `dir`

Proxmox VE can use local directories or locally mounted shares for storage. A directory is a file level storage, so you can store any content type like virtual disk images, containers, templates, ISO images or backup files.

**Note**
You can mount additional storages via standard linux `/etc/fstab`, and then define a directory storage for that mount point. This way you can use any file system supported by Linux.

This backend assumes that the underlying directory is POSIX compatible, but nothing else. This implies that you cannot create snapshots at the storage level. But there exists a workaround for VM images using the `qcow2` file format, because that format supports snapshots internally.

> **Tip**
> Some storage types do not support `O_DIRECT`, so you can't use cache mode `none` with such storages. Simply use cache mode `writeback` instead.

We use a predefined directory layout to store different content types into different sub-directories. This layout is used by all file level storage backends.

Table 8.2: Directory layout

| Content type | Subdir |
|---|---|
| VM images | `images/<VMID>/` |
| ISO images | `template/iso/` |
| Container templates | `template/cache/` |
| Backup files | `dump/` |

### 8.5.1  Configuration

This backend supports all common storage properties, and adds an additional property called `path` to specify the directory. This needs to be an absolute file system path.

**Configuration Example (/etc/pve/storage.cfg)**

```
dir: backup
        path /mnt/backup
        content backup
        maxfiles 7
```

Above configuration defines a storage pool called `backup`. That pool can be used to store up to 7 backups (`maxfiles 7`) per VM. The real path for the backup files is `/mnt/backup/dump/....`

### 8.5.2  File naming conventions

This backend uses a well defined naming scheme for VM images:

```
vm-<VMID>-<NAME>.<FORMAT>
```

**\<VMID\>**
    This specifies the owner VM.

**<NAME>**
> This can be an arbitrary name (`ascii`) without white space. The backend uses `disk-[N]` as default, where `[N]` is replaced by an integer to make the name unique.

**<FORMAT>**
> Specifies the image format (`raw`|`qcow2`|`vmdk`).

When you create a VM template, all VM images are renamed to indicate that they are now read-only, and can be used as a base image for clones:

```
base-<VMID>-<NAME>.<FORMAT>
```

---

**Note**

Such base images are used to generate cloned images. So it is important that those files are read-only, and never get modified. The backend changes the access mode to `0444`, and sets the immutable flag (`chattr +i`) if the storage supports that.

---

### 8.5.3 Storage Features

As mentioned above, most file systems do not support snapshots out of the box. To workaround that problem, this backend is able to use `qcow2` internal snapshot capabilities.

Same applies to clones. The backend uses the `qcow2` base image feature to create clones.

Table 8.3: Storage features for backend `dir`

| Content types | Image formats | Shared | Snapshots | Clones |
|---|---|---|---|---|
| images rootdir vztempl iso backup | raw qcow2 vmdk subvol | no | qcow2 | qcow2 |

### 8.5.4 Examples

Please use the following command to allocate a 4GB image on storage `local`:

```
# pvesm alloc local 100 vm-100-disk10.raw 4G
Formatting '/var/lib/vz/images/100/vm-100-disk10.raw', fmt=raw size ↩
   =4294967296
successfully created 'local:100/vm-100-disk10.raw'
```

---

**Note**

The image name must conform to above naming conventions.

---

The real file system path is shown with:

```
# pvesm path local:100/vm-100-disk10.raw
/var/lib/vz/images/100/vm-100-disk10.raw
```

And you can remove the image with:

```
# pvesm free local:100/vm-100-disk10.raw
```

## 8.6 NFS Backend

Storage pool type: `nfs`

The NFS backend is based on the directory backend, so it shares most properties. The directory layout and the file naming conventions are the same. The main advantage is that you can directly configure the NFS server properties, so the backend can mount the share automatically. There is no need to modify `/etc/fstab`. The backend can also test if the server is online, and provides a method to query the server for exported shares.

### 8.6.1 Configuration

The backend supports all common storage properties, except the shared flag, which is always set. Additionally, the following properties are used to configure the NFS server:

**server**
> Server IP or DNS name. To avoid DNS lookup delays, it is usually preferable to use an IP address instead of a DNS name - unless you have a very reliable DNS server, or list the server in the local `/etc/hosts` file.

**export**
> NFS export path (as listed by `pvesm nfsscan`).

You can also set NFS mount options:

**path**
> The local mount point (defaults to `/mnt/pve/<STORAGE_ID>/`).

**options**
> NFS mount options (see `man nfs`).

**Configuration Example (/etc/pve/storage.cfg)**

```
nfs: iso-templates
        path /mnt/pve/iso-templates
        server 10.0.0.10
        export /space/iso-templates
        options vers=3,soft
        content iso,vztmpl
```

---

**Tip**
After an NFS request times out, NFS request are retried indefinitely by default. This can lead to unexpected hangs on the client side. For read-only content, it is worth to consider the NFS `soft` option, which limits the number of retries to three.

---

### 8.6.2  Storage Features

NFS does not support snapshots, but the backend uses `qcow2` features to implement snapshots and cloning.

Table 8.4: Storage features for backend `nfs`

| Content types | Image formats | Shared | Snapshots | Clones |
|---|---|---|---|---|
| images<br>rootdir<br>vztempl iso<br>backup | raw qcow2<br>vmdk subvol | yes | qcow2 | qcow2 |

### 8.6.3  Examples

You can get a list of exported NFS shares with:

```
# pvesm nfsscan <server>
```

## 8.7  GlusterFS Backend

Storage pool type: `glusterfs`

GlusterFS is a scalable network file system. The system uses a modular design, runs on commodity hardware, and can provide a highly available enterprise storage at low costs. Such system is capable of scaling to several petabytes, and can handle thousands of clients.

---

**Note**
After a node/brick crash, GlusterFS does a full `rsync` to make sure data is consistent. This can take a very long time with large files, so this backend is not suitable to store large VM images.

---

### 8.7.1  Configuration

The backend supports all common storage properties, and adds the following GlusterFS specific options:

**server**
GlusterFS volfile server IP or DNS name.

---

**server2**
> Backup volfile server IP or DNS name.

**volume**
> GlusterFS Volume.

**transport**
> GlusterFS transport: `tcp`, `unix` or `rdma`

**Configuration Example (/etc/pve/storage.cfg)**

```
glusterfs: Gluster
        server 10.2.3.4
        server2 10.2.3.5
        volume glustervol
        content images,iso
```

### 8.7.2 File naming conventions

The directory layout and the file naming conventions are inherited from the `dir` backend.

### 8.7.3 Storage Features

The storage provides a file level interface, but no native snapshot/clone implementation.

Table 8.5: Storage features for backend `glusterfs`

| Content types | Image formats | Shared | Snapshots | Clones |
|---|---|---|---|---|
| images vztempl iso backup | raw qcow2 vmdk | yes | qcow2 | qcow2 |

## 8.8 Local ZFS Pool Backend

Storage pool type: `zfspool`

This backend allows you to access local ZFS pools (or ZFS file systems inside such pools).

### 8.8.1 Configuration

The backend supports the common storage properties `content`, `nodes`, `disable`, and the following ZFS specific properties:

**pool**

Select the ZFS pool/filesystem. All allocations are done within that pool.

**blocksize**

Set ZFS blocksize parameter.

**sparse**

Use ZFS thin-provisioning. A sparse volume is a volume whose reservation is not equal to the volume size.

**Configuration Example (/etc/pve/storage.cfg)**

```
zfspool: vmdata
        pool tank/vmdata
        content rootdir,images
        sparse
```

### 8.8.2   File naming conventions

The backend uses the following naming scheme for VM images:

```
vm-<VMID>-<NAME>        // normal VM images
base-<VMID>-<NAME>      // template VM image (read-only)
subvol-<VMID>-<NAME>   // subvolumes (ZFS filesystem for containers)
```

**<VMID>**

This specifies the owner VM.

**<NAME>**

This can be an arbitrary name (ascii) without white space. The backend uses disk[N] as default, where [N] is replaced by an integer to make the name unique.

### 8.8.3   Storage Features

ZFS is probably the most advanced storage type regarding snapshot and cloning. The backend uses ZFS datasets for both VM images (format raw) and container data (format subvol). ZFS properties are inherited from the parent dataset, so you can simply set defaults on the parent dataset.

Table 8.6: Storage features for backend zfs

| Content types | Image formats | Shared | Snapshots | Clones |
|---|---|---|---|---|
| images<br>rootdir | raw subvol | no | yes | yes |

### 8.8.4  Examples

It is recommended to create an extra ZFS file system to store your VM images:

```
# zfs create tank/vmdata
```

To enable compression on that newly allocated file system:

```
# zfs set compression=on tank/vmdata
```

You can get a list of available ZFS filesystems with:

```
# pvesm zfsscan
```

# 8.9  LVM Backend

Storage pool type: `lvm`

LVM is a light software layer on top of hard disks and partitions. It can be used to split available disk space into smaller logical volumes. LVM is widely used on Linux and makes managing hard drives easier.

Another use case is to put LVM on top of a big iSCSI LUN. That way you can easily manage space on that iSCSI LUN, which would not be possible otherwise, because the iSCSI specification does not define a management interface for space allocation.

### 8.9.1  Configuration

The LVM backend supports the common storage properties `content`, `nodes`, `disable`, and the following LVM specific properties:

**vgname**
> LVM volume group name. This must point to an existing volume group.

**base**
> Base volume. This volume is automatically activated before accessing the storage. This is mostly useful when the LVM volume group resides on a remote iSCSI server.

**saferemove**
> Zero-out data when removing LVs. When removing a volume, this makes sure that all data gets erased.

**saferemove_throughput**
> Wipe throughput (`cstream -t` parameter value).

**Configuration Example (/etc/pve/storage.cfg)**

```
lvm: myspace
        vgname myspace
        content rootdir,images
```

### 8.9.2  File naming conventions

The backend use basically the same naming conventions as the ZFS pool backend.

```
vm-<VMID>-<NAME>        // normal VM images
```

### 8.9.3  Storage Features

LVM is a typical block storage, but this backend does not support snapshot and clones. Unfortunately, normal LVM snapshots are quite inefficient, because they interfere all writes on the whole volume group during snapshot time.

One big advantage is that you can use it on top of a shared storage, for example an iSCSI LUN. The backend itself implement proper cluster wide locking.

---

**Tip**

The newer LVM-thin backend allows snapshot and clones, but does not support shared storage.

---

Table 8.7: Storage features for backend `lvm`

| Content types | Image formats | Shared | Snapshots | Clones |
|---|---|---|---|---|
| images<br>rootdir | raw | possible | no | no |

### 8.9.4  Examples

List available volume groups:

```
# pvesm lvmscan
```

## 8.10  LVM thin Backend

Storage pool type: `lvmthin`

LVM normally allocates blocks when you create a volume. LVM thin pools instead allocates blocks when they are written. This behaviour is called thin-provisioning, because volumes can be much larger than physically available space.

You can use the normal LVM command line tools to manage and create LVM thin pools (see `man lvmthin` for details). Assuming you already have a LVM volume group called `pve`, the following commands create a new LVM thin pool (size 100G) called `data`:

```
lvcreate -L 100G -n data pve
lvconvert --type thin-pool pve/data
```

### 8.10.1 Configuration

The LVM thin backend supports the common storage properties `content`, `nodes`, `disable`, and the following LVM specific properties:

**vgname**
> LVM volume group name. This must point to an existing volume group.

**thinpool**
> The name of the LVM thin pool.

**Configuration Example (/etc/pve/storage.cfg)**

```
lvmthin: local-lvm
        thinpool data
        vgname pve
        content rootdir,images
```

### 8.10.2 File naming conventions

The backend use basically the same naming conventions as the ZFS pool backend.

```
vm-<VMID>-<NAME>        // normal VM images
```

### 8.10.3 Storage Features

LVM thin is a block storage, but fully supports snapshots and clones efficiently. New volumes are automatically initialized with zero.

It must be mentioned that LVM thin pools cannot be shared across multiple nodes, so you can only use them as local storage.

Table 8.8: Storage features for backend `lvmthin`

| Content types | Image formats | Shared | Snapshots | Clones |
|---|---|---|---|---|
| images rootdir | raw | no | yes | yes |

### 8.10.4 Examples

List available LVM thin pools on volume group `pve`:

```
# pvesm lvmthinscan pve
```

## 8.11  Open-iSCSI initiator

Storage pool type: `iscsi`

iSCSI is a widely employed technology used to connect to storage servers. Almost all storage vendors support iSCSI. There are also open source iSCSI target solutions available, e.g. OpenMediaVault, which is based on Debian.

To use this backend, you need to install the `open-iscsi` package. This is a standard Debian package, but it is not installed by default to save resources.

```
# apt-get install open-iscsi
```

Low-level iscsi management task can be done using the `iscsiadm` tool.

### 8.11.1  Configuration

The backend supports the common storage properties `content`, `nodes`, `disable`, and the following iSCSI specific properties:

**portal**
> iSCSI portal (IP or DNS name with optional port).

**target**
> iSCSI target.

**Configuration Example (/etc/pve/storage.cfg)**

```
iscsi: mynas
     portal 10.10.10.1
     target iqn.2006-01.openfiler.com:tsn.dcb5aaaddd
     content none
```

---

**Tip**
If you want to use LVM on top of iSCSI, it make sense to set `content none`. That way it is not possible to create VMs using iSCSI LUNs directly.

---

### 8.11.2  File naming conventions

The iSCSI protocol does not define an interface to allocate or delete data. Instead, that needs to be done on the target side and is vendor specific. The target simply exports them as numbered LUNs. So Proxmox VE iSCSI volume names just encodes some information about the LUN as seen by the linux kernel.

### 8.11.3  Storage Features

iSCSI is a block level type storage, and provides no management interface. So it is usually best to export one big LUN, and setup LVM on top of that LUN. You can then use the LVM plugin to manage the storage on that iSCSI LUN.

Table 8.9: Storage features for backend `iscsi`

| Content types | Image formats | Shared | Snapshots | Clones |
|---|---|---|---|---|
| images none | raw | yes | no | no |

### 8.11.4  Examples

Scan a remote iSCSI portal, and returns a list of possible targets:

```
pvesm iscsiscan -portal <HOST[:PORT]>
```

## 8.12   User Mode iSCSI Backend

Storage pool type: `iscsidirect`

This backend provides basically the same functionality as the Open-iSCSI backed, but uses a user-level library (package `libiscsi2`) to implement it.

It should be noted that there are no kernel drivers involved, so this can be viewed as performance optimization. But this comes with the drawback that you cannot use LVM on top of such iSCSI LUN. So you need to manage all space allocations at the storage server side.

### 8.12.1  Configuration

The user mode iSCSI backend uses the same configuration options as the Open-iSCSI backed.

**Configuration Example (/etc/pve/storage.cfg)**

```
iscsidirect: faststore
    portal 10.10.10.1
    target iqn.2006-01.openfiler.com:tsn.dcb5aaaddd
```

### 8.12.2  Storage Features

---

**Note**
This backend works with VMs only. Containers cannot use this driver.

---

Table 8.10: Storage features for backend `iscsidirect`

| Content types | Image formats | Shared | Snapshots | Clones |
|---|---|---|---|---|
| images | raw | yes | no | no |

## 8.13    Ceph RADOS Block Devices (RBD)

Storage pool type: `rbd`

Ceph is a distributed object store and file system designed to provide excellent performance, reliability and scalability. RADOS block devices implement a feature rich block level storage, and you get the following advantages:

- thin provisioning

- resizable volumes

- distributed and redundant (striped over multiple OSDs)

- full snapshot and clone capabilities

- self healing

- no single point of failure

- scalable to the exabyte level

- kernel and user space implementation available

---

**Note**

For smaller deployments, it is also possible to run Ceph services directly on your Proxmox VE nodes. Recent hardware has plenty of CPU power and RAM, so running storage services and VMs on same node is possible.

---

### 8.13.1    Configuration

This backend supports the common storage properties `nodes`, `disable`, `content`, and the following `rbd` specific properties:

**monhost**
> List of monitor daemon IPs.

**pool**
> Ceph pool name.

**username**
> RBD user Id.

**krbd**
> Access rbd through krbd kernel module. This is required if you want to use the storage for containers.

**Configuration Example (/etc/pve/storage.cfg)**

```
rbd: ceph3
        monhost 10.1.1.20 10.1.1.21 10.1.1.22
        pool ceph3
        content images
        username admin
```

---

**Tip**

You can use the `rbd` utility to do low-level management tasks.

---

## 8.13.2 Authentication

If you use `cephx` authentication, you need to copy the keyfile from Ceph to Proxmox VE host.

Create the directory `/etc/pve/priv/ceph` with

```
mkdir /etc/pve/priv/ceph
```

Then copy the keyring

```
scp <cephserver>:/etc/ceph/ceph.client.admin.keyring /etc/pve/priv/ ↩
   ceph/<STORAGE_ID>.keyring
```

The keyring must be named to match your `<STORAGE_ID>`. Copying the keyring generally requires root privileges.

## 8.13.3 Storage Features

The `rbd` backend is a block level storage, and implements full snapshot and clone functionality.

Table 8.11: Storage features for backend `rbd`

| Content types | Image formats | Shared | Snapshots | Clones |
|---|---|---|---|---|
| images<br>rootdir | raw | yes | yes | yes |

# Chapter 9

# Storage Replication

The `pvesr` command line tool manages the Proxmox VE storage replication framework. Storage replication brings redundancy for guests using local storage and reduces migration time.

It replicates guest volumes to another node so that all data is available without using shared storage. Replication uses snapshots to minimize traffic sent over the network. Therefore, new data is sent only incrementally after an initial full sync. In the case of a node failure, your guest data is still available on the replicated node.

The replication will be done automatically in configurable intervals. The minimum replication interval is one minute and the maximal interval is once a week. The format used to specify those intervals is a subset of `systemd` calendar events, see Schedule Format Section 9.2 section:

Every guest can be replicated to multiple target nodes, but a guest cannot get replicated twice to the same target node.

Each replications bandwidth can be limited, to avoid overloading a storage or server.

Virtual guest with active replication cannot currently use online migration. Offline migration is supported in general. If you migrate to a node where the guests data is already replicated only the changes since the last synchronisation (so called `delta`) must be sent, this reduces the required time significantly. In this case the replication direction will also switch nodes automatically after the migration finished.

For example: VM100 is currently on `nodeA` and gets replicated to `nodeB`. You migrate it to `nodeB`, so now it gets automatically replicated back from `nodeB` to `nodeA`.

If you migrate to a node where the guest is not replicated, the whole disk data must send over. After the migration the replication job continues to replicate this guest to the configured nodes.

---

**Important**

High-Availability is allowed in combination with storage replication, but it has the following implications:

- redistributing services after a more preferred node comes online will lead to errors.

- recovery works, but there may be some data loss between the last synced time and the time a node failed.

---

## 9.1 Supported Storage Types

Table 9.1: Storage Types

| Description | PVE type | Snapshots | Stable |
|---|---|---|---|
| ZFS (local) | zfspool | yes | yes |

## 9.2 Schedule Format

Proxmox VE has a very flexible replication scheduler. It is based on the systemd time calendar event format.[1] Calendar events may be used to refer to one or more points in time in a single expression.

Such a calendar event uses the following format:

```
[day(s)] [[start-time(s)][/repetition-time(s)]]
```

This allows you to configure a set of days on which the job should run. You can also set one or more start times, it tells the replication scheduler the moments in time when a job should start. With this information we could create a job which runs every workday at 10 PM: `'mon,tue,wed,thu,fri 22'` which could be abbreviated to: `'mon..fri 22'`, most reasonable schedules can be written quite intuitive this way.

---

**Note**
Hours are set in 24h format.

---

To allow easier and shorter configuration one or more repetition times can be set. They indicate that on the start-time(s) itself and the start-time(s) plus all multiples of the repetition value replications will be done. If you want to start replication at 8 AM and repeat it every 15 minutes until 9 AM you would use: `'8:00/15'`

Here you see also that if no hour separation (`:`) is used the value gets interpreted as minute. If such a separation is used the value on the left denotes the hour(s) and the value on the right denotes the minute(s). Further, you can use `*` to match all possible values.

To get additional ideas look at more Examples below Section 9.2.2.

### 9.2.1 Detailed Specification

**days**

> Days are specified with an abbreviated English version: sun, mon, tue, wed, thu, fri and sat. You may use multiple days as a comma-separated list. A range of days can also be set by specifying the start and end day separated by "..", for example mon..fri. Those formats can be also mixed. If omitted `'*'` is assumed.

**time-format**

> A time format consists of hours and minutes interval lists. Hours and minutes are separated by `':'`. Both, hour and minute, can be list and ranges of values, using the same format as days. First come hours then minutes, hours can be omitted if not needed, in this case `'*'` is assumed for the value of hours. The valid range for values is 0-23 for hours and 0-59 for minutes.

---

[1] see man 7 sytemd.time for more information

### 9.2.2 Examples:

Table 9.2: Schedule Examples

| Schedule String | Alternative | Meaning |
|---|---|---|
| mon,tue,wed,thu,fri | mon..fri | All working days at 0:00 |
| sat,sun | sat..sun | Only on weekend at 0:00 |
| mon,wed,fri | — | Only on Monday, Wednesday and Friday at 0:00 |
| 12:05 | 12:05 | All weekdays at 12:05 PM |
| */5 | 0/5 | Every day all five minutes |
| mon..wed 30/10 | mon,tue,wed 30/10 | Monday, Tuesday, Wednesday 30, 40 and 50 minutes after every full hour |
| mon..fri 8..17,22:0/15 | — | All working days every 15 minutes between 8 AM and 6 PM and between 10 PM and 11 PM |
| fri 12..13:5/20 | fri 12,13:5/20 | Friday at 12:05, 12:25, 12:45, 13:05, 13:25 and 13:45 |
| 12,14,16,18,20,22:5 | 12/2:5 | Every day starting at 12:05 until 22:05 all 2 hours |
| * | */1 | Every minute (minimum interval) |

## 9.3 Error Handling

If a replication job encounters problems it will be placed in error state. In this state the configured replication intervals get suspended temporarily. Then we retry the failed replication in a 30 minute interval, once this succeeds the original schedule gets activated again.

### 9.3.1 Possible issues

This represents only the most common issues possible, depending on your setup there may be also another cause.

• Network is not working.

• No free space left on the replication target storage.

• Storage with same storage ID available on target node

---

**Note**
You can always use the replication log to get hints about a problems cause.

---

### 9.3.2  Migrating a guest in case of Error

In the case of a grave error a virtual guest may get stuck on a failed node. You then need to move it manually to a working node again.

### 9.3.3  Example

Lets assume that you have two guests (VM 100 and CT 200) running on node A and replicate to node B. Node A failed and can not get back online. Now you have to migrate the guest to Node B manually.

- connect to node B over ssh or open its shell via the WebUI

- check if that the cluster is quorate

```
# pvecm status
```

- If you have no quorum we strongly advise to fix this first and make the node operable again. Only if this is not possible at the moment you may use the following command to enforce quorum on the current node:

```
# pvecm expected 1
```

**Warning**
If expected votes are set avoid changes which affect the cluster (for example adding/removing nodes, storages, virtual guests) at all costs. Only use it to get vital guests up and running again or to resolve to quorum issue itself.

- move both guest configuration files form the origin node A to node B:

```
# mv /etc/pve/node/A/qemu-server/100.conf /etc/pve/node/B/qemu-server ←
    /100.conf
# mv /etc/pve/node/A/lxc/200.conf /etc/pve/node/B/lxc/200.conf
```

- Now you can start the guests again:

```
# qm start 100
# pct start 200
```

Remember to replace the VMIDs and node names with your respective values.

## 9.4   Managing Jobs

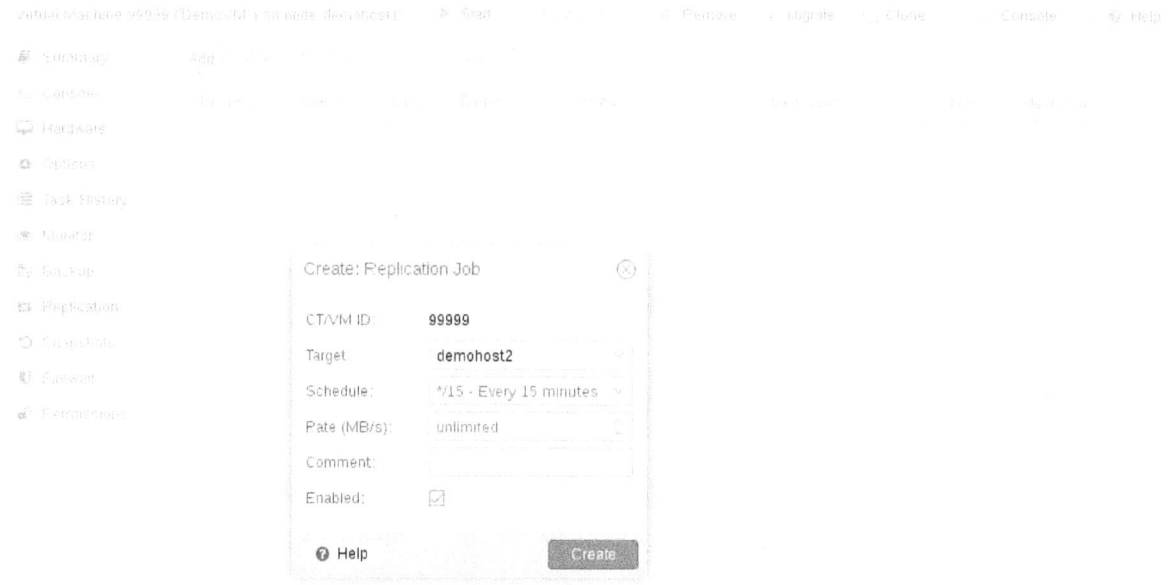

You can use the web GUI to create, modify and remove replication jobs easily. Additionally the command line interface (CLI) tool pvesr can be used to do this.

You can find the replication panel on all levels (datacenter, node, virtual guest) in the web GUI. They differ in what jobs get shown: all, only node specific or only guest specific jobs.

Once adding a new job you need to specify the virtual guest (if not already selected) and the target node. The replication schedule Section 9.2 can be set if the default of all 15 minutes is not desired. You may also impose rate limiting on a replication job, this can help to keep the storage load acceptable.

A replication job is identified by an cluster-wide unique ID. This ID is composed of the VMID in addition to an job number. This ID must only be specified manually if the CLI tool is used.

## 9.5   Command Line Interface Examples

Create a replication job which will run all 5 min with limited bandwidth of 10 mbps (megabytes per second) for the guest with guest ID 100.

```
# pvesr create-local-job 100-0 pve1 --schedule "*/5" --rate 10
```

Disable an active job with ID 100-0

```
# pvesr disable 100-0
```

Enable a deactivated job with ID 100-0

```
# pvesr enable 100-0
```

Change the schedule interval of the job with ID 100-0 to once a hour

```
# pvesr update 100-0 --schedule '*/00'
```

# Chapter 10

# Qemu/KVM Virtual Machines

Qemu (short form for Quick Emulator) is an open source hypervisor that emulates a physical computer. From the perspective of the host system where Qemu is running, Qemu is a user program which has access to a number of local resources like partitions, files, network cards which are then passed to an emulated computer which sees them as if they were real devices.

A guest operating system running in the emulated computer accesses these devices, and runs as it were running on real hardware. For instance you can pass an iso image as a parameter to Qemu, and the OS running in the emulated computer will see a real CDROM inserted in a CD drive.

Qemu can emulate a great variety of hardware from ARM to Sparc, but Proxmox VE is only concerned with 32 and 64 bits PC clone emulation, since it represents the overwhelming majority of server hardware. The emulation of PC clones is also one of the fastest due to the availability of processor extensions which greatly speed up Qemu when the emulated architecture is the same as the host architecture.

---

**Note**

You may sometimes encounter the term *KVM* (Kernel-based Virtual Machine). It means that Qemu is running with the support of the virtualization processor extensions, via the Linux kvm module. In the context of Proxmox VE *Qemu* and *KVM* can be used interchangeably as Qemu in Proxmox VE will always try to load the kvm module.

---

Qemu inside Proxmox VE runs as a root process, since this is required to access block and PCI devices.

## 10.1   Emulated devices and paravirtualized devices

The PC hardware emulated by Qemu includes a mainboard, network controllers, scsi, ide and sata controllers, serial ports (the complete list can be seen in the `kvm(1)` man page) all of them emulated in software. All these devices are the exact software equivalent of existing hardware devices, and if the OS running in the guest has the proper drivers it will use the devices as if it were running on real hardware. This allows Qemu to runs *unmodified* operating systems.

This however has a performance cost, as running in software what was meant to run in hardware involves a lot of extra work for the host CPU. To mitigate this, Qemu can present to the guest operating system *paravirtualized devices*, where the guest OS recognizes it is running inside Qemu and cooperates with the hypervisor.

Qemu relies on the virtio virtualization standard, and is thus able to presente paravirtualized virtio devices, which includes a paravirtualized generic disk controller, a paravirtualized network card, a paravirtualized serial port, a paravirtualized SCSI controller, etc ...

It is highly recommended to use the virtio devices whenever you can, as they provide a big performance improvement. Using the virtio generic disk controller versus an emulated IDE controller will double the sequential write throughput, as measured with `bonnie++(8)`. Using the virtio network interface can deliver up to three times the throughput of an emulated Intel E1000 network card, as measured with `iperf` `(1)`. [1]

## 10.2  Virtual Machines Settings

Generally speaking Proxmox VE tries to choose sane defaults for virtual machines (VM). Make sure you understand the meaning of the settings you change, as it could incur a performance slowdown, or putting your data at risk.

### 10.2.1  General Settings

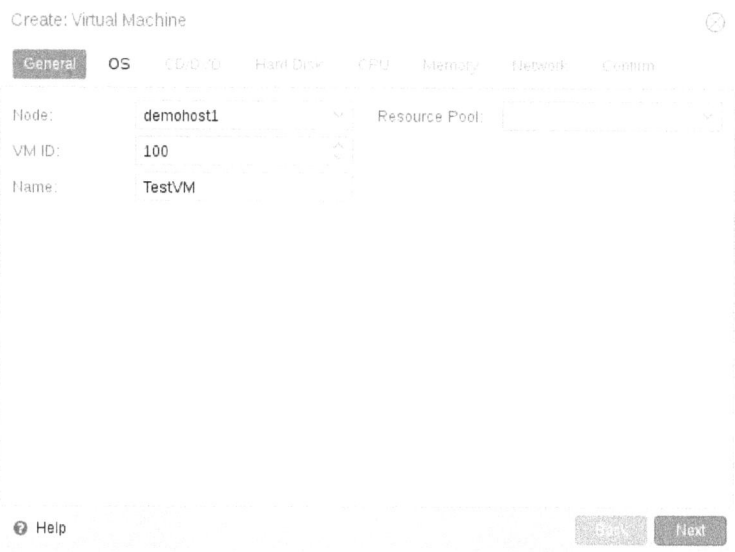

General settings of a VM include

- the **Node** : the physical server on which the VM will run

- the **VM ID**: a unique number in this Proxmox VE installation used to identify your VM

- **Name**: a free form text string you can use to describe the VM

- **Resource Pool**: a logical group of VMs

---

[1] See this benchmark on the KVM wiki http://www.linux-kvm.org/page/Using_VirtIO_NIC

## 10.2.2   OS Settings

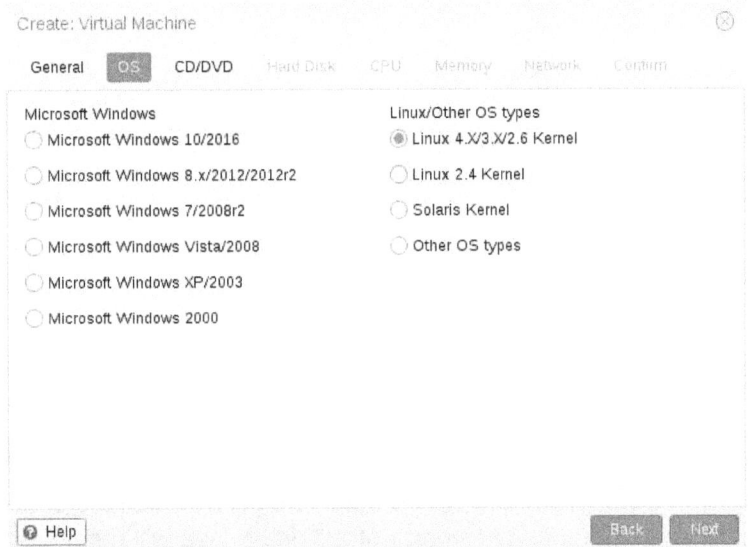

When creating a VM, setting the proper Operating System(OS) allows Proxmox VE to optimize some low level parameters. For instance Windows OS expect the BIOS clock to use the local time, while Unix based OS expect the BIOS clock to have the UTC time.

## 10.2.3   Hard Disk

Qemu can emulate a number of storage controllers:

* the **IDE** controller, has a design which goes back to the 1984 PC/AT disk controller. Even if this controller has been superseded by more more designs, each and every OS you can think of has support for it, making it a great choice if you want to run an OS released before 2003. You can connect up to 4 devices on this controller.

* the **SATA** (Serial ATA) controller, dating from 2003, has a more modern design, allowing higher throughput and a greater number of devices to be connected. You can connect up to 6 devices on this controller.

* the **SCSI** controller, designed in 1985, is commonly found on server grade hardware, and can connect up to 14 storage devices. Proxmox VE emulates by default a LSI 53C895A controller.

  A SCSI controller of type *VirtIO SCSI* is the recommended setting if you aim for performance and is automatically selected for newly created Linux VMs since Proxmox VE 4.3. Linux distributions have support for this controller since 2012, and FreeBSD since 2014. For Windows OSes, you need to provide an extra iso containing the drivers during the installation. If you aim at maximum performance, you can select a SCSI controller of type *VirtIO SCSI single* which will allow you to select the **IO Thread** option. When selecting *VirtIO SCSI single* Qemu will create a new controller for each disk, instead of adding all disks to the same controller.

* The **Virtio** controller, also called virtio-blk to distinguish from the VirtIO SCSI controller, is an older type of paravirtualized controller which has been superseded in features by the Virtio SCSI Controller.

On each controller you attach a number of emulated hard disks, which are backed by a file or a block device residing in the configured storage. The choice of a storage type will determine the format of the hard disk image. Storages which present block devices (LVM, ZFS, Ceph) will require the **raw disk image format**, whereas files based storages (Ext4, NFS, GlusterFS) will let you to choose either the **raw disk image format** or the **QEMU image format**.

- the **QEMU image format** is a copy on write format which allows snapshots, and thin provisioning of the disk image.

- the **raw disk image** is a bit-to-bit image of a hard disk, similar to what you would get when executing the dd command on a block device in Linux. This format do not support thin provisioning or snapshotting by itself, requiring cooperation from the storage layer for these tasks. It is however 10% faster than the **QEMU image format**. [2]

- the **VMware image format** only makes sense if you intend to import/export the disk image to other hyper-visors.

Setting the **Cache** mode of the hard drive will impact how the host system will notify the guest systems of block write completions. The **No cache** default means that the guest system will be notified that a write is complete when each block reaches the physical storage write queue, ignoring the host page cache. This provides a good balance between safety and speed.

If you want the Proxmox VE backup manager to skip a disk when doing a backup of a VM, you can set the **No backup** option on that disk.

If you want the Proxmox VE storage replication mechanism to skip a disk when starting a replication job, you can set the **Skip replication** option on that disk. As of Proxmox VE 5.0, replication requires the disk images to be on a storage of type zfspool, so adding a disk image to other storages when the VM has replication configured requires to skip replication for this disk image.

If your storage supports *thin provisioning* (see the storage chapter in the Proxmox VE guide), and your VM has a **SCSI** controller you can activate the **Discard** option on the hard disks connected to that controller. With **Discard** enabled, when the filesystem of a VM marks blocks as unused after removing files, the emulated SCSI controller will relay this information to the storage, which will then shrink the disk image accordingly.

[2] See this benchmark for details http://events.linuxfoundation.org/sites/events/files/slides/-CloudOpen2013_Khoa_Huynh_v3.pdf

**IO Thread**

The option **IO Thread** can only be used when using a disk with the **VirtIO** controller, or with the **SCSI** controller, when the emulated controller type is **VirtIO SCSI single**. With this enabled, Qemu creates one I/O thread per storage controller, instead of a single thread for all I/O, so it increases performance when multiple disks are used and each disk has its own storage controller. Note that backups do not currently work with **IO Thread** enabled.

## 10.2.4 CPU

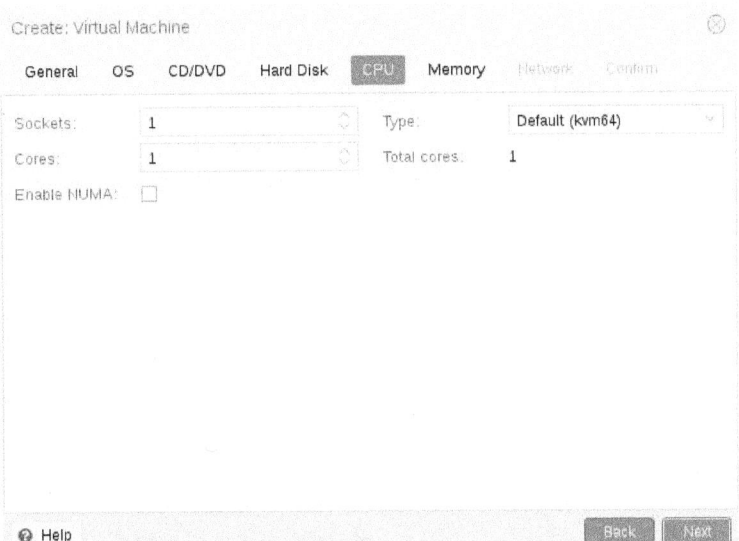

A **CPU socket** is a physical slot on a PC motherboard where you can plug a CPU. This CPU can then contain one or many **cores**, which are independent processing units. Whether you have a single CPU socket with 4 cores, or two CPU sockets with two cores is mostly irrelevant from a performance point of view. However some software is licensed depending on the number of sockets you have in your machine, in that case it makes sense to set the number of of sockets to what the license allows you, and increase the number of cores.

Increasing the number of virtual cpus (cores and sockets) will usually provide a performance improvement though that is heavily dependent on the use of the VM. Multithreaded applications will of course benefit from a large number of virtual cpus, as for each virtual cpu you add, Qemu will create a new thread of execution on the host system. If you're not sure about the workload of your VM, it is usually a safe bet to set the number of **Total cores** to 2.

---

**Note**
It is perfectly safe to set the *overall* number of total cores in all your VMs to be greater than the number of of cores you have on your server (ie. 4 VMs with each 4 Total cores running in a 8 core machine is OK) In that case the host system will balance the Qemu execution threads between your server cores just like if you were running a standard multithreaded application. However Proxmox VE will prevent you to allocate on a *single* machine more vcpus than physically available, as this will only bring the performance down due to the cost of context switches.

---

Qemu can emulate a number different of **CPU types** from 486 to the latest Xeon processors. Each new processor generation adds new features, like hardware assisted 3d rendering, random number generation, memory protection, etc ... Usually you should select for your VM a processor type which closely matches the CPU of the host system, as it means that the host CPU features (also called *CPU flags* ) will be available in your VMs. If you want an exact match, you can set the CPU type to **host** in which case the VM will have exactly the same CPU flags as your host system.

This has a downside though. If you want to do a live migration of VMs between different hosts, your VM might end up on a new system with a different CPU type. If the CPU flags passed to the guest are missing, the qemu process will stop. To remedy this Qemu has also its own CPU type **kvm64**, that Proxmox VE uses by defaults. kvm64 is a Pentium 4 look a like CPU type, which has a reduced CPU flags set, but is guaranteed to work everywhere.

In short, if you care about live migration and moving VMs between nodes, leave the kvm64 default. If you don't care about live migration, set the CPU type to host, as in theory this will give your guests maximum performance.

You can also optionally emulate a **NUMA** architecture in your VMs. The basics of the NUMA architecture mean that instead of having a global memory pool available to all your cores, the memory is spread into local banks close to each socket. This can bring speed improvements as the memory bus is not a bottleneck anymore. If your system has a NUMA architecture [3] we recommend to activate the option, as this will allow proper distribution of the VM resources on the host system. This option is also required in Proxmox VE to allow hotplugging of cores and RAM to a VM.

If the NUMA option is used, it is recommended to set the number of sockets to the number of sockets of the host system.

### 10.2.5  Memory

For each VM you have the option to set a fixed size memory or asking Proxmox VE to dynamically allocate memory based on the current RAM usage of the host.

**Fixed Memory Allocation**

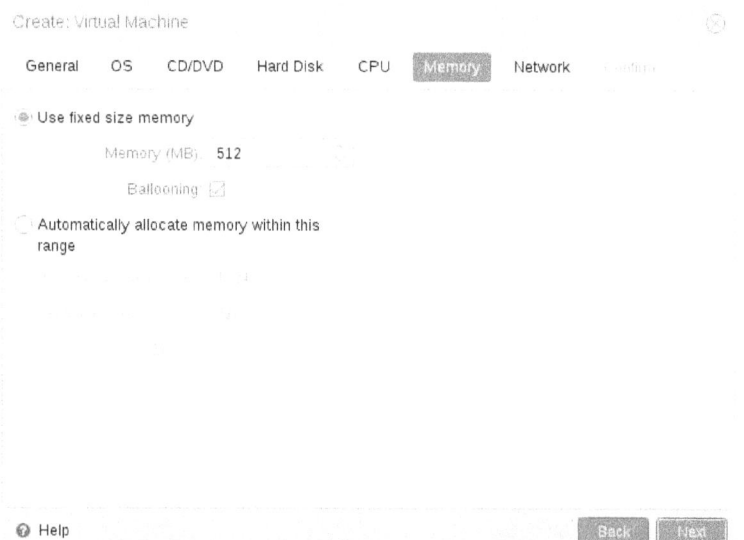

When choosing a **fixed size memory** Proxmox VE will simply allocate what you specify to your VM.

---

[3] if the command `numactl --hardware` | `grep available` returns more than one node, then your host system has a NUMA architecture

Even when using a fixed memory size, the ballooning device gets added to the VM, because it delivers useful information such as how much memory the guest really uses. In general, you should leave **ballooning** enabled, but if you want to disable it (e.g. for debugging purposes), simply uncheck **Ballooning** or set

```
balloon: 0
```

in the configuration.

### Automatic Memory Allocation

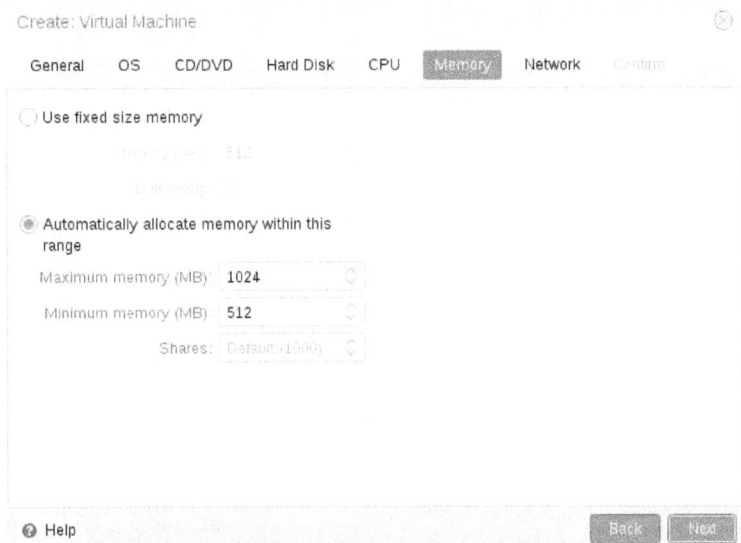

When choosing to **automatically allocate memory**, Proxmox VE will make sure that the minimum amount you specified is always available to the VM, and if RAM usage on the host is below 80%, will dynamically add memory to the guest up to the maximum memory specified.

When the host is becoming short on RAM, the VM will then release some memory back to the host, swapping running processes if needed and starting the oom killer in last resort. The passing around of memory between host and guest is done via a special `balloon` kernel driver running inside the guest, which will grab or release memory pages from the host. [4]

When multiple VMs use the autoallocate facility, it is possible to set a **Shares** coefficient which indicates the relative amount of the free host memory that each VM shoud take. Suppose for instance you have four VMs, three of them running a HTTP server and the last one is a database server. To cache more database blocks in the database server RAM, you would like to prioritize the database VM when spare RAM is available. For this you assign a Shares property of 3000 to the database VM, leaving the other VMs to the Shares default setting of 1000. The host server has 32GB of RAM, and is curring using 16GB, leaving 32 * 80/100 - 16 = 9GB RAM to be allocated to the VMs. The database VM will get 9 * 3000 / (3000 + 1000 + 1000 + 1000) = 4.5 GB extra RAM and each HTTP server will get 1/5 GB.

All Linux distributions released after 2010 have the balloon kernel driver included. For Windows OSes, the balloon driver needs to be added manually and can incur a slowdown of the guest, so we don't recommend using it on critical systems.

When allocating RAMs to your VMs, a good rule of thumb is always to leave 1GB of RAM available to the host.

---

[4] A good explanation of the inner workings of the balloon driver can be found here https://rwmj.wordpress.com/2010/07/-17/virtio-balloon/

## 10.2.6  Network Device

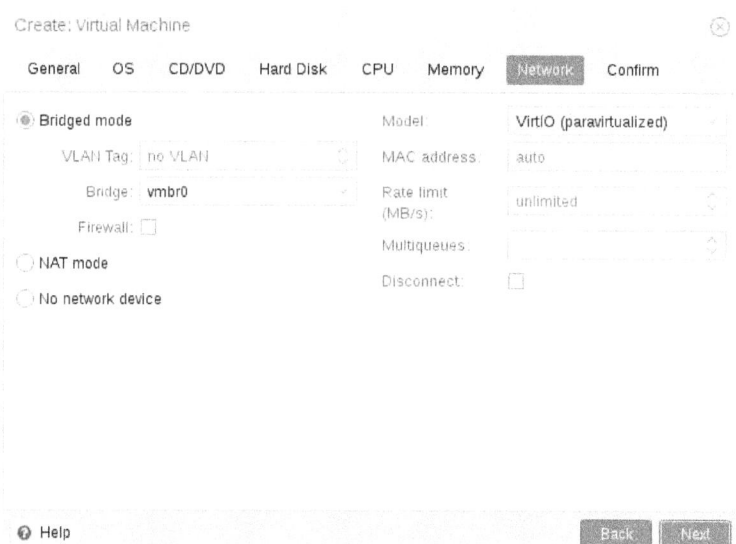

Each VM can have many *Network interface controllers* (NIC), of four different types:

- **Intel E1000** is the default, and emulates an Intel Gigabit network card.

- the **VirtIO** paravirtualized NIC should be used if you aim for maximum performance. Like all VirtIO devices, the guest OS should have the proper driver installed.

- the **Realtek 8139** emulates an older 100 MB/s network card, and should only be used when emulating older operating systems ( released before 2002 )

- the **vmxnet3** is another paravirtualized device, which should only be used when importing a VM from another hypervisor.

Proxmox VE will generate for each NIC a random **MAC address**, so that your VM is addressable on Ethernet networks.

The NIC you added to the VM can follow one of two differents models:

- in the default **Bridged mode** each virtual NIC is backed on the host by a *tap device*, ( a software loopback device simulating an Ethernet NIC ). This tap device is added to a bridge, by default vmbr0 in Proxmox VE. In this mode, VMs have direct access to the Ethernet LAN on which the host is located.

- in the alternative **NAT mode**, each virtual NIC will only communicate with the Qemu user networking stack, where a builting router and DHCP server can provide network access. This built-in DHCP will serve adresses in the private 10.0.2.0/24 range. The NAT mode is much slower than the bridged mode, and should only be used for testing.

You can also skip adding a network device when creating a VM by selecting **No network device**.

### Multiqueue

If you are using the VirtIO driver, you can optionally activate the **Multiqueue** option. This option allows the guest OS to process networking packets using multiple virtual CPUs, providing an increase in the total number of packets transfered.

When using the VirtIO driver with Proxmox VE, each NIC network queue is passed to the host kernel, where the queue will be processed by a kernel thread spawn by the vhost driver. With this option activated, it is possible to pass *multiple* network queues to the host kernel for each NIC.

When using Multiqueue, it is recommended to set it to a value equal to the number of Total Cores of your guest. You also need to set in the VM the number of multi-purpose channels on each VirtIO NIC with the ethtool command:

```
ethtool -L ens1 combined X
```

where X is the number of the number of vcpus of the VM.

You should note that setting the Multiqueue parameter to a value greater than one will increase the CPU load on the host and guest systems as the traffic increases. We recommend to set this option only when the VM has to process a great number of incoming connections, such as when the VM is running as a router, reverse proxy or a busy HTTP server doing long polling.

### 10.2.7  USB Passthrough

There are two different types of USB passthrough devices:

- Host USB passtrough

- SPICE USB passthrough

Host USB passthrough works by giving a VM a USB device of the host. This can either be done via the vendor- and product-id, or via the host bus and port.

The vendor/product-id looks like this: **0123:abcd**, where **0123** is the id of the vendor, and **abcd** is the id of the product, meaning two pieces of the same usb device have the same id.

The bus/port looks like this: **1-2.3.4**, where **1** is the bus and **2.3.4** is the port path. This represents the physical ports of your host (depending of the internal order of the usb controllers).

If a device is present in a VM configuration when the VM starts up, but the device is not present in the host, the VM can boot without problems. As soon as the device/port ist available in the host, it gets passed through.

---

 **Warning**
Using this kind of USB passthrough means that you cannot move a VM online to another host, since the hardware is only available on the host the VM is currently residing.

---

The second type of passthrough is SPICE USB passthrough. This is useful if you use a SPICE client which supports it. If you add a SPICE USB port to your VM, you can passthrough a USB device from where your SPICE client is, directly to the VM (for example an input device or hardware dongle).

### 10.2.8  BIOS and UEFI

In order to properly emulate a computer, QEMU needs to use a firmware. By default QEMU uses **SeaBIOS** for this, which is an open-source, x86 BIOS implementation. SeaBIOS is a good choice for most standard setups.

There are, however, some scenarios in which a BIOS is not a good firmware to boot from, e.g. if you want to do VGA passthrough. [5] In such cases, you should rather use **OVMF**, which is an open-source UEFI implemenation. [6]

If you want to use OVMF, there are several things to consider:

In order to save things like the **boot order**, there needs to be an EFI Disk. This disk will be included in backups and snapshots, and there can only be one.

You can create such a disk with the following command:

```
qm set <vmid> -efidisk0 <storage>:1,format=<format>
```

Where **<storage>** is the storage where you want to have the disk, and **<format>** is a format which the storage supports. Alternatively, you can create such a disk through the web interface with *Add → EFI Disk* in the hardware section of a VM.

When using OVMF with a virtual display (without VGA passthrough), you need to set the client resolution in the OVMF menu(which you can reach with a press of the ESC button during boot), or you have to choose SPICE as the display type.

### 10.2.9   Automatic Start and Shutdown of Virtual Machines

After creating your VMs, you probably want them to start automatically when the host system boots. For this you need to select the option *Start at boot* from the *Options* Tab of your VM in the web interface, or set it with the following command:

```
qm set <vmid> -onboot 1
```

**Start and Shutdown Order**

In some case you want to be able to fine tune the boot order of your VMs, for instance if one of your VM is providing firewalling or DHCP to other guest systems. For this you can use the following parameters:

- **Start/Shutdown order**: Defines the start order priority. E.g. set it to 1 if you want the VM to be the first to be started. (We use the reverse startup order for shutdown, so a machine with a start order of 1 would be the last to be shut down)

- **Startup delay**: Defines the interval between this VM start and subsequent VMs starts . E.g. set it to 240 if you want to wait 240 seconds before starting other VMs.

---

[5] Alex Williamson has a very good blog entry about this. http://vfio.blogspot.co.at/2014/08/primary-graphics-assignment-without-vga.html

[6] See the OVMF Project http://www.tianocore.org/ovmf/

- **Shutdown timeout**: Defines the duration in seconds Proxmox VE should wait for the VM to be offline after issuing a shutdown command. By default this value is set to 60, which means that Proxmox VE will issue a shutdown request, wait 60s for the machine to be offline, and if after 60s the machine is still online will notify that the shutdown action failed.

---

**Note**

VMs managed by the HA stack do not follow the *start on boot* and *boot order* options currently. Those VMs will be skipped by the startup and shutdown algorithm as the HA manager itself ensures that VMs get started and stopped.

---

Please note that machines without a Start/Shutdown order parameter will always start after those where the parameter is set, and this parameter only makes sense between the machines running locally on a host, and not cluster-wide.

## 10.3  Migration

If you have a cluster, you can migrate your VM to another host with

```
qm migrate <vmid> <target>
```

There are generally two mechanisms for this

- Online Migration (aka Live Migration)

- Offline Migration

### 10.3.1  Online Migration

When your VM is running and it has no local resources defined (such as disks on local storage, passed through devices, etc.) you can initiate a live migration with the -online flag.

**How it works**

This starts a Qemu Process on the target host with the *incoming* flag, which means that the process starts and waits for the memory data and device states from the source Virtual Machine (since all other resources, e.g. disks, are shared, the memory content and device state are the only things left to transmit).

Once this connection is established, the source begins to send the memory content asynchronously to the target. If the memory on the source changes, those sections are marked dirty and there will be another pass of sending data. This happens until the amount of data to send is so small that it can pause the VM on the source, send the remaining data to the target and start the VM on the target in under a second.

**Requirements**

For Live Migration to work, there are some things required:

- The VM has no local resources (e.g. passed through devices, local disks, etc.)

- The hosts are in the same Proxmox VE cluster.

- The hosts have a working (and reliable) network connection.

- The target host must have the same or higher versions of the Proxmox VE packages. (It **might** work the other way, but this is never guaranteed)

### 10.3.2  Offline Migration

If you have local resources, you can still offline migrate your VMs, as long as all disk are on storages, which are defined on both hosts. Then the migration will copy the disk over the network to the target host.

## 10.4   Copies and Clones

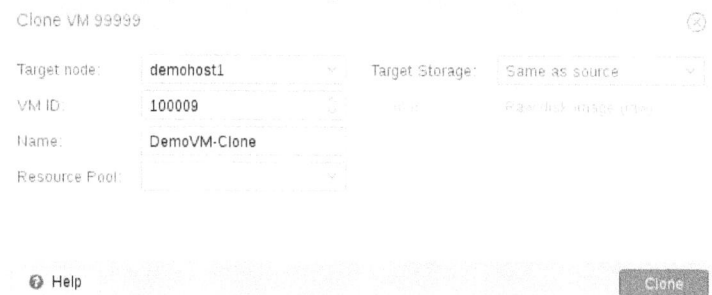

VM installation is usually done using an installation media (CD-ROM) from the operation system vendor. Depending on the OS, this can be a time consuming task one might want to avoid.

An easy way to deploy many VMs of the same type is to copy an existing VM. We use the term *clone* for such copies, and distinguish between *linked* and *full* clones.

**Full Clone**
> The result of such copy is an independent VM. The new VM does not share any storage resources with the original.
>
> It is possible to select a **Target Storage**, so one can use this to migrate a VM to a totally different storage. You can also change the disk image **Format** if the storage driver supports several formats.
>
> ---
> **Note**
> A full clone need to read and copy all VM image data. This is usually much slower than creating a linked clone.
>
> ---
>
> Some storage types allows to copy a specific **Snapshot**, which defaults to the *current* VM data. This also means that the final copy never includes any additional snapshots from the original VM.

**Linked Clone**

Modern storage drivers supports a way to generate fast linked clones. Such a clone is a writable copy whose initial contents are the same as the original data. Creating a linked clone is nearly instantaneous, and initially consumes no additional space.

They are called *linked* because the new image still refers to the original. Unmodified data blocks are read from the original image, but modification are written (and afterwards read) from a new location. This technique is called *Copy-on-write*.

This requires that the original volume is read-only. With Proxmox VE one can convert any VM into a read-only Template). Such templates can later be used to create linked clones efficiently.

---

**Note**

You cannot delete the original template while linked clones exists.

---

It is not possible to change the **Target storage** for linked clones, because this is a storage internal feature.

The **Target node** option allows you to create the new VM on a different node. The only restriction is that the VM is on shared storage, and that storage is also available on the target node.

To avoid resource conflicts, all network interface MAC addresses gets randomized, and we generate a new *UUID* for the VM BIOS (smbios1) setting.

## 10.5   Virtual Machine Templates

One can convert a VM into a Template. Such templates are read-only, and you can use them to create linked clones.

---

**Note**

It is not possible to start templates, because this would modify the disk images. If you want to change the template, create a linked clone and modify that.

---

## 10.6   Importing Virtual Machines from foreign hypervisors

A VM export from a foreign hypervisor takes usually the form of one or more disk images, with a configuration file describing the settings of the VM (RAM, number of cores).

The disk images can be in the vmdk format, if the disks come from VMware or VirtualBox, or qcow2 if the disks come from a KVM hypervisor. The most popular configuration format for VM exports is the OVF standard, but in practice interoperation is limited because many settings are not implemented in the standard itself, and hypervisors export the supplementary information in non-standard extensions.

Besides the problem of format, importing disk images from other hypervisors may fail if the emulated hardware changes too much from one hypervisor to another. Windows VMs are particularly concerned by this, as the OS is very picky about any changes of hardware. This problem may be solved by installing the MergeIDE.zip utility available from the Internet before exporting and choosing a hard disk type of **IDE** before booting the imported Windows VM.

Finally there is the question of paravirtualized drivers, which improve the speed of the emulated system and are specific to the hypervisor. GNU/Linux and other free Unix OSes have all the necessary drivers installed by default and you can switch to the paravirtualized drivers right after importing the VM. For Windows VMs, you need to install the Windows paravirtualized drivers by yourself.

GNU/Linux and other free Unix can usually be imported without hassle. Note that we cannot guarantee a successful import/export of Windows WM in all cases due to the problems above.

### 10.6.1  Step-by-step example of a Windows disk image import

Microsoft provides Virtual Machines exports in different formats for browser testing. We are going to use one of these to demonstrate a VMDK import.

#### Download the export zip

After getting informed about the user agreement, choose the *Microsoft Edge on Windows 10 Virtual Machine* for the VMware platform, and download the zip.

#### Extract the disk image from the zip

Using the unzip utility or any archiver of your choice, unpack the zip, and copy via ssh/scp the vmdk file to your Proxmox VE host.

#### Create a new virtual machine and import the disk

Create a virtual machine with 2 cores, 2GB RAM, and one NIC on the default `vmbr0` bridge:

```
qm create 999 -net0 e1000,bridge=vmbr0 -name Win10 -memory 2048 - ↩
   bootdisk sata0
```

Import the disk image to the `local-lvm` storage:

```
qm importdisk 999 MSEdge "MSEdge - Win10_preview.vmdk" local-lvm
```

The disk will be marked as **Unused** in the VM 999 configuration. After that you can go in the GUI, in the VM **Hardware**, **Edit** the unused disk and set the **Bus/Device** to **SATA/0**. The VM is ready to be started.

## 10.7  Managing Virtual Machines with qm

qm is the tool to manage Qemu/Kvm virtual machines on Proxmox VE. You can create and destroy virtual machines, and control execution (start/stop/suspend/resume). Besides that, you can use qm to set parameters in the associated config file. It is also possible to create and delete virtual disks.

### 10.7.1   CLI Usage Examples

Using an iso file uploaded on the *local* storage, create a VM with a 4 GB IDE disk on the *local-lvm* storage

```
qm create 300 -ide0 local-lvm:4 -net0 e1000 -cdrom local:iso/proxmox ↩
    -mailgateway_2.1.iso
```

Start the new VM

```
qm start 300
```

Send a shutdown request, then wait until the VM is stopped.

```
qm shutdown 300 && qm wait 300
```

Same as above, but only wait for 40 seconds.

```
qm shutdown 300 && qm wait 300 -timeout 40
```

## 10.8   Configuration

VM configuration files are stored inside the Proxmox cluster file system, and can be accessed at `/etc/pve/qemu-server/<VMID>.conf`. Like other files stored inside `/etc/pve/`, they get automatically replicated to all other cluster nodes.

---

**Note**
VMIDs < 100 are reserved for internal purposes, and VMIDs need to be unique cluster wide.

---

**Example VM Configuration**

```
cores: 1
sockets: 1
memory: 512
name: webmail
ostype: l26
bootdisk: virtio0
net0: e1000=EE:D2:28:5F:B6:3E,bridge=vmbr0
virtio0: local:vm-100-disk-1,size=32G
```

Those configuration files are simple text files, and you can edit them using a normal text editor (`vi`, `nano`, ...). This is sometimes useful to do small corrections, but keep in mind that you need to restart the VM to apply such changes.

For that reason, it is usually better to use the `qm` command to generate and modify those files, or do the whole thing using the GUI. Our toolkit is smart enough to instantaneously apply most changes to running VM. This feature is called "hot plug", and there is no need to restart the VM in that case.

### 10.8.1 File Format

VM configuration files use a simple colon separated key/value format. Each line has the following format:

```
# this is a comment
OPTION: value
```

Blank lines in those files are ignored, and lines starting with a # character are treated as comments and are also ignored.

### 10.8.2 Snapshots

When you create a snapshot, qm stores the configuration at snapshot time into a separate snapshot section within the same configuration file. For example, after creating a snapshot called "testsnapshot", your configuration file will look like this:

**VM configuration with snapshot**

```
memory: 512
swap: 512
parent: testsnaphot
...

[testsnaphot]
memory: 512
swap: 512
snaptime: 1457170803
...
```

There are a few snapshot related properties like `parent` and `snaptime`. The `parent` property is used to store the parent/child relationship between snapshots. `snaptime` is the snapshot creation time stamp (Unix epoch).

### 10.8.3 Options

**acpi: <boolean> (*default* = 1)**
    Enable/disable ACPI.

**agent: <boolean> (*default* = 0)**
    Enable/disable Qemu GuestAgent.

**args: <string>**
    Arbitrary arguments passed to kvm, for example:

    args: -no-reboot -no-hpet

---

**Note**
this option is for experts only.

---

**autostart: <boolean>** (*default* = 0)

Automatic restart after crash (currently ignored).

**balloon: <integer>** (0 - N)

Amount of target RAM for the VM in MB. Using zero disables the ballon driver.

**bios: <ovmf | seabios>** (*default* = seabios)

Select BIOS implementation.

**boot: [acdn]{1,4}** (*default* = cdn)

Boot on floppy (a), hard disk (c), CD-ROM (d), or network (n).

**bootdisk: (ide|sata|scsi|virtio)\d+**

Enable booting from specified disk.

**cdrom: <volume>**

This is an alias for option -ide2

**cores: <integer>** (1 - N) (*default* = 1)

The number of cores per socket.

**cpu: [cputype=]<enum> [,hidden=<1|0>]**

Emulated CPU type.

> **cputype=<486 | Broadwell | Broadwell-noTSX | Conroe | Haswell | Haswell-noTSX | IvyBridge | Nehalem | Opteron_G1 | Opteron_G2 | Opteron_G3 | Opteron_G4 | Opteron_G5 | Penryn | SandyBridge | Skylake-Client | Westmere | athlon | core2duo | coreduo | host | kvm32 | kvm64 | pentium | pentium2 | pentium3 | phenom | qemu32 | qemu64>** (*default* = kvm64)
>
> Emulated CPU type.

> **hidden=<boolean>** (*default* = 0)
>
> Do not identify as a KVM virtual machine.

**cpulimit: <number>** (0 - 128) (*default* = 0)

Limit of CPU usage.

---

**Note**

If the computer has 2 CPUs, it has total of *2* CPU time. Value *0* indicates no CPU limit.

---

**cpuunits: <integer>** (0 - 500000) (*default* = 1024)

CPU weight for a VM. Argument is used in the kernel fair scheduler. The larger the number is, the more CPU time this VM gets. Number is relative to weights of all the other running VMs.

**Note**
You can disable fair-scheduler configuration by setting this to 0.

**description: <string>**
Description for the VM. Only used on the configuration web interface. This is saved as comment inside the configuration file.

**efidisk0: [file=]<volume> [,format=<enum>] [,size=<DiskSize>]**
Configure a Disk for storing EFI vars

**file=<volume>**
The drive's backing volume.

**format=<cloop | cow | qcow | qcow2 | qed | raw | vmdk>**
The drive's backing file's data format.

**size=<DiskSize>**
Disk size. This is purely informational and has no effect.

**freeze: <boolean>**
Freeze CPU at startup (use *c* monitor command to start execution).

**hostpci[n]: [host=]<HOSTPCIID[;HOSTPCIID2...]> [,pcie=<1|0>] [,rombar=<1|0>] [,romfile=<string>] [,x-vga=<1|0>]**
Map host PCI devices into guest.

**Note**
This option allows direct access to host hardware. So it is no longer possible to migrate such machines - use with special care.

 **Caution**
Experimental! User reported problems with this option.

**host=<HOSTPCIID[;HOSTPCIID2...]>**
Host PCI device pass through. The PCI ID of a host's PCI device or a list of PCI virtual functions of the host. HOSTPCIID syntax is:
*bus:dev.func* (hexadecimal numbers)
You can us the *lspci* command to list existing PCI devices.

**pcie=<boolean> (*default = 0*)**
Choose the PCI-express bus (needs the *q35* machine model).

**rombar=<boolean> (*default = 1*)**
Specify whether or not the device's ROM will be visible in the guest's memory map.

**romfile=<string>**
  Custom pci device rom filename (must be located in /usr/share/kvm/).

**x-vga=<boolean> (*default* = 0)**
  Enable vfio-vga device support.

**hotplug: <string> (*default* = network,disk,usb)**
  Selectively enable hotplug features. This is a comma separated list of hotplug features: *network*, *disk*, *cpu*, *memory* and *usb*. Use *0* to disable hotplug completely. Value *1* is an alias for the default *network,disk,usb*.

**hugepages: <1024 | 2 | any>**
  Enable/disable hugepages memory.

**ide[n]: [file=]<volume> [,aio=<native|threads>] [,backup=<1|0>] [,bps=<bps>] [,bps_max_length=<seconds>] [,bps_rd=<bps>] [,bps_rd_max_length=<seconds>] [,bps_wr=<bps>] [,bps_wr_max_length= <seconds>] [,cache=<enum>] [,cyls=<integer>] [,detect_zeroes=<1|0>] [,discard=<ignore|on>] [,format=<enum>] [,heads=<integer>] [,iops= <iops>] [,iops_max=<iops>] [,iops_max_length=<seconds>] [,iops_rd= <iops>] [,iops_rd_max=<iops>] [,iops_rd_max_length=<seconds>] [,iops_wr=<iops>] [,iops_wr_max=<iops>] [,iops_wr_max_length= <seconds>] [,mbps=<mbps>] [,mbps_max=<mbps>] [,mbps_rd=<mbps>] [,mbps_rd_max=<mbps>] [,mbps_wr=<mbps>] [,mbps_wr_max=<mbps>] [,media=<cdrom|disk>] [,model=<model>] [,replicate=<1|0>] [,rerror= <ignore|report|stop>] [,secs=<integer>] [,serial=<serial>] [,size= <DiskSize>] [,snapshot=<1|0>] [,trans=<none|lba|auto>] [,werror= <enum>]**
  Use volume as IDE hard disk or CD-ROM (n is 0 to 3).

  **aio=<native | threads>**
    AIO type to use.

  **backup=<boolean>**
    Whether the drive should be included when making backups.

  **bps=<bps>**
    Maximum r/w speed in bytes per second.

  **bps_max_length=<seconds>**
    Maximum length of I/O bursts in seconds.

  **bps_rd=<bps>**
    Maximum read speed in bytes per second.

  **bps_rd_max_length=<seconds>**
    Maximum length of read I/O bursts in seconds.

  **bps_wr=<bps>**
    Maximum write speed in bytes per second.

`bps_wr_max_length=<seconds>`
Maximum length of write I/O bursts in seconds.

`cache=<directsync | none | unsafe | writeback | writethrough>`
The drive's cache mode

`cyls=<integer>`
Force the drive's physical geometry to have a specific cylinder count.

`detect_zeroes=<boolean>`
Controls whether to detect and try to optimize writes of zeroes.

`discard=<ignore | on>`
Controls whether to pass discard/trim requests to the underlying storage.

`file=<volume>`
The drive's backing volume.

`format=<cloop | cow | qcow | qcow2 | qed | raw | vmdk>`
The drive's backing file's data format.

`heads=<integer>`
Force the drive's physical geometry to have a specific head count.

`iops=<iops>`
Maximum r/w I/O in operations per second.

`iops_max=<iops>`
Maximum unthrottled r/w I/O pool in operations per second.

`iops_max_length=<seconds>`
Maximum length of I/O bursts in seconds.

`iops_rd=<iops>`
Maximum read I/O in operations per second.

`iops_rd_max=<iops>`
Maximum unthrottled read I/O pool in operations per second.

`iops_rd_max_length=<seconds>`
Maximum length of read I/O bursts in seconds.

`iops_wr=<iops>`
Maximum write I/O in operations per second.

`iops_wr_max=<iops>`
Maximum unthrottled write I/O pool in operations per second.

`iops_wr_max_length=<seconds>`
Maximum length of write I/O bursts in seconds.

`mbps=<mbps>`
Maximum r/w speed in megabytes per second.

**mbps_max=<mbps>**
    Maximum unthrottled r/w pool in megabytes per second.

**mbps_rd=<mbps>**
    Maximum read speed in megabytes per second.

**mbps_rd_max=<mbps>**
    Maximum unthrottled read pool in megabytes per second.

**mbps_wr=<mbps>**
    Maximum write speed in megabytes per second.

**mbps_wr_max=<mbps>**
    Maximum unthrottled write pool in megabytes per second.

**media=<cdrom | disk>** (*default = disk*)
    The drive's media type.

**model=<model>**
    The drive's reported model name, url-encoded, up to 40 bytes long.

**replicate=<boolean>** (*default = 1*)
    Whether the drive should considered for replication jobs.

**rerror=<ignore | report | stop>**
    Read error action.

**secs=<integer>**
    Force the drive's physical geometry to have a specific sector count.

**serial=<serial>**
    The drive's reported serial number, url-encoded, up to 20 bytes long.

**size=<DiskSize>**
    Disk size. This is purely informational and has no effect.

**snapshot=<boolean>**
    Whether the drive should be included when making snapshots.

**trans=<auto | lba | none>**
    Force disk geometry bios translation mode.

**werror=<enospc | ignore | report | stop>**
    Write error action.

**keyboard: <da | de | de-ch | en-gb | en-us | es | fi | fr | fr-be |
fr-ca | fr-ch | hu | is | it | ja | lt | mk | nl | no | pl | pt |
pt-br | sl | sv | tr>** (*default = en-us*)
    Keybord layout for vnc server. Default is read from the */etc/pve/datacenter.conf* configuration file.

**kvm: <boolean>** (*default = 1*)
    Enable/disable KVM hardware virtualization.

**localtime: <boolean>**
> Set the real time clock to local time. This is enabled by default if ostype indicates a Microsoft OS.

**lock: <backup | migrate | rollback | snapshot>**
> Lock/unlock the VM.

**machine: (pc|pc(-i440fx)?-\d+\.\d+(\.pxe)?|q35|pc-q35-\d+\.\d+(\.pxe)?)**
> Specific the Qemu machine type.

**memory: <integer> (16 - N)** (*default* = 512)
> Amount of RAM for the VM in MB. This is the maximum available memory when you use the balloon device.

**migrate_downtime: <number> (0 - N)** (*default* = 0.1)
> Set maximum tolerated downtime (in seconds) for migrations.

**migrate_speed: <integer> (0 - N)** (*default* = 0)
> Set maximum speed (in MB/s) for migrations. Value 0 is no limit.

**name: <string>**
> Set a name for the VM. Only used on the configuration web interface.

**net[n]: [model=]<enum> [,bridge=<bridge>] [,firewall=<1|0>] [,link_down=<1|0>] [,macaddr=<XX:XX:XX:XX:XX:XX>] [,queues= <integer>] [,rate=<number>] [,tag=<integer>] [,trunks=<vlanid[; vlanid...]>] [,<model>=<macaddr>]**
> Specify network devices.

> **bridge=<bridge>**
>> Bridge to attach the network device to. The Proxmox VE standard bridge is called *vmbr0*.
>>
>> If you do not specify a bridge, we create a kvm user (NATed) network device, which provides DHCP and DNS services. The following addresses are used:
>>
>> ```
>> 10.0.2.2    Gateway
>> 10.0.2.3    DNS Server
>> 10.0.2.4    SMB Server
>> ```
>>
>> The DHCP server assign addresses to the guest starting from 10.0.2.15.

> **firewall=<boolean>**
>> Whether this interface should be protected by the firewall.

> **link_down=<boolean>**
>> Whether this interface should be disconnected (like pulling the plug).

> **macaddr=<XX:XX:XX:XX:XX:XX>**
>> MAC address. That address must be unique withing your network. This is automatically generated if not specified.

> **model=<e1000 | e1000-82540em | e1000-82544gc | e1000-82545em | i82551 | i82557b | i82559er | ne2k_isa | ne2k_pci | pcnet | rtl8139 | virtio | vmxnet3>**
> Network Card Model. The *virtio* model provides the best performance with very low CPU overhead. If your guest does not support this driver, it is usually best to use *e1000*.
>
> **queues=<integer> (0 - 16)**
> Number of packet queues to be used on the device.
>
> **rate=<number> (0 - N)**
> Rate limit in mbps (megabytes per second) as floating point number.
>
> **tag=<integer> (1 - 4094)**
> VLAN tag to apply to packets on this interface.
>
> **trunks=<vlanid[;vlanid...]>**
> VLAN trunks to pass through this interface.

**numa: <boolean> (*default* = 0)**
Enable/disable NUMA.

**numa[n]: cpus=<id[-id];...> [,hostnodes=<id[-id];...>] [,memory= <number>] [,policy=<preferred|bind|interleave>]**
NUMA topology.

> **cpus=<id[-id];...>**
> CPUs accessing this NUMA node.
>
> **hostnodes=<id[-id];...>**
> Host NUMA nodes to use.
>
> **memory=<number>**
> Amount of memory this NUMA node provides.
>
> **policy=<bind | interleave | preferred>**
> NUMA allocation policy.

**onboot: <boolean> (*default* = 0)**
Specifies whether a VM will be started during system bootup.

**ostype: <l24 | l26 | other | solaris | w2k | w2k3 | w2k8 | win10 | win7 | win8 | wvista | wxp>**
Specify guest operating system. This is used to enable special optimization/features for specific operating systems:

other            unspecified OS

wxp              Microsoft Windows XP

| w2k | Microsoft Windows 2000 |
| w2k3 | Microsoft Windows 2003 |
| w2k8 | Microsoft Windows 2008 |
| wvista | Microsoft Windows Vista |
| win7 | Microsoft Windows 7 |
| win8 | Microsoft Windows 8/2012 |
| l24 | Linux 2.4 Kernel |
| l26 | Linux 2.6/3.X Kernel |
| solaris | Solaris/OpenSolaris/OpenIndiania kernel |

**parallel[n]: /dev/parport\d+|/dev/usb/lp\d+**
Map host parallel devices (n is 0 to 2).

---
**Note**

This option allows direct access to host hardware. So it is no longer possible to migrate such machines - use with special care.

---

---
 **Caution**

Experimental! User reported problems with this option.

---

**protection: <boolean> (*default* = 0)**
Sets the protection flag of the VM. This will disable the remove VM and remove disk operations.

**reboot: <boolean> (*default* = 1)**
Allow reboot. If set to *0* the VM exit on reboot.

```
sata[n]: [file=]<volume> [,aio=<native|threads>] [,backup=<1|0>]
[,bps=<bps>] [,bps_max_length=<seconds>] [,bps_rd=<bps>]
[,bps_rd_max_length=<seconds>] [,bps_wr=<bps>] [,bps_wr_max_length=
<seconds>] [,cache=<enum>] [,cyls=<integer>] [,detect_zeroes=<1|0>]
[,discard=<ignore|on>] [,format=<enum>] [,heads=<integer>] [,iops=
<iops>] [,iops_max=<iops>] [,iops_max_length=<seconds>] [,iops_rd=
<iops>] [,iops_rd_max=<iops>] [,iops_rd_max_length=<seconds>]
[,iops_wr=<iops>] [,iops_wr_max=<iops>] [,iops_wr_max_length=
<seconds>] [,mbps=<mbps>] [,mbps_max=<mbps>] [,mbps_rd=<mbps>]
[,mbps_rd_max=<mbps>] [,mbps_wr=<mbps>] [,mbps_wr_max=<mbps>]
[,media=<cdrom|disk>] [,replicate=<1|0>] [,rerror=
<ignore|report|stop>] [,secs=<integer>] [,serial=<serial>] [,size=
<DiskSize>] [,snapshot=<1|0>] [,trans=<none|lba|auto>] [,werror=
<enum>]
```
Use volume as SATA hard disk or CD-ROM (n is 0 to 5).

**aio=<native | threads>**
AIO type to use.

**backup=<boolean>**
Whether the drive should be included when making backups.

**bps=<bps>**
Maximum r/w speed in bytes per second.

**bps_max_length=<seconds>**
Maximum length of I/O bursts in seconds.

**bps_rd=<bps>**
Maximum read speed in bytes per second.

**bps_rd_max_length=<seconds>**
Maximum length of read I/O bursts in seconds.

**bps_wr=<bps>**
Maximum write speed in bytes per second.

**bps_wr_max_length=<seconds>**
Maximum length of write I/O bursts in seconds.

**cache=<directsync | none | unsafe | writeback | writethrough>**
The drive's cache mode

**cyls=<integer>**
Force the drive's physical geometry to have a specific cylinder count.

**detect_zeroes=<boolean>**
Controls whether to detect and try to optimize writes of zeroes.

**discard=<ignore | on>**
Controls whether to pass discard/trim requests to the underlying storage.

**file=<volume>**
The drive's backing volume.

**format=<cloop | cow | qcow | qcow2 | qed | raw | vmdk>**
The drive's backing file's data format.

**heads=<integer>**
Force the drive's physical geometry to have a specific head count.

**iops=<iops>**
Maximum r/w I/O in operations per second.

**iops_max=<iops>**
Maximum unthrottled r/w I/O pool in operations per second.

**iops_max_length=<seconds>**
Maximum length of I/O bursts in seconds.

**iops_rd=<iops>**
Maximum read I/O in operations per second.

**iops_rd_max=<iops>**
Maximum unthrottled read I/O pool in operations per second.

**iops_rd_max_length=<seconds>**
Maximum length of read I/O bursts in seconds.

**iops_wr=<iops>**
Maximum write I/O in operations per second.

**iops_wr_max=<iops>**
Maximum unthrottled write I/O pool in operations per second.

**iops_wr_max_length=<seconds>**
Maximum length of write I/O bursts in seconds.

**mbps=<mbps>**
Maximum r/w speed in megabytes per second.

**mbps_max=<mbps>**
Maximum unthrottled r/w pool in megabytes per second.

**mbps_rd=<mbps>**
Maximum read speed in megabytes per second.

**mbps_rd_max=<mbps>**
Maximum unthrottled read pool in megabytes per second.

**mbps_wr=<mbps>**
Maximum write speed in megabytes per second.

**mbps_wr_max=<mbps>**
Maximum unthrottled write pool in megabytes per second.

**media=<cdrom | disk>** (*default* = disk)

The drive's media type.

**replicate=<boolean>** (*default* = 1)

Whether the drive should considered for replication jobs.

**rerror=<ignore | report | stop>**

Read error action.

**secs=<integer>**

Force the drive's physical geometry to have a specific sector count.

**serial=<serial>**

The drive's reported serial number, url-encoded, up to 20 bytes long.

**size=<DiskSize>**

Disk size. This is purely informational and has no effect.

**snapshot=<boolean>**

Whether the drive should be included when making snapshots.

**trans=<auto | lba | none>**

Force disk geometry bios translation mode.

**werror=<enospc | ignore | report | stop>**

Write error action.

**scsi[n]: [file=]<volume> [,aio=<native|threads>] [,backup=<1|0>] [,bps=<bps>] [,bps_max_length=<seconds>] [,bps_rd=<bps>] [,bps_rd_max_length=<seconds>] [,bps_wr=<bps>] [,bps_wr_max_length= <seconds>] [,cache=<enum>] [,cyls=<integer>] [,detect_zeroes=<1|0>] [,discard=<ignore|on>] [,format=<enum>] [,heads=<integer>] [,iops= <iops>] [,iops_max=<iops>] [,iops_max_length=<seconds>] [,iops_rd= <iops>] [,iops_rd_max=<iops>] [,iops_rd_max_length=<seconds>] [,iops_wr=<iops>] [,iops_wr_max=<iops>] [,iops_wr_max_length= <seconds>] [,iothread=<1|0>] [,mbps=<mbps>] [,mbps_max=<mbps>] [,mbps_rd=<mbps>] [,mbps_rd_max=<mbps>] [,mbps_wr=<mbps>] [,mbps_wr_max=<mbps>] [,media=<cdrom|disk>] [,queues=<integer>] [,replicate=<1|0>] [,rerror=<ignore|report|stop>] [,scsiblock= <1|0>] [,secs=<integer>] [,serial=<serial>] [,size=<DiskSize>] [,snapshot=<1|0>] [,trans=<none|lba|auto>] [,werror=<enum>]**

Use volume as SCSI hard disk or CD-ROM (n is 0 to 13).

**aio=<native | threads>**

AIO type to use.

**backup=<boolean>**

Whether the drive should be included when making backups.

**bps=<bps>**

Maximum r/w speed in bytes per second.

**bps_max_length=<seconds>**
Maximum length of I/O bursts in seconds.

**bps_rd=<bps>**
Maximum read speed in bytes per second.

**bps_rd_max_length=<seconds>**
Maximum length of read I/O bursts in seconds.

**bps_wr=<bps>**
Maximum write speed in bytes per second.

**bps_wr_max_length=<seconds>**
Maximum length of write I/O bursts in seconds.

**cache=<directsync | none | unsafe | writeback | writethrough>**
The drive's cache mode

**cyls=<integer>**
Force the drive's physical geometry to have a specific cylinder count.

**detect_zeroes=<boolean>**
Controls whether to detect and try to optimize writes of zeroes.

**discard=<ignore | on>**
Controls whether to pass discard/trim requests to the underlying storage.

**file=<volume>**
The drive's backing volume.

**format=<cloop | cow | qcow | qcow2 | qed | raw | vmdk>**
The drive's backing file's data format.

**heads=<integer>**
Force the drive's physical geometry to have a specific head count.

**iops=<iops>**
Maximum r/w I/O in operations per second.

**iops_max=<iops>**
Maximum unthrottled r/w I/O pool in operations per second.

**iops_max_length=<seconds>**
Maximum length of I/O bursts in seconds.

**iops_rd=<iops>**
Maximum read I/O in operations per second.

**iops_rd_max=<iops>**
Maximum unthrottled read I/O pool in operations per second.

**iops_rd_max_length=<seconds>**
Maximum length of read I/O bursts in seconds.

**iops_wr=<iops>**
    Maximum write I/O in operations per second.

**iops_wr_max=<iops>**
    Maximum unthrottled write I/O pool in operations per second.

**iops_wr_max_length=<seconds>**
    Maximum length of write I/O bursts in seconds.

**iothread=<boolean>**
    Whether to use iothreads for this drive

**mbps=<mbps>**
    Maximum r/w speed in megabytes per second.

**mbps_max=<mbps>**
    Maximum unthrottled r/w pool in megabytes per second.

**mbps_rd=<mbps>**
    Maximum read speed in megabytes per second.

**mbps_rd_max=<mbps>**
    Maximum unthrottled read pool in megabytes per second.

**mbps_wr=<mbps>**
    Maximum write speed in megabytes per second.

**mbps_wr_max=<mbps>**
    Maximum unthrottled write pool in megabytes per second.

**media=<cdrom | disk> (*default* = disk)**
    The drive's media type.

**queues=<integer>  (2 - N)**
    Number of queues.

**replicate=<boolean> (*default* = 1)**
    Whether the drive should considered for replication jobs.

**rerror=<ignore | report | stop>**
    Read error action.

**scsiblock=<boolean> (*default* = 0)**
    whether to use scsi-block for full passthrough of host block device

---

 **Warning**
    can lead to I/O errors in combination with low memory or high memory fragmentation
    on host

---

**secs=<integer>**
    Force the drive's physical geometry to have a specific sector count.

**serial=<serial>**
>    The drive's reported serial number, url-encoded, up to 20 bytes long.

**size=<DiskSize>**
>    Disk size. This is purely informational and has no effect.

**snapshot=<boolean>**
>    Whether the drive should be included when making snapshots.

**trans=<auto | lba | none>**
>    Force disk geometry bios translation mode.

**werror=<enospc | ignore | report | stop>**
>    Write error action.

**scsihw: <lsi | lsi53c810 | megasas | pvscsi | virtio-scsi-pci | virtio-scsi-single>** (*default* = lsi)
>    SCSI controller model

**serial[n]: (/dev/.+|socket)**
>    Create a serial device inside the VM (n is 0 to 3), and pass through a host serial device (i.e. /dev/ttyS0), or create a unix socket on the host side (use *qm terminal* to open a terminal connection).

---

**Note**

If you pass through a host serial device, it is no longer possible to migrate such machines - use with special care.

---

 **Caution**

Experimental! User reported problems with this option.

---

**shares: <integer>  (0 - 50000) (*default* = 1000)**
>    Amount of memory shares for auto-ballooning. The larger the number is, the more memory this VM gets. Number is relative to weights of all other running VMs. Using zero disables auto-ballooning

**smbios1: [family=<string>] [,manufacturer=<string>] [,product=<string>] [,serial=<string>] [,sku=<string>] [,uuid=<UUID>] [,version=<string>]**
>    Specify SMBIOS type 1 fields.

**family=<string>**
>    Set SMBIOS1 family string.

**manufacturer=<string>**
>    Set SMBIOS1 manufacturer.

**product=<string>**
    Set SMBIOS1 product ID.

**serial=<string>**
    Set SMBIOS1 serial number.

**sku=<string>**
    Set SMBIOS1 SKU string.

**uuid=<UUID>**
    Set SMBIOS1 UUID.

**version=<string>**
    Set SMBIOS1 version.

**smp: <integer> (1 - N) (*default* = 1)**
    The number of CPUs. Please use option -sockets instead.

**sockets: <integer> (1 - N) (*default* = 1)**
    The number of CPU sockets.

**startdate: (now | YYYY-MM-DD | YYYY-MM-DDTHH:MM:SS) (*default* = now)**
    Set the initial date of the real time clock. Valid format for date are: *now* or *2006-06-17T16:01:21* or *2006-06-17*.

**startup: `[[order=]\d+] [,up=\d+] [,down=\d+]`**
    Startup and shutdown behavior. Order is a non-negative number defining the general startup order. Shutdown in done with reverse ordering. Additionally you can set the *up* or *down* delay in seconds, which specifies a delay to wait before the next VM is started or stopped.

**tablet: <boolean> (*default* = 1)**
    Enable/disable the USB tablet device. This device is usually needed to allow absolute mouse positioning with VNC. Else the mouse runs out of sync with normal VNC clients. If you're running lots of console-only guests on one host, you may consider disabling this to save some context switches. This is turned off by default if you use spice (-vga=qxl).

**tdf: <boolean> (*default* = 0)**
    Enable/disable time drift fix.

**template: <boolean> (*default* = 0)**
    Enable/disable Template.

**unused[n]: <string>**
    Reference to unused volumes. This is used internally, and should not be modified manually.

**usb[n]: [host=]<HOSTUSBDEVICE|spice> [,usb3=<1|0>]**
    Configure an USB device (n is 0 to 4).

**host=<HOSTUSBDEVICE|spice>**

>   The Host USB device or port or the value *spice*. HOSTUSBDEVICE syntax is:

>   ```
>   'bus-port(.port)*' (decimal numbers) or
>   'vendor_id:product_id' (hexadeciaml numbers) or
>   'spice'
>   ```

>   You can use the *lsusb -t* command to list existing usb devices.

>   **Note**
>
>   This option allows direct access to host hardware. So it is no longer possible to migrate such machines - use with special care.

>   The value *spice* can be used to add a usb redirection devices for spice.

**usb3=<boolean>** (*default = 0*)

>   Specifies whether if given host option is a USB3 device or port (this does currently not work reliably with spice redirection and is then ignored).

**vcpus: <integer>  (1 - N)** (*default = 0*)

>   Number of hotplugged vcpus.

**vga: <cirrus | qxl | qxl2 | qxl3 | qxl4 | serial0 | serial1 | serial2 | serial3 | std | vmware>**

>   Select the VGA type. If you want to use high resolution modes (>= 1280x1024x16) then you should use the options *std* or *vmware*. Default is *std* for win8/win7/w2k8, and *cirrus* for other OS types. The *qxl* option enables the SPICE display sever. For win* OS you can select how many independent displays you want, Linux guests can add displays them self. You can also run without any graphic card, using a serial device as terminal.

**virtio[n]: [file=]<volume> [,aio=<native|threads>] [,backup=<1|0>] [,bps=<bps>] [,bps_max_length=<seconds>] [,bps_rd=<bps>] [,bps_rd_max_length=<seconds>] [,bps_wr=<bps>] [,bps_wr_max_length= <seconds>] [,cache=<enum>] [,cyls=<integer>] [,detect_zeroes=<1|0>] [,discard=<ignore|on>] [,format=<enum>] [,heads=<integer>] [,iops= <iops>] [,iops_max=<iops>] [,iops_max_length=<seconds>] [,iops_rd= <iops>] [,iops_rd_max=<iops>] [,iops_rd_max_length=<seconds>] [,iops_wr=<iops>] [,iops_wr_max=<iops>] [,iops_wr_max_length= <seconds>] [,iothread=<1|0>] [,mbps=<mbps>] [,mbps_max=<mbps>] [,mbps_rd=<mbps>] [,mbps_rd_max=<mbps>] [,mbps_wr=<mbps>] [,mbps_wr_max=<mbps>] [,media=<cdrom|disk>] [,replicate=<1|0>] [,rerror=<ignore|report|stop>] [,secs=<integer>] [,serial=<serial>] [,size=<DiskSize>] [,snapshot=<1|0>] [,trans=<none|lba|auto>] [,werror=<enum>]**

>   Use volume as VIRTIO hard disk (n is 0 to 15).

>   **aio=<native | threads>**
>
>   >   AIO type to use.

**backup=<boolean>**
> Whether the drive should be included when making backups.

**bps=<bps>**
> Maximum r/w speed in bytes per second.

**bps_max_length=<seconds>**
> Maximum length of I/O bursts in seconds.

**bps_rd=<bps>**
> Maximum read speed in bytes per second.

**bps_rd_max_length=<seconds>**
> Maximum length of read I/O bursts in seconds.

**bps_wr=<bps>**
> Maximum write speed in bytes per second.

**bps_wr_max_length=<seconds>**
> Maximum length of write I/O bursts in seconds.

**cache=<directsync | none | unsafe | writeback | writethrough>**
> The drive's cache mode

**cyls=<integer>**
> Force the drive's physical geometry to have a specific cylinder count.

**detect_zeroes=<boolean>**
> Controls whether to detect and try to optimize writes of zeroes.

**discard=<ignore | on>**
> Controls whether to pass discard/trim requests to the underlying storage.

**file=<volume>**
> The drive's backing volume.

**format=<cloop | cow | qcow | qcow2 | qed | raw | vmdk>**
> The drive's backing file's data format.

**heads=<integer>**
> Force the drive's physical geometry to have a specific head count.

**iops=<iops>**
> Maximum r/w I/O in operations per second.

**iops_max=<iops>**
> Maximum unthrottled r/w I/O pool in operations per second.

**iops_max_length=<seconds>**
> Maximum length of I/O bursts in seconds.

**iops_rd=<iops>**
> Maximum read I/O in operations per second.

**iops_rd_max=<iops>**
Maximum unthrottled read I/O pool in operations per second.

**iops_rd_max_length=<seconds>**
Maximum length of read I/O bursts in seconds.

**iops_wr=<iops>**
Maximum write I/O in operations per second.

**iops_wr_max=<iops>**
Maximum unthrottled write I/O pool in operations per second.

**iops_wr_max_length=<seconds>**
Maximum length of write I/O bursts in seconds.

**iothread=<boolean>**
Whether to use iothreads for this drive

**mbps=<mbps>**
Maximum r/w speed in megabytes per second.

**mbps_max=<mbps>**
Maximum unthrottled r/w pool in megabytes per second.

**mbps_rd=<mbps>**
Maximum read speed in megabytes per second.

**mbps_rd_max=<mbps>**
Maximum unthrottled read pool in megabytes per second.

**mbps_wr=<mbps>**
Maximum write speed in megabytes per second.

**mbps_wr_max=<mbps>**
Maximum unthrottled write pool in megabytes per second.

**media=<cdrom | disk>** (*default* = **disk**)
The drive's media type.

**replicate=<boolean>** (*default* = 1)
Whether the drive should considered for replication jobs.

**rerror=<ignore | report | stop>**
Read error action.

**secs=<integer>**
Force the drive's physical geometry to have a specific sector count.

**serial=<serial>**
The drive's reported serial number, url-encoded, up to 20 bytes long.

**size=<DiskSize>**
Disk size. This is purely informational and has no effect.

**snapshot=<boolean>**
> Whether the drive should be included when making snapshots.

**trans=<auto | lba | none>**
> Force disk geometry bios translation mode.

**werror=<enospc | ignore | report | stop>**
> Write error action.

**watchdog: [[model=]<i6300esb|ib700>] [,action=<enum>]**
> Create a virtual hardware watchdog device. Once enabled (by a guest action), the watchdog must be periodically polled by an agent inside the guest or else the watchdog will reset the guest (or execute the respective action specified)

**action=<debug | none | pause | poweroff | reset | shutdown>**
> The action to perform if after activation the guest fails to poll the watchdog in time.

**model=<i6300esb | ib700> (default = i6300esb)**
> Watchdog type to emulate.

## 10.9 Locks

Online migrations, snapshots and backups (vzdump) set a lock to prevent incompatible concurrent actions on the affected VMs. Sometimes you need to remove such a lock manually (e.g., after a power failure).

```
qm unlock <vmid>
```

 **Caution**
Only do that if you are sure the action which set the lock is no longer running.

# Chapter 11

# Proxmox Container Toolkit

Containers are a lightweight alternative to fully virtualized VMs. Instead of emulating a complete Operating System (OS), containers simply use the OS of the host they run on. This implies that all containers use the same kernel, and that they can access resources from the host directly.

This is great because containers do not waste CPU power nor memory due to kernel emulation. Container run-time costs are close to zero and usually negligible. But there are also some drawbacks you need to consider:

- You can only run Linux based OS inside containers, i.e. it is not possible to run FreeBSD or MS Windows inside.

- For security reasons, access to host resources needs to be restricted. This is done with AppArmor, Sec-Comp filters and other kernel features. Be prepared that some syscalls are not allowed inside containers.

Proxmox VE uses LXC as underlying container technology. We consider LXC as low-level library, which provides countless options. It would be too difficult to use those tools directly. Instead, we provide a small wrapper called pct, the "Proxmox Container Toolkit".

The toolkit is tightly coupled with Proxmox VE. That means that it is aware of the cluster setup, and it can use the same network and storage resources as fully virtualized VMs. You can even use the Proxmox VE firewall, or manage containers using the HA framework.

Our primary goal is to offer an environment as one would get from a VM, but without the additional overhead. We call this "System Containers".

---

**Note**
If you want to run micro-containers (with docker, rkt, ...), it is best to run them inside a VM.

---

## 11.1  Technology Overview

- LXC (https://linuxcontainers.org/)

- Integrated into Proxmox VE graphical user interface (GUI)

- Easy to use command line tool pct

- Access via Proxmox VE REST API

- lxcfs to provide containerized /proc file system

- AppArmor/Seccomp to improve security

- CRIU: for live migration (planned)

- Use latest available kernels (4.4.X)

- Image based deployment (templates)

- Use Proxmox VE storage library

- Container setup from host (network, DNS, storage, ... )

## 11.2   Security Considerations

Containers use the same kernel as the host, so there is a big attack surface for malicious users. You should consider this fact if you provide containers to totally untrusted people. In general, fully virtualized VMs provide better isolation.

The good news is that LXC uses many kernel security features like AppArmor, CGroups and PID and user namespaces, which makes containers usage quite secure.

## 11.3   Guest Operating System Configuration

We normally try to detect the operating system type inside the container, and then modify some files inside the container to make them work as expected. Here is a short list of things we do at container startup:

**set /etc/hostname**
> to set the container name

**modify /etc/hosts**
> to allow lookup of the local hostname

**network setup**
> pass the complete network setup to the container

**configure DNS**
> pass information about DNS servers

**adapt the init system**
> for example, fix the number of spawned getty processes

**set the root password**
> when creating a new container

**rewrite ssh_host_keys**
>   so that each container has unique keys

**randomize crontab**
>   so that cron does not start at the same time on all containers

Changes made by Proxmox VE are enclosed by comment markers:

```
# --- BEGIN PVE ---
<data>
# --- END PVE ---
```

Those markers will be inserted at a reasonable location in the file. If such a section already exists, it will be updated in place and will not be moved.

Modification of a file can be prevented by adding a `.pve-ignore.` file for it. For instance, if the file `/etc/.pve-ignore.hosts` exists then the `/etc/hosts` file will not be touched. This can be a simple empty file creatd via:

```
# touch /etc/.pve-ignore.hosts
```

Most modifications are OS dependent, so they differ between different distributions and versions. You can completely disable modifications by manually setting the `ostype` to `unmanaged`.

OS type detection is done by testing for certain files inside the container:

**Ubuntu**
>   inspect /etc/lsb-release (`DISTRIB_ID=Ubuntu`)

**Debian**
>   test /etc/debian_version

**Fedora**
>   test /etc/fedora-release

**RedHat or CentOS**
>   test /etc/redhat-release

**ArchLinux**
>   test /etc/arch-release

**Alpine**
>   test /etc/alpine-release

**Gentoo**
>   test /etc/gentoo-release

---

**Note**

Container start fails if the configured `ostype` differs from the auto detected type.

---

## 11.4 Container Images

Container images, sometimes also referred to as "templates" or "appliances", are `tar` archives which contain everything to run a container. You can think of it as a tidy container backup. Like most modern container toolkits, `pct` uses those images when you create a new container, for example:

```
pct create 999 local:vztmpl/debian-8.0-standard_8.0-1_amd64.tar.gz
```

Proxmox VE itself ships a set of basic templates for most common operating systems, and you can download them using the `pveam` (short for Proxmox VE Appliance Manager) command line utility. You can also download TurnKey Linux containers using that tool (or the graphical user interface).

Our image repositories contain a list of available images, and there is a cron job run each day to download that list. You can trigger that update manually with:

```
pveam update
```

After that you can view the list of available images using:

```
pveam available
```

You can restrict this large list by specifying the `section` you are interested in, for example basic `system` images:

**List available system images**

```
# pveam available --section system
system          archlinux-base_2015-24-29-1_x86_64.tar.gz
system          centos-7-default_20160205_amd64.tar.xz
system          debian-6.0-standard_6.0-7_amd64.tar.gz
system          debian-7.0-standard_7.0-3_amd64.tar.gz
system          debian-8.0-standard_8.0-1_amd64.tar.gz
system          ubuntu-12.04-standard_12.04-1_amd64.tar.gz
system          ubuntu-14.04-standard_14.04-1_amd64.tar.gz
system          ubuntu-15.04-standard_15.04-1_amd64.tar.gz
system          ubuntu-15.10-standard_15.10-1_amd64.tar.gz
```

Before you can use such a template, you need to download them into one of your storages. You can simply use storage `local` for that purpose. For clustered installations, it is preferred to use a shared storage so that all nodes can access those images.

```
pveam download local debian-8.0-standard_8.0-1_amd64.tar.gz
```

You are now ready to create containers using that image, and you can list all downloaded images on storage `local` with:

```
# pveam list local
local:vztmpl/debian-8.0-standard_8.0-1_amd64.tar.gz   190.20MB
```

The above command shows you the full Proxmox VE volume identifiers. They include the storage name, and most other Proxmox VE commands can use them. For example you can delete that image later with:

```
pveam remove local:vztmpl/debian-8.0-standard_8.0-1_amd64.tar.gz
```

## 11.5 Container Storage

Traditional containers use a very simple storage model, only allowing a single mount point, the root file system. This was further restricted to specific file system types like `ext4` and `nfs`. Additional mounts are often done by user provided scripts. This turned out to be complex and error prone, so we try to avoid that now.

Our new LXC based container model is more flexible regarding storage. First, you can have more than a single mount point. This allows you to choose a suitable storage for each application. For example, you can use a relatively slow (and thus cheap) storage for the container root file system. Then you can use a second mount point to mount a very fast, distributed storage for your database application. See section Mount Points for further details.

The second big improvement is that you can use any storage type supported by the Proxmox VE storage library. That means that you can store your containers on local `lvmthin` or `zfs`, shared `iSCSI` storage, or even on distributed storage systems like `ceph`. It also enables us to use advanced storage features like snapshots and clones. `vzdump` can also use the snapshot feature to provide consistent container backups.

Last but not least, you can also mount local devices directly, or mount local directories using bind mounts. That way you can access local storage inside containers with zero overhead. Such bind mounts also provide an easy way to share data between different containers.

### 11.5.1 FUSE Mounts

**Warning**
Because of existing issues in the Linux kernel's freezer subsystem the usage of FUSE mounts inside a container is strongly advised against, as containers need to be frozen for suspend or snapshot mode backups.

If FUSE mounts cannot be replaced by other mounting mechanisms or storage technologies, it is possible to establish the FUSE mount on the Proxmox host and use a bind mount point to make it accessible inside the container.

### 11.5.2 Using Quotas Inside Containers

Quotas allow to set limits inside a container for the amount of disk space that each user can use. This only works on ext4 image based storage types and currently does not work with unprivileged containers.

Activating the `quota` option causes the following mount options to be used for a mount point: `usrjquota=aquota.user,grpjquota=aquota.group,jqfmt=vfsv0`

This allows quotas to be used like you would on any other system. You can initialize the `/aquota.user` and `/aquota.group` files by running

```
quotacheck -cmug /
quotaon /
```

and edit the quotas via the `edquota` command. Refer to the documentation of the distribution running inside the container for details.

---

**Note**

You need to run the above commands for every mount point by passing the mount point's path instead of just /.

---

### 11.5.3  Using ACLs Inside Containers

The standard Posix **A**ccess **C**ontrol **L**ists are also available inside containers. ACLs allow you to set more detailed file ownership than the traditional user/ group/others model.

### 11.5.4  Backup of Containers mount points

By default additional mount points besides the RootDisk mount point are not included in backups. You can reverse this default behavior by setting the * Backup* option on a mount point.

### 11.5.5  Replication of Containers mount points

By default additional mount points are replicated when the RootDisk is replicated. If you want the Proxmox VE storage replication mechanism to skip a mount point when starting a replication job, you can set the **Skip replication** option on that mount point.
As of Proxmox VE 5.0, replication requires a storage of type `zfspool`, so adding a mount point to a different type of storage when the container has replication configured requires to **Skip replication** for that mount point.

## 11.6  Container Settings

### 11.6.1  General Settings

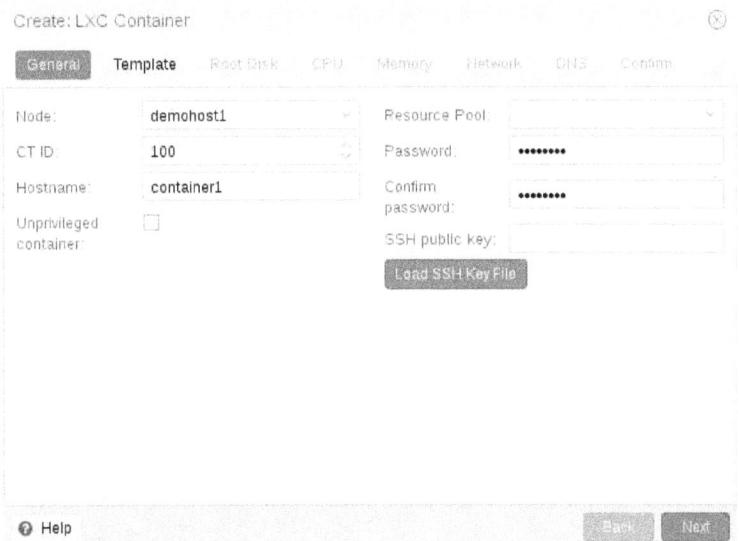

General settings of a container include

- the **Node** : the physical server on which the container will run

- the **CT ID**: a unique number in this Proxmox VE installation used to identify your container

- **Hostname**: the hostname of the container

- **Resource Pool**: a logical group of containers and VMs

- **Password**: the root password of the container

- **SSH Public Key**: a public key for connecting to the root account over SSH

- **Unprivileged container**: this option allows to choose at creation time if you want to create a privileged or unprivileged container.

### Privileged Containers

Security is done by dropping capabilities, using mandatory access control (AppArmor), SecComp filters and namespaces. The LXC team considers this kind of container as unsafe, and they will not consider new container escape exploits to be security issues worthy of a CVE and quick fix. So you should use this kind of containers only inside a trusted environment, or when no untrusted task is running as root in the container.

### Unprivileged Containers

This kind of containers use a new kernel feature called user namespaces. The root UID 0 inside the container is mapped to an unprivileged user outside the container. This means that most security issues (container escape, resource abuse, . . . ) in those containers will affect a random unprivileged user, and so would be a generic kernel security bug rather than an LXC issue. The LXC team thinks unprivileged containers are safe by design.

**Note**

If the container uses systemd as an init system, please be aware the systemd version running inside the container should be equal or greater than 220.

## 11.6.2 CPU

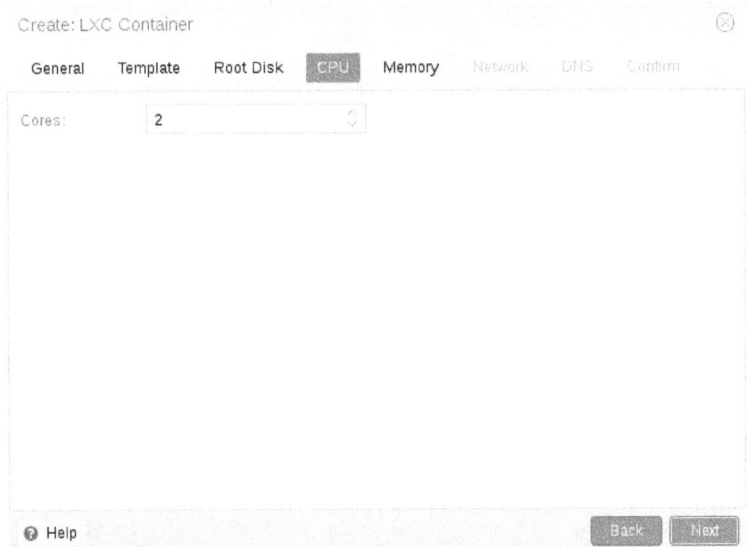

You can restrict the number of visible CPUs inside the container using the `cores` option. This is implemented using the Linux *cpuset* cgroup (**control group**). A special task inside `pvestatd` tries to distribute running containers among available CPUs. You can view the assigned CPUs using the following command:

```
# pct cpusets
 -------------------
 102:               6 7
 105:       2 3 4 5
 108:   0 1
 -------------------
```

Containers use the host kernel directly, so all task inside a container are handled by the host CPU scheduler. Proxmox VE uses the Linux *CFS* (**C**ompletely **F**air **S**cheduler) scheduler by default, which has additional bandwidth control options.

cpulimit:    You can use this option to further limit assigned CPU time. Please note that this is a floating point number, so it is perfectly valid to assign two cores to a container, but restrict overall CPU consumption to half a core.

```
cores: 2
cpulimit: 0.5
```

cpuunits:    This is a relative weight passed to the kernel scheduler. The larger the number is, the more CPU time this container gets. Number is relative to the weights of all the other running containers. The default is 1024. You can use this setting to prioritize some containers.

### 11.6.3 Memory

Container memory is controlled using the cgroup memory controller.

memory: Limit overall memory usage. This corresponds to the `memory.limit_in_bytes` cgroup setting.

swap: Allows the container to use additional swap memory from the host swap space. This corresponds to the `memory.memsw.limit_in_bytes` cgroup setting, which is set to the sum of both value (`memory + swap`).

### 11.6.4 Mount Points

The root mount point is configured with the `rootfs` property, and you can configure up to 10 additional mount points. The corresponding options are called `mp0` to `mp9`, and they can contain the following setting:

```
rootfs: [volume=]<volume> [,acl=<1|0>] [,quota=<1|0>] [,replicate=
<1|0>] [,ro=<1|0>] [,shared=<1|0>] [,size=<DiskSize>]
```
   Use volume as container root. See below for a detailed description of all options.

```
mp[n]: [volume=]<volume> ,mp=<Path> [,acl=<1|0>] [,backup=<1|0>]
[,quota=<1|0>] [,replicate=<1|0>] [,ro=<1|0>] [,shared=<1|0>]
[,size=<DiskSize>]
```
   Use volume as container mount point.

    `acl=<boolean>`
   Explicitly enable or disable ACL support.

    `backup=<boolean>`
   Whether to include the mount point in backups (only used for volume mount points).

    `mp=<Path>`
   Path to the mount point as seen from inside the container.

> **Note**
> Must not contain any symlinks for security reasons.

    `quota=<boolean>`
   Enable user quotas inside the container (not supported with zfs subvolumes)

    `replicate=<boolean>` (*default = 1*)
   Will include this volume to a storage replica job.

    `ro=<boolean>`
   Read-only mount point

    `shared=<boolean>` (*default = 0*)
   Mark this non-volume mount point as available on all nodes.

 **Warning**
This option does not share the mount point automatically, it assumes it is shared already!

    `size=<DiskSize>`
   Volume size (read only value).

    `volume=<volume>`
   Volume, device or directory to mount into the container.

Currently there are basically three types of mount points: storage backed mount points, bind mounts and device mounts.

### Typical container rootfs configuration

```
rootfs: thin1:base-100-disk-1,size=8G
```

### Storage Backed Mount Points

Storage backed mount points are managed by the Proxmox VE storage subsystem and come in three different flavors:

- Image based: these are raw images containing a single ext4 formatted file system.

- ZFS subvolumes: these are technically bind mounts, but with managed storage, and thus allow resizing and snapshotting.

- Directories: passing `size=0` triggers a special case where instead of a raw image a directory is created.

### Bind Mount Points

Bind mounts allow you to access arbitrary directories from your Proxmox VE host inside a container. Some potential use cases are:

- Accessing your home directory in the guest

- Accessing an USB device directory in the guest

- Accessing an NFS mount from the host in the guest

Bind mounts are considered to not be managed by the storage subsystem, so you cannot make snapshots or deal with quotas from inside the container. With unprivileged containers you might run into permission problems caused by the user mapping and cannot use ACLs.

---

**Note**

The contents of bind mount points are not backed up when using `vzdump`.

---

**Warning**

For security reasons, bind mounts should only be established using source directories especially reserved for this purpose, e.g., a directory hierarchy under `/mnt/bindmounts`. Never bind mount system directories like `/`, `/var` or `/etc` into a container - this poses a great security risk.

---

**Note**

The bind mount source path must not contain any symlinks.

---

For example, to make the directory `/mnt/bindmounts/shared` accessible in the container with ID `100` under the path `/shared`, use a configuration line like `mp0: /mnt/bindmounts/shared,mp=/shared` in `/etc/pve/lxc/100.conf`. Alternatively, use `pct set 100 -mp0 /mnt/bindmounts/shared,mp=/shared` to achieve the same result.

**Device Mount Points**

Device mount points allow to mount block devices of the host directly into the container. Similar to bind mounts, device mounts are not managed by Proxmox VE's storage subsystem, but the `quota` and `acl` options will be honored.

---

**Note**

Device mount points should only be used under special circumstances. In most cases a storage backed mount point offers the same performance and a lot more features.

---

**Note**

The contents of device mount points are not backed up when using `vzdump`.

---

## 11.6.5 Network

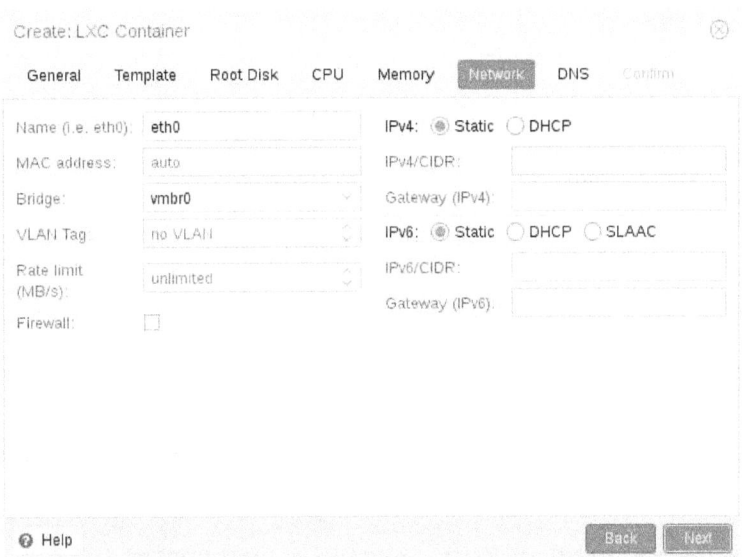

You can configure up to 10 network interfaces for a single container. The corresponding options are called `net0` to `net9`, and they can contain the following setting:

```
net[n]: name=<string> [,bridge=<bridge>] [,firewall=<1|0>] [,gw=
<GatewayIPv4>] [,gw6=<GatewayIPv6>] [,hwaddr=<XX:XX:XX:XX:XX:XX>]
[,ip=<IPv4Format/CIDR>] [,ip6=<IPv6Format/CIDR>] [,mtu=<integer>]
[,rate=<mbps>] [,tag=<integer>] [,trunks=<vlanid[;vlanid...]>]
[,type=<veth>]
```
Specifies network interfaces for the container.

> **bridge=<bridge>**
> Bridge to attach the network device to.

> **firewall=<boolean>**
> Controls whether this interface's firewall rules should be used.

**gw=<GatewayIPv4>**
Default gateway for IPv4 traffic.

**gw6=<GatewayIPv6>**
Default gateway for IPv6 traffic.

**hwaddr=<XX:XX:XX:XX:XX:XX>**
The interface MAC address. This is dynamically allocated by default, but you can set that statically if needed, for example to always have the same link-local IPv6 address. (lxc.network.hwaddr)

**ip=<IPv4Format/CIDR>**
IPv4 address in CIDR format.

**ip6=<IPv6Format/CIDR>**
IPv6 address in CIDR format.

**mtu=<integer> (64 - N)**
Maximum transfer unit of the interface. (lxc.network.mtu)

**name=<string>**
Name of the network device as seen from inside the container. (lxc.network.name)

**rate=<mbps>**
Apply rate limiting to the interface

**tag=<integer> (1 - 4094)**
VLAN tag for this interface.

**trunks=<vlanid[;vlanid...]>**
VLAN ids to pass through the interface

**type=<veth>**
Network interface type.

## 11.6.6  Automatic Start and Shutdown of Containers

After creating your containers, you probably want them to start automatically when the host system boots. For this you need to select the option *Start at boot* from the *Options* Tab of your container in the web interface, or set it with the following command:

```
pct set <ctid> -onboot 1
```

### Start and Shutdown Order

If you want to fine tune the boot order of your containers, you can use the following parameters :

- **Start/Shutdown order**: Defines the start order priority. E.g. set it to 1 if you want the CT to be the first to be started. (We use the reverse startup order for shutdown, so a container with a start order of 1 would be the last to be shut down)

- **Startup delay**: Defines the interval between this container start and subsequent containers starts . E.g. set it to 240 if you want to wait 240 seconds before starting other containers.

- **Shutdown timeout**: Defines the duration in seconds Proxmox VE should wait for the container to be offline after issuing a shutdown command. By default this value is set to 60, which means that Proxmox VE will issue a shutdown request, wait 60s for the machine to be offline, and if after 60s the machine is still online will notify that the shutdown action failed.

Please note that containers without a Start/Shutdown order parameter will always start after those where the parameter is set, and this parameter only makes sense between the machines running locally on a host, and not cluster-wide.

## 11.7  Backup and Restore

### 11.7.1  Container Backup

It is possible to use the `vzdump` tool for container backup. Please refer to the `vzdump` manual page for details.

### 11.7.2  Restoring Container Backups

Restoring container backups made with `vzdump` is possible using the `pct restore` command. By default, `pct restore` will attempt to restore as much of the backed up container configuration as possible. It is possible to override the backed up configuration by manually setting container options on the command line (see the `pct` manual page for details).

---

**Note**

`pvesm extractconfig` can be used to view the backed up configuration contained in a vzdump archive.

---

There are two basic restore modes, only differing by their handling of mount points:

#### "Simple" Restore Mode

If neither the `rootfs` parameter nor any of the optional `mpX` parameters are explicitly set, the mount point configuration from the backed up configuration file is restored using the following steps:

1. Extract mount points and their options from backup

2. Create volumes for storage backed mount points (on storage provided with the `storage` parameter, or default local storage if unset)

3. Extract files from backup archive

4. Add bind and device mount points to restored configuration (limited to root user)

---

**Note**

Since bind and device mount points are never backed up, no files are restored in the last step, but only the configuration options. The assumption is that such mount points are either backed up with another mechanism (e.g., NFS space that is bind mounted into many containers), or not intended to be backed up at all.

---

This simple mode is also used by the container restore operations in the web interface.

### "Advanced" Restore Mode

By setting the `rootfs` parameter (and optionally, any combination of `mpX` parameters), the `pct rest ore` command is automatically switched into an advanced mode. This advanced mode completely ignores the `rootfs` and `mpX` configuration options contained in the backup archive, and instead only uses the options explicitly provided as parameters.

This mode allows flexible configuration of mount point settings at restore time, for example:

• Set target storages, volume sizes and other options for each mount point individually

• Redistribute backed up files according to new mount point scheme

• Restore to device and/or bind mount points (limited to root user)

## 11.8 Managing Containers with `pct`

`pct` is the tool to manage Linux Containers on Proxmox VE. You can create and destroy containers, and control execution (start, stop, migrate, ...). You can use pct to set parameters in the associated config file, like network configuration or memory limits.

### 11.8.1 CLI Usage Examples

Create a container based on a Debian template (provided you have already downloaded the template via the web interface)

```
pct create 100 /var/lib/vz/template/cache/debian-8.0-standard_8.0-1 ↵
   _amd64.tar.gz
```

Start container 100

```
pct start 100
```

Start a login session via getty

```
pct console 100
```

Enter the LXC namespace and run a shell as root user

```
pct enter 100
```

Display the configuration

```
pct config 100
```

Add a network interface called eth0, bridged to the host bridge vmbr0, set the address and gateway, while it's running

```
pct set 100 -net0 name=eth0,bridge=vmbr0,ip=192.168.15.147/24,gw ↩
   =192.168.15.1
```

Reduce the memory of the container to 512MB

```
pct set 100 -memory 512
```

### 11.8.2  Obtaining Debugging Logs

In case pct start is unable to start a specific container, it might be helpful to collect debugging output by running lxc-start (replace ID with the container's ID):

```
lxc-start -n ID -F -l DEBUG -o /tmp/lxc-ID.log
```

This command will attempt to start the container in foreground mode, to stop the container run pct shutdown ID or pct stop ID in a second terminal.

The collected debug log is written to /tmp/lxc-ID.log.

---

**Note**
If you have changed the container's configuration since the last start attempt with pct start, you need to run pct start at least once to also update the configuration used by lxc-start.

---

## 11.9  Migration

If you have a cluster, you can migrate your Containers with

```
pct migrate <vmid> <target>
```

This works as long as your Container is offline. If it has local volumes or mountpoints defined, the migration will copy the content over the network to the target host if there is the same storage defined.

If you want to migrate online Containers, the only way is to use restart migration. This can be initiated with the -restart flag and the optional -timeout parameter.

A restart migration will shut down the Container and kill it after the specified timeout (the default is 180 seconds). Then it will migrate the Container like an offline migration and when finished, it starts the Container on the target node.

## 11.10   Configuration

The `/etc/pve/lxc/<CTID>.conf` file stores container configuration, where `<CTID>` is the numeric ID of the given container. Like all other files stored inside `/etc/pve/`, they get automatically replicated to all other cluster nodes.

---

**Note**

CTIDs < 100 are reserved for internal purposes, and CTIDs need to be unique cluster wide.

---

**Example Container Configuration**

```
ostype: debian
arch: amd64
hostname: www
memory: 512
swap: 512
net0: bridge=vmbr0,hwaddr=66:64:66:64:64:36,ip=dhcp,name=eth0,type=veth
rootfs: local:107/vm-107-disk-1.raw,size=7G
```

Those configuration files are simple text files, and you can edit them using a normal text editor (`vi`, `nano`, ...). This is sometimes useful to do small corrections, but keep in mind that you need to restart the container to apply such changes.

For that reason, it is usually better to use the `pct` command to generate and modify those files, or do the whole thing using the GUI. Our toolkit is smart enough to instantaneously apply most changes to running containers. This feature is called "hot plug", and there is no need to restart the container in that case.

### 11.10.1   File Format

Container configuration files use a simple colon separated key/value format. Each line has the following format:

```
# this is a comment
OPTION: value
```

Blank lines in those files are ignored, and lines starting with a # character are treated as comments and are also ignored.

It is possible to add low-level, LXC style configuration directly, for example:

```
lxc.init_cmd: /sbin/my_own_init
```

or

```
lxc.init_cmd = /sbin/my_own_init
```

Those settings are directly passed to the LXC low-level tools.

## 11.10.2 Snapshots

When you create a snapshot, `pct` stores the configuration at snapshot time into a separate snapshot section within the same configuration file. For example, after creating a snapshot called "testsnapshot", your configuration file will look like this:

**Container configuration with snapshot**

```
memory: 512
swap: 512
parent: testsnaphot
...

[testsnaphot]
memory: 512
swap: 512
snaptime: 1457170803
...
```

There are a few snapshot related properties like `parent` and `snaptime`. The `parent` property is used to store the parent/child relationship between snapshots. `snaptime` is the snapshot creation time stamp (Unix epoch).

## 11.10.3 Options

**arch: <amd64 | i386>** (*default* = `amd64`)
  OS architecture type.

**cmode: <console | shell | tty>** (*default* = `tty`)
  Console mode. By default, the console command tries to open a connection to one of the available tty devices. By setting cmode to *console* it tries to attach to /dev/console instead. If you set cmode to *shell*, it simply invokes a shell inside the container (no login).

**console: <boolean>** (*default* = 1)
  Attach a console device (/dev/console) to the container.

**cores: <integer>** (1 – 128)
  The number of cores assigned to the container. A container can use all available cores by default.

**cpulimit: <number>** (0 – 128) (*default* = 0)
  Limit of CPU usage.

---

**Note**
If the computer has 2 CPUs, it has a total of *2* CPU time. Value *0* indicates no CPU limit.

---

**cpuunits: <integer> (0 — 500000) (*default* = 1024)**
CPU weight for a VM. Argument is used in the kernel fair scheduler. The larger the number is, the more CPU time this VM gets. Number is relative to the weights of all the other running VMs.

---

**Note**
You can disable fair-scheduler configuration by setting this to 0.

---

**description: <string>**
Container description. Only used on the configuration web interface.

**hostname: <string>**
Set a host name for the container.

**lock: <backup | migrate | rollback | snapshot>**
Lock/unlock the VM.

**memory: <integer>  (16 — N) (*default* = 512)**
Amount of RAM for the VM in MB.

**mp[n]: [volume=]<volume> ,mp=<Path> [,acl=<1|0>] [,backup=<1|0>] [,quota=<1|0>] [,replicate=<1|0>] [,ro=<1|0>] [,shared=<1|0>] [,size=<DiskSize>]**
Use volume as container mount point.

**acl=<boolean>**
Explicitly enable or disable ACL support.

**backup=<boolean>**
Whether to include the mount point in backups (only used for volume mount points).

**mp=<Path>**
Path to the mount point as seen from inside the container.

---

**Note**
Must not contain any symlinks for security reasons.

---

**quota=<boolean>**
Enable user quotas inside the container (not supported with zfs subvolumes)

**replicate=<boolean> (*default* = 1)**
Will include this volume to a storage replica job.

**ro=<boolean>**
Read-only mount point

**shared=<boolean> (*default* = 0)**
Mark this non-volume mount point as available on all nodes.

**Warning**
This option does not share the mount point automatically, it assumes it is shared already!

**size=<DiskSize>**
Volume size (read only value).

**volume=<volume>**
Volume, device or directory to mount into the container.

**nameserver: <string>**
Sets DNS server IP address for a container. Create will automatically use the setting from the host if you neither set searchdomain nor nameserver.

**net[n]: name=<string> [,bridge=<bridge>] [,firewall=<1|0>] [,gw= <GatewayIPv4>] [,gw6=<GatewayIPv6>] [,hwaddr=<XX:XX:XX:XX:XX:XX>] [,ip=<IPv4Format/CIDR>] [,ip6=<IPv6Format/CIDR>] [,mtu=<integer>] [,rate=<mbps>] [,tag=<integer>] [,trunks=<vlanid[;vlanid...]>] [,type=<veth>]**
Specifies network interfaces for the container.

**bridge=<bridge>**
Bridge to attach the network device to.

**firewall=<boolean>**
Controls whether this interface's firewall rules should be used.

**gw=<GatewayIPv4>**
Default gateway for IPv4 traffic.

**gw6=<GatewayIPv6>**
Default gateway for IPv6 traffic.

**hwaddr=<XX:XX:XX:XX:XX:XX>**
The interface MAC address. This is dynamically allocated by default, but you can set that statically if needed, for example to always have the same link-local IPv6 address. (lxc.network.hwaddr)

**ip=<IPv4Format/CIDR>**
IPv4 address in CIDR format.

**ip6=<IPv6Format/CIDR>**
IPv6 address in CIDR format.

**mtu=<integer> (64 - N)**
Maximum transfer unit of the interface. (lxc.network.mtu)

**name=<string>**
Name of the network device as seen from inside the container. (lxc.network.name)

`rate=<mbps>`
Apply rate limiting to the interface

`tag=<integer> (1 - 4094)`
VLAN tag for this interface.

`trunks=<vlanid[;vlanid...]>`
VLAN ids to pass through the interface

`type=<veth>`
Network interface type.

`onboot: <boolean>` (*default* = 0)
Specifies whether a VM will be started during system bootup.

`ostype: <alpine | archlinux | centos | debian | fedora | gentoo | opensuse | ubuntu | unmanaged>`
OS type. This is used to setup configuration inside the container, and corresponds to lxc setup scripts in /usr/share/lxc/config/<ostype>.common.conf. Value *unmanaged* can be used to skip and OS specific setup.

`protection: <boolean>` (*default* = 0)
Sets the protection flag of the container. This will prevent the CT or CT's disk remove/update operation.

`rootfs: [volume=]<volume> [,acl=<1|0>] [,quota=<1|0>] [,replicate= <1|0>] [,ro=<1|0>] [,shared=<1|0>] [,size=<DiskSize>]`
Use volume as container root.

`acl=<boolean>`
Explicitly enable or disable ACL support.

`quota=<boolean>`
Enable user quotas inside the container (not supported with zfs subvolumes)

`replicate=<boolean>` (*default* = 1)
Will include this volume to a storage replica job.

`ro=<boolean>`
Read-only mount point

`shared=<boolean>` (*default* = 0)
Mark this non-volume mount point as available on all nodes.

 **Warning**
This option does not share the mount point automatically, it assumes it is shared already!

`size=<DiskSize>`
Volume size (read only value).

**`volume=<volume>`**
>    Volume, device or directory to mount into the container.

**`searchdomain: <string>`**
>    Sets DNS search domains for a container. Create will automatically use the setting from the host if you neither set searchdomain nor nameserver.

**`startup: `[[order=]\d+] [,up=\d+] [,down=\d+] `**
>    Startup and shutdown behavior. Order is a non-negative number defining the general startup order. Shutdown in done with reverse ordering. Additionally you can set the *up* or *down* delay in seconds, which specifies a delay to wait before the next VM is started or stopped.

**`swap: <integer>  (0 - N)` (*default* = 512)**
>    Amount of SWAP for the VM in MB.

**`template: <boolean>` (*default* = 0)**
>    Enable/disable Template.

**`tty: <integer>  (0 - 6)` (*default* = 2)**
>    Specify the number of tty available to the container

**`unprivileged: <boolean>` (*default* = 0)**
>    Makes the container run as unprivileged user. (Should not be modified manually.)

**`unused[n]: <string>`**
>    Reference to unused volumes. This is used internally, and should not be modified manually.

## 11.11  Locks

Container migrations, snapshots and backups (`vzdump`) set a lock to prevent incompatible concurrent actions on the affected container. Sometimes you need to remove such a lock manually (e.g., after a power failure).

```
pct unlock <CTID>
```

**Caution**
Only do that if you are sure the action which set the lock is no longer running.

# Chapter 12

# Proxmox VE Firewall

Proxmox VE Firewall provides an easy way to protect your IT infrastructure. You can setup firewall rules for all hosts inside a cluster, or define rules for virtual machines and containers. Features like firewall macros, security groups, IP sets and aliases help to make that task easier.

While all configuration is stored on the cluster file system, the `iptables`-based firewall runs on each cluster node, and thus provides full isolation between virtual machines. The distributed nature of this system also provides much higher bandwidth than a central firewall solution.

The firewall has full support for IPv4 and IPv6. IPv6 support is fully transparent, and we filter traffic for both protocols by default. So there is no need to maintain a different set of rules for IPv6.

## 12.1 Zones

The Proxmox VE firewall groups the network into the following logical zones:

**Host**
Traffic from/to a cluster node

**VM**
Traffic from/to a specific VM

For each zone, you can define firewall rules for incoming and/or outgoing traffic.

## 12.2 Configuration Files

All firewall related configuration is stored on the proxmox cluster file system. So those files are automatically distributed to all cluster nodes, and the `pve-firewall` service updates the underlying `iptables` rules automatically on changes.

You can configure anything using the GUI (i.e. **Datacenter** → **Firewall**, or on a **Node** → **Firewall**), or you can edit the configuration files directly using your preferred editor.

Firewall configuration files contains sections of key-value pairs. Lines beginning with a # and blank lines are considered comments. Sections starts with a header line containing the section name enclosed in [ and ].

## 12.2.1  Cluster Wide Setup

The cluster wide firewall configuration is stored at:

```
/etc/pve/firewall/cluster.fw
```

The configuration can contain the following sections:

**[OPTIONS]**
This is used to set cluster wide firewall options.

**enable: <integer>  (0 - N)**
Enable or disable the firewall cluster wide.

**policy_in: <ACCEPT | DROP | REJECT>**
Input policy.

**policy_out: <ACCEPT | DROP | REJECT>**
Output policy.

**[RULES]**
This sections contains cluster wide firewall rules for all nodes.

**[IPSET <name>]**
Cluster wide IP set definitions.

**[GROUP <name>]**
Cluster wide security group definitions.

**[ALIASES]**
Cluster wide Alias definitions.

### Enabling the Firewall

The firewall is completely disabled by default, so you need to set the enable option here:

```
[OPTIONS]
# enable firewall (cluster wide setting, default is disabled)
enable: 1
```

---

 **Important**
If you enable the firewall, traffic to all hosts is blocked by default. Only exceptions is WebGUI(8006) and ssh(22) from your local network.

---

If you want to administrate your Proxmox VE hosts from remote, you need to create rules to allow traffic from those remote IPs to the web GUI (port 8006). You may also want to allow ssh (port 22), and maybe SPICE (port 3128).

**Tip**

Please open a SSH connection to one of your Proxmox VE hosts before enabling the firewall. That way you still have access to the host if something goes wrong .

To simplify that task, you can instead create an IPSet called "management", and add all remote IPs there. This creates all required firewall rules to access the GUI from remote.

## 12.2.2   Host Specific Configuration

Host related configuration is read from:

`/etc/pve/nodes/<nodename>/host.fw`

This is useful if you want to overwrite rules from `cluster.fw` config. You can also increase log verbosity, and set netfilter related options. The configuration can contain the following sections:

**[OPTIONS]**
  This is used to set host related firewall options.

**enable: <boolean>**
  Enable host firewall rules.

**log_level_in: <alert | crit | debug | emerg | err | info | nolog | notice | warning>**
  Log level for incoming traffic.

**log_level_out: <alert | crit | debug | emerg | err | info | nolog | notice | warning>**
  Log level for outgoing traffic.

**ndp: <boolean>**
  Enable NDP.

**nf_conntrack_max: <integer> (32768 — N)**
  Maximum number of tracked connections.

**nf_conntrack_tcp_timeout_established: <integer> (7875 — N)**
  Conntrack established timeout.

**nosmurfs: <boolean>**
  Enable SMURFS filter.

**smurf_log_level: <alert | crit | debug | emerg | err | info | nolog | notice | warning>**
  Log level for SMURFS filter.

`tcp_flags_log_level: <alert | crit | debug | emerg | err | info | nolog | notice | warning>`

Log level for illegal tcp flags filter.

`tcpflags: <boolean>`

Filter illegal combinations of TCP flags.

`[RULES]`

This sections contains host specific firewall rules.

## 12.2.3 VM/Container Configuration

VM firewall configuration is read from:

`/etc/pve/firewall/<VMID>.fw`

and contains the following data:

`[OPTIONS]`

This is used to set VM/Container related firewall options.

`dhcp: <boolean>`

Enable DHCP.

`enable: <boolean>`

Enable/disable firewall rules.

`ipfilter: <boolean>`

Enable default IP filters. This is equivalent to adding an empty ipfilter-net<id> ipset for every interface. Such ipsets implicitly contain sane default restrictions such as restricting IPv6 link local addresses to the one derived from the interface's MAC address. For containers the configured IP addresses will be implicitly added.

`log_level_in: <alert | crit | debug | emerg | err | info | nolog | notice | warning>`

Log level for incoming traffic.

`log_level_out: <alert | crit | debug | emerg | err | info | nolog | notice | warning>`

Log level for outgoing traffic.

`macfilter: <boolean>`

Enable/disable MAC address filter.

`ndp: <boolean>`

Enable NDP.

**policy_in: <ACCEPT | DROP | REJECT>**
Input policy.

**policy_out: <ACCEPT | DROP | REJECT>**
Output policy.

**radv: <boolean>**
Allow sending Router Advertisement.

**[RULES]**
This sections contains VM/Container firewall rules.

**[IPSET <name>]**
IP set definitions.

**[ALIASES]**
IP Alias definitions.

### Enabling the Firewall for VMs and Containers

Each virtual network device has its own firewall enable flag. So you can selectively enable the firewall for each interface. This is required in addition to the general firewall `enable` option.

The firewall requires a special network device setup, so you need to restart the VM/container after enabling the firewall on a network interface.

## 12.3 Firewall Rules

Firewall rules consists of a direction (IN or OUT) and an action (ACCEPT, DENY, REJECT). You can also specify a macro name. Macros contain predefined sets of rules and options. Rules can be disabled by prefixing them with |.

### Firewall rules syntax

```
[RULES]

DIRECTION ACTION [OPTIONS]
|DIRECTION ACTION [OPTIONS] # disabled rule

DIRECTION MACRO(ACTION) [OPTIONS] # use predefined macro
```

The following options can be used to refine rule matches.

**-dest <string>**
Restrict packet destination address. This can refer to a single IP address, an IP set (*+ipsetname*) or an IP alias definition. You can also specify an address range like *20.34.101.207-201.3.9.99*, or a list of IP addresses and networks (entries are separated by comma). Please do not mix IPv4 and IPv6 addresses inside such lists.

**-dport <string>**

> Restrict TCP/UDP destination port. You can use service names or simple numbers (0-65535), as defined in */etc/services*. Port ranges can be specified with *\d+:\d+*, for example *80:85*, and you can use comma separated list to match several ports or ranges.

**-iface <string>**

> Network interface name. You have to use network configuration key names for VMs and containers (*net\d+*). Host related rules can use arbitrary strings.

**-proto <string>**

> IP protocol. You can use protocol names (*tcp/udp*) or simple numbers, as defined in */etc/protocols*.

**-source <string>**

> Restrict packet source address. This can refer to a single IP address, an IP set (*+ipsetname*) or an IP alias definition. You can also specify an address range like *20.34.101.207-201.3.9.99*, or a list of IP addresses and networks (entries are separated by comma). Please do not mix IPv4 and IPv6 addresses inside such lists.

**-sport <string>**

> Restrict TCP/UDP source port. You can use service names or simple numbers (0-65535), as defined in */etc/services*. Port ranges can be specified with *\d+:\d+*, for example *80:85*, and you can use comma separated list to match several ports or ranges.

Here are some examples:

```
[RULES]
IN SSH(ACCEPT) -i net0
IN SSH(ACCEPT) -i net0 # a comment
IN SSH(ACCEPT) -i net0 -source 192.168.2.192 # only allow SSH from ↩
    192.168.2.192
IN SSH(ACCEPT) -i net0 -source 10.0.0.1-10.0.0.10 # accept SSH for ip range
IN SSH(ACCEPT) -i net0 -source 10.0.0.1,10.0.0.2,10.0.0.3 #accept ssh for ↩
    ip list
IN SSH(ACCEPT) -i net0 -source +mynetgroup # accept ssh for ipset ↩
    mynetgroup
IN SSH(ACCEPT) -i net0 -source myserveralias #accept ssh for alias ↩
    myserveralias

|IN SSH(ACCEPT) -i net0 # disabled rule

IN  DROP # drop all incoming packages
OUT ACCEPT # accept all outgoing packages
```

# 12.4 Security Groups

A security group is a collection of rules, defined at cluster level, which can be used in all VMs' rules. For example you can define a group named "webserver" with rules to open the *http* and *https* ports.

```
# /etc/pve/firewall/cluster.fw

[group webserver]
IN  ACCEPT -p tcp -dport 80
IN  ACCEPT -p tcp -dport 443
```

Then, you can add this group to a VM's firewall

```
# /etc/pve/firewall/<VMID>.fw

[RULES]
GROUP webserver
```

## 12.5  IP Aliases

IP Aliases allow you to associate IP addresses of networks with a name. You can then refer to those names:

- inside IP set definitions

- in source and dest properties of firewall rules

### 12.5.1  Standard IP Alias `local_network`

This alias is automatically defined. Please use the following command to see assigned values:

```
# pve-firewall localnet
local hostname: example
local IP address: 192.168.2.100
network auto detect: 192.168.0.0/20
using detected local_network: 192.168.0.0/20
```

The firewall automatically sets up rules to allow everything needed for cluster communication (corosync, API, SSH) using this alias.

The user can overwrite these values in the cluster.fw alias section. If you use a single host on a public network, it is better to explicitly assign the local IP address

```
#   /etc/pve/firewall/cluster.fw
[ALIASES]
local_network 1.2.3.4 # use the single ip address
```

## 12.6  IP Sets

IP sets can be used to define groups of networks and hosts. You can refer to them with '+name` in the firewall rules' source and dest properties.

The following example allows HTTP traffic from the management IP set.

```
IN HTTP(ACCEPT) -source +management
```

### 12.6.1  Standard IP set `management`

This IP set applies only to host firewalls (not VM firewalls). Those IPs are allowed to do normal management tasks (PVE GUI, VNC, SPICE, SSH).

The local cluster network is automatically added to this IP set (alias `cluster_network`), to enable inter-host cluster communication. (multicast,ssh,...)

```
# /etc/pve/firewall/cluster.fw

[IPSET management]
192.168.2.10
192.168.2.10/24
```

### 12.6.2  Standard IP set `blacklist`

Traffic from these IPs is dropped by every host's and VM's firewall.

```
# /etc/pve/firewall/cluster.fw

[IPSET blacklist]
77.240.159.182
213.87.123.0/24
```

### 12.6.3  Standard IP set `ipfilter-net*`

These filters belong to a VM's network interface and are mainly used to prevent IP spoofing. If such a set exists for an interface then any outgoing traffic with a source IP not matching its interface's corresponding ipfilter set will be dropped.

For containers with configured IP addresses these sets, if they exist (or are activated via the general `IP Filter` option in the VM's firewall's **options** tab), implicitly contain the associated IP addresses.

For both virtual machines and containers they also implicitly contain the standard MAC-derived IPv6 link-local address in order to allow the neighbor discovery protocol to work.

```
/etc/pve/firewall/<VMID>.fw

[IPSET ipfilter-net0] # only allow specified IPs on net0
192.168.2.10
```

## 12.7  Services and Commands

The firewall runs two service daemons on each node:

- pvefw-logger: NFLOG daemon (ulogd replacement).

- pve-firewall: updates iptables rules

There is also a CLI command named `pve-firewall`, which can be used to start and stop the firewall service:

```
# pve-firewall start
# pve-firewall stop
```

To get the status use:

```
# pve-firewall status
```

The above command reads and compiles all firewall rules, so you will see warnings if your firewall configuration contains any errors.

If you want to see the generated iptables rules you can use:

```
# iptables-save
```

## 12.8  Tips and Tricks

### 12.8.1  How to allow FTP

FTP is an old style protocol which uses port 21 and several other dynamic ports. So you need a rule to accept port 21. In addition, you need to load the `ip_conntrack_ftp` module. So please run:

```
modprobe ip_conntrack_ftp
```

and add `ip_conntrack_ftp` to `/etc/modules` (so that it works after a reboot).

### 12.8.2  Suricata IPS integration

If you want to use the Suricata IPS (Intrusion Prevention System), it's possible.

Packets will be forwarded to the IPS only after the firewall ACCEPTed them.

Rejected/Dropped firewall packets don't go to the IPS.

Install suricata on proxmox host:

```
# apt-get install suricata
# modprobe nfnetlink_queue
```

Don't forget to add `nfnetlink_queue` to `/etc/modules` for next reboot.

Then, enable IPS for a specific VM with:

```
# /etc/pve/firewall/<VMID>.fw

[OPTIONS]
ips: 1
ips_queues: 0
```

`ips_queues` will bind a specific cpu queue for this VM.

Available queues are defined in

```
# /etc/default/suricata
NFQUEUE=0
```

## 12.9   Notes on IPv6

The firewall contains a few IPv6 specific options. One thing to note is that IPv6 does not use the ARP protocol anymore, and instead uses NDP (Neighbor Discovery Protocol) which works on IP level and thus needs IP addresses to succeed. For this purpose link-local addresses derived from the interface's MAC address are used. By default the `NDP` option is enabled on both host and VM level to allow neighbor discovery (NDP) packets to be sent and received.

Beside neighbor discovery NDP is also used for a couple of other things, like autoconfiguration and advertising routers.

By default VMs are allowed to send out router solicitation messages (to query for a router), and to receive router advertisement packets. This allows them to use stateless auto configuration. On the other hand VMs cannot advertise themselves as routers unless the "Allow Router Advertisement" (`radv:    1`) option is set.

As for the link local addresses required for NDP, there's also an "IP Filter" (`ipfilter:    1`) option which can be enabled which has the same effect as adding an `ipfilter-net*` ipset for each of the VM's network interfaces containing the corresponding link local addresses. (See the Standard IP set ipfilter-net* section for details.)

## 12.10   Ports used by Proxmox VE

- Web interface: 8006

- VNC Web console: 5900-5999

- SPICE proxy: 3128

- sshd (used for cluster actions): 22

- rpcbind: 111

- corosync multicast (if you run a cluster): 5404, 5405 UDP

# Chapter 13

# User Management

Proxmox VE supports multiple authentication sources, e.g. Linux PAM, an integrated Proxmox VE authentication server, LDAP, Microsoft Active Directory.

By using the role based user- and permission management for all objects (VMs, storages, nodes, etc.) granular access can be defined.

## 13.1   Users

Proxmox VE stores user attributes in `/etc/pve/user.cfg`. Passwords are not stored here, users are instead associated with authentication realms described below. Therefore a user is internally often identified by its name and realm in the form `<userid>@<realm>`.

Each user entry in this file contains the following information:

• First name

• Last name

• E-mail address

• Group memberships

• An optional Expiration date

• A comment or note about this user

• Whether this user is enabled or disabled

• Optional two factor authentication keys

### 13.1.1   System administrator

The system's root user can always log in via the Linux PAM realm and is an unconfined administrator. This user cannot be deleted, but attributes can still be changed and system mails will be sent to the email address assigned to this user.

### 13.1.2 Groups

Each user can be member of several groups. Groups are the preferred way to organize access permissions. You should always grant permission to groups instead of using individual users. That way you will get a much shorter access control list which is easier to handle.

## 13.2 Authentication Realms

As Proxmox VE users are just counterparts for users existing on some external realm, the realms have to be configured in `/etc/pve/domains.cfg`. The following realms (authentication methods) are available:

**Linux PAM standard authentication**
>    In this case a system user has to exist (eg. created via the `adduser` command) on all nodes the user is allowed to login, and the user authenticates with their usual system password.

```
useradd heinz
passwd heinz
groupadd watchman
usermod -a -G watchman heinz
```

**Proxmox VE authentication server**
>    This is a unix like password store (`/etc/pve/priv/shadow.cfg`). Password are encrypted using the SHA-256 hash method. This is the most convenient method for for small (or even medium) installations where users do not need access to anything outside of Proxmox VE. In this case users are fully managed by Proxmox VE and are able to change their own passwords via the GUI.

**LDAP**
>    It is possible to authenticate users via an LDAP server (eq. openldap). The server and an optional fallback server can be configured and the connection can be encrypted via SSL.
>
>    Users are searched under a *Base Domain Name* (`base_dn`), with the user name found in the attribute specified in the *User Attribute Name* (`user_attr`) field.
>
>    For instance, if a user is represented via the following ldif dataset:

```
# user1 of People at ldap-test.com
dn: uid=user1,ou=People,dc=ldap-test,dc=com
objectClass: top
objectClass: person
objectClass: organizationalPerson
objectClass: inetOrgPerson
uid: user1
cn: Test User 1
sn: Testers
description: This is the first test user.
```

>    The *Base Domain Name* would be `ou=People,dc=ldap-test,dc=com` and the user attribute would be `uid`.
>
>    If Proxmox VE needs to authenticate (bind) to the ldap server before being able to query and authenticate users, a bind domain name can be configured via the `bind_dn` property in `/etc/pve/`

`domains.cfg`. Its password then has to be stored in `/etc/pve/priv/ldap/<realmname>.pw` (eg. `/etc/pve/priv/ldap/my-ldap.pw`). This file should contain a single line containing the raw password.

### Microsoft Active Directory

A server and authentication domain need to be specified. Like with ldap an optional fallback server, optional port, and SSL encryption can be configured.

## 13.3 Two factor authentication

Each realm can optionally be secured additionally by two factor authentication. This can be done by selecting one of the available methods via the *TFA* dropdown box when adding or editing an Authentication Realm. When a realm has TFA enabled it becomes a requirement and only users with configured TFA will be able to login.

Currently there are two methods available:

### Time based OATH (TOTP)

This uses the standard HMAC-SHA1 algorithm where the current time is hashed with the user's configured key. The time step and password length parameters are configured.

A user can have multiple keys configured (separated by spaces), and the keys can be specified in Base32 (RFC3548) or hexadecimal notation.

Proxmox VE provides a key generation tool (`oathkeygen`) which prints out a random key in Base32 notation which can be used directly with various OTP tools, such as the `oathtool` command line tool, the Google authenticator or FreeOTP Android apps.

### YubiKey OTP

For authenticating via a YubiKey a Yubico API ID, API KEY and validation server URL must be configured, and users must have a YubiKey available. In order to get the key ID from a YubiKey, you can trigger the YubiKey once after connecting it to USB and copy the first 12 characters of the typed password into the user's *Key IDs* field.

Please refer to the YubiKey OTP documentation for how to use the YubiCloud or host your own verification server.

## 13.4 Permission Management

In order for a user to perform an action (such as listing, modifying or deleting a parts of a VM configuration), the user needs to have the appropriate permissions.

Proxmox VE uses a role and path based permission management system. An entry in the permissions table allows a user or group to take on a specific role when accessing an *object* or *path*. This means an such an access rule can be represented as a triple of *(path, user, role)* or *(path, group, role)*, with the role containing a set of allowed actions, and the path representing the target of these actions.

## 13.4.1 Roles

A role is simply a list of privileges. Proxmox VE comes with a number of predefined roles which satisfies most needs.

- `Administrator`: has all privileges

- `NoAccess`: has no privileges (used to forbid access)

- `PVEAdmin`: can do most things, but miss rights to modify system settings (`Sys.PowerMgmt`, `Sys.Modify`, `Realm.Allocate`).

- `PVEAuditor`: read only access

- `PVEDatastoreAdmin`: create and allocate backup space and templates

- `PVEDatastoreUser`: allocate backup space and view storage

- `PVEPoolAdmin`: allocate pools

- `PVESysAdmin`: User ACLs, audit, system console and system logs

- `PVETemplateUser`: view and clone templates

- `PVEUserAdmin`: user administration

- `PVEVMAdmin`: fully administer VMs

- `PVEVMUser`: view, backup, config CDROM, VM console, VM power management

You can see the whole set of predefined roles on the GUI.

Adding new roles can currently only be done from the command line, like this:

```
pveum roleadd PVE_Power-only -privs "VM.PowerMgmt VM.Console"
pveum roleadd Sys_Power-only -privs "Sys.PowerMgmt Sys.Console"
```

## 13.4.2 Privileges

A privilege is the right to perform a specific action. To simplify management, lists of privileges are grouped into roles, which can then be used in the permission table. Note that privileges cannot directly be assigned to users and paths without being part of a role.

We currently use the following privileges:

**Node / System related privileges**

- `Permissions.Modify`: modify access permissions
- `Sys.PowerMgmt`: Node power management (start, stop, reset, shutdown, . . . )
- `Sys.Console`: console access to Node
- `Sys.Syslog`: view Syslog
- `Sys.Audit`: view node status/config, Corosync cluster config and HA config

- `Sys.Modify`: create/remove/modify node network parameters
- `Group.Allocate`: create/remove/modify groups
- `Pool.Allocate`: create/remove/modify a pool
- `Realm.Allocate`: create/remove/modify authentication realms
- `Realm.AllocateUser`: assign user to a realm
- `User.Modify`: create/remove/modify user access and details.

**Virtual machine related privileges**

- `VM.Allocate`: create/remove new VM to server inventory
- `VM.Migrate`: migrate VM to alternate server on cluster
- `VM.PowerMgmt`: power management (start, stop, reset, shutdown, ...)
- `VM.Console`: console access to VM
- `VM.Monitor`: access to VM monitor (kvm)
- `VM.Backup`: backup/restore VMs
- `VM.Audit`: view VM config
- `VM.Clone`: clone/copy a VM
- `VM.Config.Disk`: add/modify/delete Disks
- `VM.Config.CDROM`: eject/change CDROM
- `VM.Config.CPU`: modify CPU settings
- `VM.Config.Memory`: modify Memory settings
- `VM.Config.Network`: add/modify/delete Network devices
- `VM.Config.HWType`: modify emulated HW type
- `VM.Config.Options`: modify any other VM configuration
- `VM.Snapshot`: create/remove VM snapshots

**Storage related privileges**

- `Datastore.Allocate`: create/remove/modify a data store, delete volumes
- `Datastore.AllocateSpace`: allocate space on a datastore
- `Datastore.AllocateTemplate`: allocate/upload templates and iso images
- `Datastore.Audit`: view/browse a datastore

### 13.4.3  Objects and Paths

Access permissions are assigned to objects, such as a virtual machines, storages or pools of resources. We use file system like paths to address these objects. These paths form a natural tree, and permissions of higher levels (shorter path) can optionally be propagated down within this hierarchy.

Paths can be templated. When an API call requires permissions on a templated path, the path may contain references to parameters of the API call. These references are specified in curly braces. Some parameters are implicitly taken from the API call's URI. For instance the permission path `/nodes/{node}` when calling */nodes/mynode/status* requires permissions on `/nodes/mynode`, while the path `{path}` in a PUT request to `/access/acl` refers to the method's `path` parameter.

Some examples are:

- `/nodes/{node}`: Access to Proxmox VE server machines

- `/vms`: Covers all VMs

- `/vms/{vmid}`: Access to specific VMs

- `/storage/{storeid}`: Access to a storages

- `/pool/{poolname}`: Access to VMs part of a pool

- `/access/groups`: Group administration

- `/access/realms/{realmid}`: Administrative access to realms

**Inheritance**

As mentioned earlier, object paths form a file system like tree, and permissions can be inherited down that tree (the propagate flag is set by default). We use the following inheritance rules:

- Permissions for individual users always replace group permissions.

- Permissions for groups apply when the user is member of that group.

- Permissions replace the ones inherited from an upper level.

## 13.4.4 Pools

Pools can be used to group a set of virtual machines and data stores. You can then simply set permissions on pools (`/pool/{poolid}`), which are inherited to all pool members. This is a great way simplify access control.

## 13.4.5 What permission do I need?

The required API permissions are documented for each individual method, and can be found at http://pve.proxmox.com/-pve-docs/api-viewer/

The permissions are specified as a list which can be interpreted as a tree of logic and access-check functions:

`["and", <subtests>...]` **and** `["or", <subtests>...]`
    Each(`and`) or any(`or`) further element in the current list has to be true.

`["perm", <path>, [ <privileges>... ], <options>...]`
    The `path` is a templated parameter (see Objects and Paths). All (or , if the `any` option is used, any) of the listed privileges must be allowed on the specified path. If a `require-param` option is specified, then its specified parameter is required even if the API call's schema otherwise lists it as being optional.

**["userid-group", [ <privileges>... ], <options>...]**
The caller must have any of the listed privileges on `/access/groups`. In addition there are two possible checks depending on whether the `groups_param` option is set:

- `groups_param` is set: The API call has a non-optional `groups` parameter and the caller must have any of the listed privileges on all of the listed groups.

- `groups_param` is not set: The user passed via the `userid` parameter must exist and be part of a group on which the caller has any of the listed privileges (via the `/access/groups/<group>` path).

**["userid-param", "self"]**
The value provided for the API call's `userid` parameter must refer to the user performing the action. (Usually in conjunction with `or`, to allow users to perform an action on themselves even if they don't have elevated privileges.)

**["userid-param", "Realm.AllocateUser"]**
The user needs `Realm.AllocateUser` access to `/access/realm/<realm>`, with `<realm>` refering to the realm of the user passed via the `userid` parameter. Note that the user does not need to exist in order to be associated with a realm, since user IDs are passed in the form of `<username>@<realm>`.

**["perm-modify", <path>]**
The `path` is a templated parameter (see Objects and Paths). The user needs either the `Permissions.Modify` privilege, or, depending on the path, the following privileges as a possible substitute:

- `/storage/...`: additionally requires 'Datastore.Allocate`
- `/vms/...`: additionally requires 'VM.Allocate`
- `/pool/...`: additionally requires 'Pool.Allocate`

If the path is empty, `Permission.Modify` on `/access` is required.

## 13.5 Command Line Tool

Most users will simply use the GUI to manage users. But there is also a full featured command line tool called `pveum` (short for "**P**roxmox **VE U**ser **M**anager"). Please note that all Proxmox VE command line tools are wrappers around the API, so you can also access those function through the REST API.

Here are some simple usage examples. To show help type:

```
pveum
```

or (to show detailed help about a specific command)

```
pveum help useradd
```

Create a new user:

```
pveum useradd testuser@pve -comment "Just a test"
```

Set or Change the password (not all realms support that):

```
pveum passwd testuser@pve
```

Disable a user:

```
pveum usermod testuser@pve -enable 0
```

Create a new group:

```
pveum groupadd testgroup
```

Create a new role:

```
pveum roleadd PVE_Power-only -privs "VM.PowerMgmt VM.Console"
```

## 13.6  Real World Examples

### 13.6.1  Administrator Group

One of the most wanted features was the ability to define a group of users with full administrator rights (without using the root account).

Define the group:

```
pveum groupadd admin -comment "System Administrators"
```

Then add the permission:

```
pveum aclmod / -group admin -role Administrator
```

You can finally add users to the new *admin* group:

```
pveum usermod testuser@pve -group admin
```

### 13.6.2  Auditors

You can give read only access to users by assigning the `PVEAuditor` role to users or groups.

Example1: Allow user `joe@pve` to see everything

```
pveum aclmod / -user joe@pve -role PVEAuditor
```

Example1: Allow user `joe@pve` to see all virtual machines

```
pveum aclmod /vms -user joe@pve -role PVEAuditor
```

### 13.6.3   Delegate User Management

If you want to delegate user managenent to user `joe@pve` you can do that with:

```
pveum aclmod /access -user joe@pve -role PVEUserAdmin
```

User `joe@pve` can now add and remove users, change passwords and other user attributes. This is a very powerful role, and you most likely want to limit that to selected realms and groups. The following example allows `joe@pve` to modify users within realm `pve` if they are members of group `customers`:

```
pveum aclmod /access/realm/pve -user joe@pve -role PVEUserAdmin
pveum aclmod /access/groups/customers -user joe@pve -role PVEUserAdmin
```

---

**Note**

The user is able to add other users, but only if they are members of group `customers` and within realm `pve`.

---

### 13.6.4   Pools

An enterprise is usually structured into several smaller departments, and it is common that you want to assign resources to them and delegate management tasks. A pool is simply a set of virtual machines and data stores. You can create pools on the GUI. After that you can add resources to the pool (VMs, Storage).

You can also assign permissions to the pool. Those permissions are inherited to all pool members.

Lets assume you have a software development department, so we first create a group

```
pveum groupadd developers -comment "Our software developers"
```

Now we create a new user which is a member of that group

```
pveum useradd developer1@pve -group developers -password
```

---

**Note**
The -password parameter will prompt you for a password

---

I assume we already created a pool called "dev-pool" on the GUI. So we can now assign permission to that pool:

```
pveum aclmod /pool/dev-pool/ -group developers -role PVEAdmin
```

Our software developers can now administrate the resources assigned to that pool.

# Chapter 14

# High Availability

Our modern society depends heavily on information provided by computers over the network. Mobile devices amplified that dependency, because people can access the network any time from anywhere. If you provide such services, it is very important that they are available most of the time.

We can mathematically define the availability as the ratio of (A) the total time a service is capable of being used during a given interval to (B) the length of the interval. It is normally expressed as a percentage of uptime in a given year.

Table 14.1: Availability - Downtime per Year

| Availability % | Downtime per year |
| --- | --- |
| 99 | 3.65 days |
| 99.9 | 8.76 hours |
| 99.99 | 52.56 minutes |
| 99.999 | 5.26 minutes |
| 99.9999 | 31.5 seconds |
| 99.99999 | 3.15 seconds |

There are several ways to increase availability. The most elegant solution is to rewrite your software, so that you can run it on several host at the same time. The software itself need to have a way to detect errors and do failover. This is relatively easy if you just want to serve read-only web pages. But in general this is complex, and sometimes impossible because you cannot modify the software yourself. The following solutions works without modifying the software:

• Use reliable "server" components

---

**Note**
Computer components with same functionality can have varying reliability numbers, depending on the component quality. Most vendors sell components with higher reliability as "server" components - usually at higher price.

---

• Eliminate single point of failure (redundant components)

---

- use an uninterruptible power supply (UPS)
- use redundant power supplies on the main boards
- use ECC-RAM
- use redundant network hardware
- use RAID for local storage
- use distributed, redundant storage for VM data

- Reduce downtime

  - rapidly accessible administrators (24/7)
  - availability of spare parts (other nodes in a Proxmox VE cluster)
  - automatic error detection (provided by `ha-manager`)
  - automatic failover (provided by `ha-manager`)

Virtualization environments like Proxmox VE make it much easier to reach high availability because they remove the "hardware" dependency. They also support to setup and use redundant storage and network devices. So if one host fail, you can simply start those services on another host within your cluster.

Even better, Proxmox VE provides a software stack called `ha-manager`, which can do that automatically for you. It is able to automatically detect errors and do automatic failover.

Proxmox VE `ha-manager` works like an "automated" administrator. First, you configure what resources (VMs, containers, ...) it should manage. `ha-manager` then observes correct functionality, and handles service failover to another node in case of errors. `ha-manager` can also handle normal user requests which may start, stop, relocate and migrate a service.

But high availability comes at a price. High quality components are more expensive, and making them redundant duplicates the costs at least. Additional spare parts increase costs further. So you should carefully calculate the benefits, and compare with those additional costs.

---

**Tip**
Increasing availability from 99% to 99.9% is relatively simply. But increasing availability from 99.9999% to 99.99999% is very hard and costly. `ha-manager` has typical error detection and failover times of about 2 minutes, so you can get no more than 99.999% availability.

---

## 14.1  Requirements

You must meet the following requirements before you start with HA:

- at least three cluster nodes (to get reliable quorum)

- shared storage for VMs and containers

- hardware redundancy (everywhere)

- use reliable "server" components

- hardware watchdog - if not available we fall back to the linux kernel software watchdog (`softdog`)

- optional hardware fencing devices

## 14.2  Resources

We call the primary management unit handled by `ha-manager` a resource. A resource (also called "service") is uniquely identified by a service ID (SID), which consists of the resource type and an type specific ID, e.g.: `vm:100`. That example would be a resource of type `vm` (virtual machine) with the ID 100.

For now we have two important resources types - virtual machines and containers. One basic idea here is that we can bundle related software into such VM or container, so there is no need to compose one big service from other services, like it was done with `rgmanager`. In general, a HA managed resource should not depend on other resources.

## 14.3  Management Tasks

This section provides a short overview of common management tasks. The first step is to enable HA for a resource. This is done by adding the resource to the HA resource configuration. You can do this using the GUI, or simply use the command line tool, for example:

```
# ha-manager add vm:100
```

The HA stack now tries to start the resources and keeps it running. Please note that you can configure the "requested" resources state. For example you may want that the HA stack stops the resource:

```
# ha-manager set vm:100 --state stopped
```

and start it again later:

```
# ha-manager set vm:100 --state started
```

You can also use the normal VM and container management commands. They automatically forward the commands to the HA stack, so

```
# qm start 100
```

simply sets the requested state to `started`. Same applied to `qm stop`, which sets the requested state to `stopped`.

---

**Note**
The HA stack works fully asynchronous and needs to communicate with other cluster members. So it takes some seconds until you see the result of such actions.

---

To view the current HA resource configuration use:

```
# ha-manager config
vm:100
        state stopped
```

And you can view the actual HA manager and resource state with:

```
# ha-manager status
quorum OK
master node1 (active, Wed Nov 23 11:07:23 2016)
lrm elsa (active, Wed Nov 23 11:07:19 2016)
service vm:100 (node1, started)
```

You can also initiate resource migration to other nodes:

```
# ha-manager migrate vm:100 node2
```

This uses online migration and tries to keep the VM running. Online migration needs to transfer all used memory over the network, so it is sometimes faster to stop VM, then restart it on the new node. This can be done using the `relocate` command:

```
# ha-manager relocate vm:100 node2
```

Finally, you can remove the resource from the HA configuration using the following command:

```
# ha-manager remove vm:100
```

---

**Note**

This does not start or stop the resource.

---

But all HA related task can be done on the GUI, so there is no need to use the command line at all.

## 14.4 How It Works

This section provides a detailed description of the Proxmox VE HA manager internals. It describes all involved daemons and how they work together. To provide HA, two daemons run on each node:

**pve-ha-lrm**

The local resource manager (LRM), which controls the services running on the local node. It reads the requested states for its services from the current manager status file and executes the respective commands.

**pve-ha-crm**

The cluster resource manager (CRM), which makes the cluster wide decisions. It sends commands to the LRM, processes the results, and moves resources to other nodes if something fails. The CRM also handles node fencing.

---

**Note**

Locks are provided by our distributed configuration file system (pmxcfs). They are used to guarantee that each LRM is active once and working. As a LRM only executes actions when it holds its lock, we can mark a failed node as fenced if we can acquire its lock. This lets us then recover any failed HA services securely without any interference from the now unknown failed node. This all gets supervised by the CRM which holds currently the manager master lock.

---

## 14.4.1  Service States

The CRM use a service state enumeration to record the current service state. We display this state on the GUI and you can query it using the `ha-manager` command line tool:

```
# ha-manager status
quorum OK
master elsa (active, Mon Nov 21 07:23:29 2016)
lrm elsa (active, Mon Nov 21 07:23:22 2016)
service ct:100 (elsa, stopped)
service ct:102 (elsa, started)
service vm:501 (elsa, started)
```

Here is the list of possible states:

**stopped**

> Service is stopped (confirmed by LRM). If the LRM detects a stopped service is still running, it will stop it again.

**request_stop**

> Service should be stopped. The CRM waits for confirmation from the LRM.

**stopping**

> Pending stop request. But the CRM did not get the request so far.

**started**

> Service is active an LRM should start it ASAP if not already running. If the Service fails and is detected to be not running the LRM restarts it (see Start Failure Policy Section 14.7).

**starting**

> Pending start request. But the CRM has not got any confirmation from the LRM that the service is running.

**fence**

> Wait for node fencing (service node is not inside quorate cluster partition). As soon as node gets fenced successfully the service will be recovered to another node, if possible (see Fencing Section 14.6).

**freeze**

> Do not touch the service state. We use this state while we reboot a node, or when we restart the LRM daemon (see Package Updates Section 14.9).

**migrate**

> Migrate service (live) to other node.

**error**

> Service is disabled because of LRM errors. Needs manual intervention (see Error Recovery Section 14.8).

**queued**

Service is newly added, and the CRM has not seen it so far.

**disabled**

Service is stopped and marked as `disabled`

## 14.4.2 Local Resource Manager

The local resource manager (`pve-ha-lrm`) is started as a daemon on boot and waits until the HA cluster is quorate and thus cluster wide locks are working.

It can be in three states:

**wait for agent lock**

The LRM waits for our exclusive lock. This is also used as idle state if no service is configured.

**active**

The LRM holds its exclusive lock and has services configured.

**lost agent lock**

The LRM lost its lock, this means a failure happened and quorum was lost.

After the LRM gets in the active state it reads the manager status file in `/etc/pve/ha/manager_s tatus` and determines the commands it has to execute for the services it owns. For each command a worker gets started, this workers are running in parallel and are limited to at most 4 by default. This default setting may be changed through the datacenter configuration key `max_worker`. When finished the worker process gets collected and its result saved for the CRM.

---

**Note**

The default value of at most 4 concurrent workers may be unsuited for a specific setup. For example may 4 live migrations happen at the same time, which can lead to network congestions with slower networks and/or big (memory wise) services. Ensure that also in the worst case no congestion happens and lower the `max_worker` value if needed. In the contrary, if you have a particularly powerful high end setup you may also want to increase it.

---

Each command requested by the CRM is uniquely identifiable by an UID, when the worker finished its result will be processed and written in the LRM status file `/etc/pve/nodes/<nodename>/lrm_status`. There the CRM may collect it and let its state machine - respective the commands output - act on it.

The actions on each service between CRM and LRM are normally always synced. This means that the CRM requests a state uniquely marked by an UID, the LRM then executes this action **one time** and writes back the result, also identifiable by the same UID. This is needed so that the LRM does not executes an outdated command. With the exception of the `stop` and the `error` command, those two do not depend on the result produced and are executed always in the case of the stopped state and once in the case of the error state.

---

**Note**
The HA Stack logs every action it makes. This helps to understand what and also why something happens in the cluster. Here its important to see what both daemons, the LRM and the CRM, did. You may use `journalctl -u pve-ha-lrm` on the node(s) where the service is and the same command for the pve-ha-crm on the node which is the current master.

---

### 14.4.3  Cluster Resource Manager

The cluster resource manager (`pve-ha-crm`) starts on each node and waits there for the manager lock, which can only be held by one node at a time. The node which successfully acquires the manager lock gets promoted to the CRM master.

It can be in three states:

**wait for agent lock**
> The CRM waits for our exclusive lock. This is also used as idle state if no service is configured

**active**
> The CRM holds its exclusive lock and has services configured

**lost agent lock**
> The CRM lost its lock, this means a failure happened and quorum was lost.

It main task is to manage the services which are configured to be highly available and try to always enforce the requested state. For example, a service with the requested state *started* will be started if its not already running. If it crashes it will be automatically started again. Thus the CRM dictates the actions which the LRM needs to execute.

When an node leaves the cluster quorum, its state changes to unknown. If the current CRM then can secure the failed nodes lock, the services will be *stolen* and restarted on another node.

When a cluster member determines that it is no longer in the cluster quorum, the LRM waits for a new quorum to form. As long as there is no quorum the node cannot reset the watchdog. This will trigger a reboot after the watchdog then times out, this happens after 60 seconds.

## 14.5  Configuration

The HA stack is well integrated into the Proxmox VE API. So, for example, HA can be configured via the `ha-manager` command line interface, or the Proxmox VE web interface - both interfaces provide an easy way to manage HA. Automation tools can use the API directly.

All HA configuration files are within `/etc/pve/ha/`, so they get automatically distributed to the cluster nodes, and all nodes share the same HA configuration.

## 14.5.1 Resources

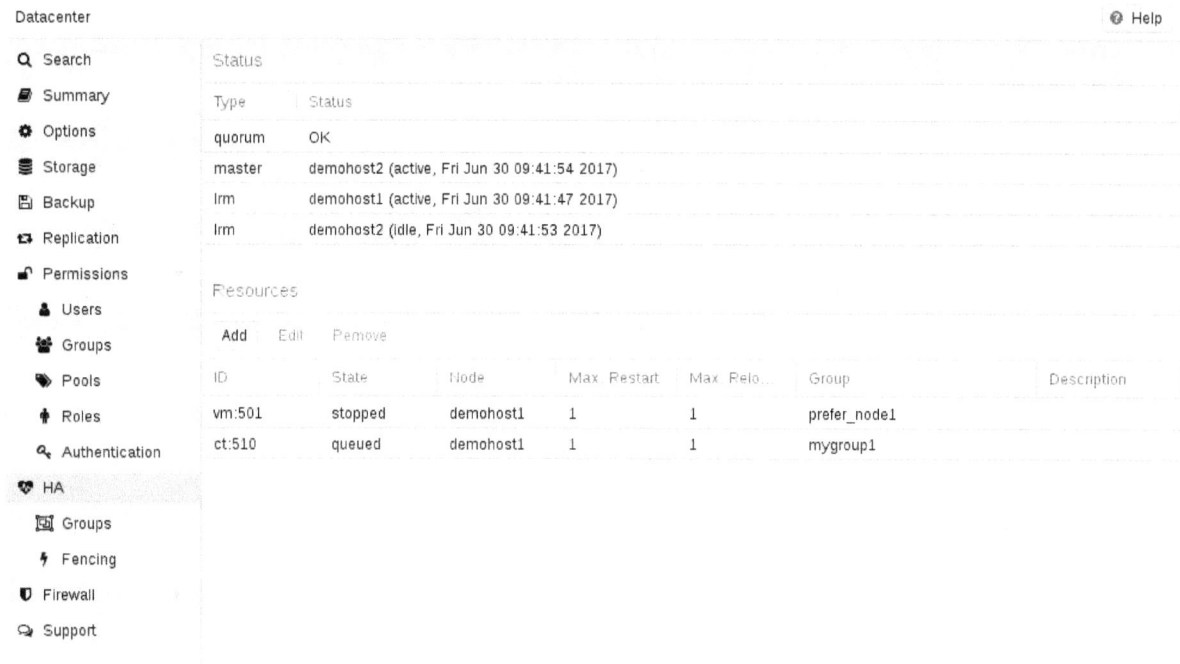

The resource configuration file `/etc/pve/ha/resources.cfg` stores the list of resources managed by `ha-manager`. A resource configuration inside that list look like this:

```
<type>: <name>
        <property> <value>
        ...
```

It starts with a resource type followed by a resource specific name, separated with colon. Together this forms the HA resource ID, which is used by all `ha-manager` commands to uniquely identify a resource (example: `vm:100` or `ct:101`). The next lines contain additional properties:

**comment: <string>**
Description.

**group: <string>**
The HA group identifier.

**max_relocate: <integer>  (0 − N) (*default* = 1)**
Maximal number of service relocate tries when a service failes to start.

**max_restart: <integer>  (0 − N) (*default* = 1)**
Maximal number of tries to restart the service on a node after its start failed.

**state: <disabled | enabled | started | stopped> (*default* = started)**
Requested resource state. The CRM reads this state and acts accordingly. Please note that `enabled` is just an alias for `started`.

**started**
> The CRM tries to start the resource. Service state is set to `started` after successful start. On node failures, or when start fails, it tries to recover the resource. If everything fails, service state it set to `error`.

**stopped**
> The CRM tries to keep the resource in `stopped` state, but it still tries to relocate the resources on node failures.

**disabled**
> The CRM tries to put the resource in `stopped` state, but does not try to relocate the resources on node failures. The main purpose of this state is error recovery, because it is the only way to move a resource out of the `error` state.

Here is a real world example with one VM and one container. As you see, the syntax of those files is really simple, so it is even posiible to read or edit those files using your favorite editor:

**Configuration Example (/etc/pve/ha/resources.cfg)**

```
vm: 501
    state started
    max_relocate 2

ct: 102
    # Note: use default settings for everything
```

Above config was generated using the `ha-manager` command line tool:

```
# ha-manager add vm:501 --state started --max_relocate 2
# ha-manager add ct:102
```

## 14.5.2 Groups

| Datacenter | | | | | | @ Help |
|---|---|---|---|---|---|---|
| Q Search | Create | Edit | Remove | | | |
| Summary | Group ↑ | restricted | nofailback | Nodes | Comment | |
| Options | mygroup1 | No | No | node3:1,node4,node2:1,node1:2 | complex group | |
| Storage | mygroup2 | Yes | No | node1,node2 | simple restricted group | |
| Backup | prefer_node1 | No | No | node1 | prefer node1 | |
| Replication | | | | | | |
| Permissions | | | | | | |
| Users | | | | | | |
| Groups | | | | | | |
| Pools | | | | | | |
| Roles | | | | | | |
| Authentication | | | | | | |
| HA | | | | | | |
| Groups | | | | | | |
| Fencing | | | | | | |
| Firewall | | | | | | |
| Support | | | | | | |

The HA group configuration file `/etc/pve/ha/groups.cfg` is used to define groups of cluster nodes. A resource can be restricted to run only on the members of such group. A group configuration look like this:

```
group: <group>
       nodes <node_list>
       <property> <value>
       ...
```

**comment: <string>**
Description.

**nodes: <node>[:<pri>]{,<node>[:<pri>]}\***
List of cluster node members, where a priority can be given to each node. A resource bound to a group will run on the available nodes with the highest priority. If there are more nodes in the highest priority class, the services will get distributed to those nodes. The priorities have a relative meaning only.

**nofailback: <boolean> (*default* = 0)**
The CRM tries to run services on the node with the highest priority. If a node with higher priority comes online, the CRM migrates the service to that node. Enabling nofailback prevents that behavior.

**restricted: <boolean> (*default* = 0)**
Resources bound to restricted groups may only run on nodes defined by the group. The resource will be placed in the stopped state if no group node member is online. Resources on unrestricted groups may run on any cluster node if all group members are offline, but they will migrate back as soon as a group member comes online. One can implement a *preferred node* behavior using an unrestricted group with only one member.

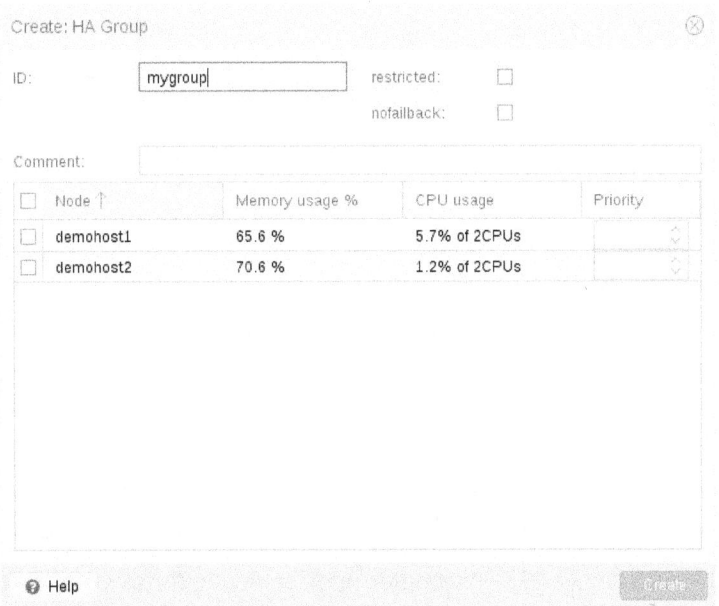

A common requirement is that a resource should run on a specific node. Usually the resource is able to run on other nodes, so you can define an unrestricted group with a single member:

```
# ha-manager groupadd prefer_node1 --nodes node1
```

For bigger clusters, it makes sense to define a more detailed failover behavior. For example, you may want to run a set of services on `node1` if possible. If `node1` is not available, you want to run them equally splitted on `node2` and `node3`. If those nodes also fail the services should run on `node4`. To achieve this you could set the node list to:

```
# ha-manager groupadd mygroup1 -nodes "node1:2,node2:1,node3:1,node4"
```

Another use case is if a resource uses other resources only available on specific nodes, lets say `node1` and `node2`. We need to make sure that HA manager does not use other nodes, so we need to create a restricted group with said nodes:

```
# ha-manager groupadd mygroup2 -nodes "node1,node2" -restricted
```

Above commands created the following group configuration fils:

**Configuration Example (/etc/pve/ha/groups.cfg)**

```
group: prefer_node1
        nodes node1

group: mygroup1
        nodes node2:1,node4,node1:2,node3:1

group: mygroup2
        nodes node2,node1
        restricted 1
```

The `nofailback` options is mostly useful to avoid unwanted resource movements during administration tasks. For example, if you need to migrate a service to a node which hasn't the highest priority in the group, you need to tell the HA manager to not move this service instantly back by setting the `nofailback` option.

Another scenario is when a service was fenced and it got recovered to another node. The admin tries to repair the fenced node and brings it up online again to investigate the failure cause and check if it runs stable again. Setting the `nofailback` flag prevents that the recovered services move straight back to the fenced node.

# 14.6  Fencing

On node failures, fencing ensures that the erroneous node is guaranteed to be offline. This is required to make sure that no resource runs twice when it gets recovered on another node. This is a really important task, because without, it would not be possible to recover a resource on another node.

If a node would not get fenced, it would be in an unknown state where it may have still access to shared resources. This is really dangerous! Imagine that every network but the storage one broke. Now, while not reachable from the public network, the VM still runs and writes to the shared storage.

If we then simply start up this VM on another node, we would get a dangerous race conditions because we write from both nodes. Such condition can destroy all VM data and the whole VM could be rendered unusable. The recovery could also fail if the storage protects from multiple mounts.

## 14.6.1  How Proxmox VE Fences

There are different methods to fence a node, for example, fence devices which cut off the power from the node or disable their communication completely. Those are often quite expensive and bring additional critical components into a system, because if they fail you cannot recover any service.

We thus wanted to integrate a simpler fencing method, which does not require additional external hardware. This can be done using watchdog timers.

POSSIBLE FENCING METHODS

- external power switches

- isolate nodes by disabling complete network traffic on the switch

- self fencing using watchdog timers

Watchdog timers are widely used in critical and dependable systems since the beginning of micro controllers. They are often independent and simple integrated circuits which are used to detect and recover from computer malfunctions.

During normal operation, `ha-manager` regularly resets the watchdog timer to prevent it from elapsing. If, due to a hardware fault or program error, the computer fails to reset the watchdog, the timer will elapse and triggers a reset of the whole server (reboot).

Recent server motherboards often include such hardware watchdogs, but these need to be configured. If no watchdog is available or configured, we fall back to the Linux Kernel *softdog*. While still reliable, it is not independent of the servers hardware, and thus has a lower reliability than a hardware watchdog.

### 14.6.2  Configure Hardware Watchdog

By default, all hardware watchdog modules are blocked for security reasons. They are like a loaded gun if not correctly initialized. To enable a hardware watchdog, you need to specify the module to load in */etc/default/pve-ha-manager*, for example:

```
# select watchdog module (default is softdog)
WATCHDOG_MODULE=iTCO_wdt
```

This configuration is read by the *watchdog-mux* service, which load the specified module at startup.

### 14.6.3  Recover Fenced Services

After a node failed and its fencing was successful, the CRM tries to move services from the failed node to nodes which are still online.

The selection of nodes, on which those services gets recovered, is influenced by the resource `group` settings, the list of currently active nodes, and their respective active service count.

The CRM first builds a set out of the intersection between user selected nodes (from `group` setting) and available nodes. It then choose the subset of nodes with the highest priority, and finally select the node with the lowest active service count. This minimizes the possibility of an overloaded node.

---

**Caution**
On node failure, the CRM distributes services to the remaining nodes. This increase the service count on those nodes, and can lead to high load, especially on small clusters. Please design your cluster so that it can handle such worst case scenarios.

---

## 14.7  Start Failure Policy

The start failure policy comes in effect if a service failed to start on a node once ore more times. It can be used to configure how often a restart should be triggered on the same node and how often a service should be relocated so that it gets a try to be started on another node. The aim of this policy is to circumvent temporary unavailability of shared resources on a specific node. For example, if a shared storage isn't available on a quorate node anymore, e.g. network problems, but still on other nodes, the relocate policy allows then that the service gets started nonetheless.

There are two service start recover policy settings which can be configured specific for each resource.

**max_restart**
 Maximum number of tries to restart an failed service on the actual node. The default is set to one.

**max_relocate**
 Maximum number of tries to relocate the service to a different node. A relocate only happens after the max_restart value is exceeded on the actual node. The default is set to one.

---

**Note**
The relocate count state will only reset to zero when the service had at least one successful start. That means if a service is re-started without fixing the error only the restart policy gets repeated.

---

## 14.8  Error Recovery

If after all tries the service state could not be recovered it gets placed in an error state. In this state the service won't get touched by the HA stack anymore. The only way out is disabling a service:

```
# ha-manager set vm:100 --state disabled
```

This can also be done in the web interface.

To recover from the error state you should do the following:

- bring the resource back into a safe and consistent state (e.g.: kill its process if the service could not be stopped)

- disable the resource to remove the error flag

- fix the error which led to this failures

- **after** you fixed all errors you may request that the service starts again

## 14.9  Package Updates

When updating the ha-manager you should do one node after the other, never all at once for various reasons. First, while we test our software thoughtfully, a bug affecting your specific setup cannot totally be ruled out. Upgrading one node after the other and checking the functionality of each node after finishing the update helps to recover from an eventual problems, while updating all could render you in a broken cluster state and is generally not good practice.

Also, the Proxmox VE HA stack uses a request acknowledge protocol to perform actions between the cluster and the local resource manager. For restarting, the LRM makes a request to the CRM to freeze all its services. This prevents that they get touched by the Cluster during the short time the LRM is restarting. After that the LRM may safely close the watchdog during a restart. Such a restart happens on a update and as already stated a active master CRM is needed to acknowledge the requests from the LRM, if this is not the case the update process can be too long which, in the worst case, may result in a watchdog reset.

## 14.10  Node Maintenance

It is sometimes possible to shutdown or reboot a node to do maintenance tasks. Either to replace hardware, or simply to install a new kernel image.

### 14.10.1  Shutdown

A shutdown (*poweroff*) is usually done if the node is planned to stay down for some time. The LRM stops all managed services in that case. This means that other nodes will take over those service afterwards.

---

**Note**
Recent hardware has large amounts of RAM. So we stop all resources, then restart them to avoid online migration of all that RAM. If you want to use online migration, you need to invoke that manually before you shutdown the node.

---

## 14.10.2  Reboot

Node reboots are initiated with the *reboot* command. This is usually done after installing a new kernel. Please note that this is different from "shutdown", because the node immediately starts again.

The LRM tells the CRM that it wants to restart, and waits until the CRM puts all resources into the `freeze` state (same mechanism is used for Pakage Updates Section 14.9). This prevents that those resources are moved to other nodes. Instead, the CRM start the resources after the reboot on the same node.

## 14.10.3  Manual Resource Movement

Last but not least, you can also move resources manually to other nodes before you shutdown or restart a node. The advantage is that you have full control, and you can decide if you want to use online migration or not.

---

**Note**

Please do not *kill* services like `pve-ha-crm`, `pve-ha-lrm` or `watchdog-mux`. They manage and use the watchdog, so this can result in a node reboot.

---

# Chapter 15

# Backup and Restore

Backups are a requirements for any sensible IT deployment, and Proxmox VE provides a fully integrated solution, using the capabilities of each storage and each guest system type. This allows the system administrator to fine tune via the `mode` option between consistency of the backups and downtime of the guest system.

Proxmox VE backups are always full backups - containing the VM/CT configuration and all data. Backups can be started via the GUI or via the `vzdump` command line tool.

### Backup Storage

Before a backup can run, a backup storage must be defined. Refer to the Storage documentation on how to add a storage. A backup storage must be a file level storage, as backups are stored as regular files. In most situations, using a NFS server is a good way to store backups. You can save those backups later to a tape drive, for off-site archiving.

### Scheduled Backup

Backup jobs can be scheduled so that they are executed automatically on specific days and times, for selectable nodes and guest systems. Configuration of scheduled backups is done at the Datacenter level in the GUI, which will generate a cron entry in /etc/cron.d/vzdump.

## 15.1  Backup modes

There are several ways to provide consistency (option `mode`), depending on the guest type.

BACKUP MODES FOR VMs:

**`stop` mode**
: This mode provides the highest consistency of the backup, at the cost of a downtime in the VM operation. It works by executing an orderly shutdown of the VM, and then runs a background Qemu process to backup the VM data. After the backup is complete, the Qemu process resumes the VM to full operation mode if it was previously running.

### suspend **mode**

This mode is provided for compatibility reason, and suspends the VM before calling the `snapshot` mode. Since suspending the VM results in a longer downtime and does not necessarily improve the data consistency, the use of the `snapshot` mode is recommended instead.

### snapshot **mode**

This mode provides the lowest operation downtime, at the cost of a small inconstancy risk. It works by performing a Proxmox VE live backup, in which data blocks are copied while the VM is running. If the guest agent is enabled (`agent:  1`) and running, it calls `guest-fsfreeze-freeze` and `guest-fsfreeze-thaw` to improve consistency.

A technical overview of the Proxmox VE live backup for QemuServer can be found online here.

---

**Note**

Proxmox VE live backup provides snapshot-like semantics on any storage type. It does not require that the underlying storage supports snapshots.

---

BACKUP MODES FOR CONTAINERS:

### stop **mode**

Stop the container for the duration of the backup. This potentially results in a very long downtime.

### suspend **mode**

This mode uses rsync to copy the container data to a temporary location (see option `--tmpdir`). Then the container is suspended and a second rsync copies changed files. After that, the container is started (resumed) again. This results in minimal downtime, but needs additional space to hold the container copy.

When the container is on a local file system and the target storage of the backup is an NFS server, you should set `--tmpdir` to reside on a local file system too, as this will result in a many fold performance improvement. Use of a local `tmpdir` is also required if you want to backup a local container using ACLs in suspend mode if the backup storage is an NFS server.

### snapshot **mode**

This mode uses the snapshotting facilities of the underlying storage. First, the container will be suspended to ensure data consistency. A temporary snapshot of the container's volumes will be made and the snapshot content will be archived in a tar file. Finally, the temporary snapshot is deleted again.

---

**Note**

`snapshot` mode requires that all backed up volumes are on a storage that supports snapshots. Using the `backup=no` mount point option individual volumes can be excluded from the backup (and thus this requirement).

---

**Note**

By default additional mount points besides the RootDisk mount point are not included in backups. For volume mount points you can set the **Backup** option to include the mount point in the backup. Device and bind mounts are never backed up as their content is managed outside the Proxmox VE storage library.

---

## 15.2 Backup File Names

Newer versions of vzdump encode the guest type and the backup time into the filename, for example

```
vzdump-lxc-105-2009_10_09-11_04_43.tar
```

That way it is possible to store several backup in the same directory. The parameter `maxfiles` can be used to specify the maximum number of backups to keep.

## 15.3 Restore

The resulting archive files can be restored with the following programs.

**pct restore**
    Container restore utility

**qmrestore**
    QemuServer restore utility

For details see the corresponding manual pages.

## 15.4 Configuration

Global configuration is stored in `/etc/vzdump.conf`. The file uses a simple colon separated key/value format. Each line has the following format:

```
OPTION: value
```

Blank lines in the file are ignored, and lines starting with a # character are treated as comments and are also ignored. Values from this file are used as default, and can be overwritten on the command line.

We currently support the following options:

**bwlimit: <integer> (0 − N)** (*default* = 0)
    Limit I/O bandwidth (KBytes per second).

**compress: <0 | 1 | gzip | lzo>** (*default* = 0)
    Compress dump file.

**dumpdir: <string>**
    Store resulting files to specified directory.

**exclude-path: <string>**
    Exclude certain files/directories (shell globs).

**ionice: <integer>** (0 − 8) (*default* = 7)
> Set CFQ ionice priority.

**lockwait: <integer>** (0 − N) (*default* = 180)
> Maximal time to wait for the global lock (minutes).

**mailnotification: <always | failure>** (*default* = always)
> Specify when to send an email

**mailto: <string>**
> Comma-separated list of email addresses that should receive email notifications.

**maxfiles: <integer>** (1 − N) (*default* = 1)
> Maximal number of backup files per guest system.

**mode: <snapshot | stop | suspend>** (*default* = snapshot)
> Backup mode.

**pigz: <integer>** (*default* = 0)
> Use pigz instead of gzip when N>0. N=1 uses half of cores, N>1 uses N as thread count.

**remove: <boolean>** (*default* = 1)
> Remove old backup files if there are more than *maxfiles* backup files.

**script: <string>**
> Use specified hook script.

**stdexcludes: <boolean>** (*default* = 1)
> Exclude temporary files and logs.

**stopwait: <integer>** (0 − N) (*default* = 10)
> Maximal time to wait until a guest system is stopped (minutes).

**storage: <string>**
> Store resulting file to this storage.

**tmpdir: <string>**
> Store temporary files to specified directory.

### Example vzdump.conf Configuration

```
tmpdir: /mnt/fast_local_disk
storage: my_backup_storage
mode: snapshot
bwlimit: 10000
```

## 15.5   Hook Scripts

You can specify a hook script with option `--script`. This script is called at various phases of the backup process, with parameters accordingly set. You can find an example in the documentation directory (`vzdump-hook-script.pl`).

## 15.6   File Exclusions

---
**Note**
this option is only available for container backups.

---

`vzdump` skips the following files by default (disable with the option `--stdexcludes 0`)

```
/tmp/?*
/var/tmp/?*
/var/run/?*pid
```

You can also manually specify (additional) exclude paths, for example:

```
# vzdump 777 --exclude-path /tmp/ --exclude-path '/var/foo*'
```

(only excludes tmp directories)

Configuration files are also stored inside the backup archive (in `./etc/vzdump/`) and will be correctly restored.

## 15.7   Examples

Simply dump guest 777 - no snapshot, just archive the guest private area and configuration files to the default dump directory (usually `/var/lib/vz/dump/`).

```
# vzdump 777
```

Use rsync and suspend/resume to create a snapshot (minimal downtime).

```
# vzdump 777 --mode suspend
```

Backup all guest systems and send notification mails to root and admin.

```
# vzdump --all --mode suspend --mailto root --mailto admin
```

Use snapshot mode (no downtime) and non-default dump directory.

```
# vzdump 777 --dumpdir /mnt/backup --mode snapshot
```

Backup more than one guest (selectively)

```
# vzdump 101 102 103 --mailto root
```

Backup all guests excluding 101 and 102

```
# vzdump --mode suspend --exclude 101,102
```

Restore a container to a new CT 600

```
# pct restore 600 /mnt/backup/vzdump-lxc-777.tar
```

Restore a QemuServer VM to VM 601

```
# qmrestore /mnt/backup/vzdump-qemu-888.vma 601
```

Clone an existing container 101 to a new container 300 with a 4GB root file system, using pipes

```
# vzdump 101 --stdout | pct restore --rootfs 4 300 -
```

# Chapter 16

# Important Service Daemons

## 16.1   pvedaemon - Proxmox VE API Daemon

This daemon exposes the whole Proxmox VE API on `127.0.0.1:85`. It runs as `root` and has permission to do all privileged operations.

> **Note**
> The daemon listens to a local address only, so you cannot access it from outside. The `pveproxy` daemon exposes the API to the outside world.

## 16.2   pveproxy - Proxmox VE API Proxy Daemon

This daemon exposes the whole Proxmox VE API on TCP port 8006 using HTTPS. It runs as user `www-data` and has very limited permissions. Operation requiring more permissions are forwarded to the local `pvedaemon`.

Requests targeted for other nodes are automatically forwarded to those nodes. This means that you can manage your whole cluster by connecting to a single Proxmox VE node.

### 16.2.1   Host based Access Control

It is possible to configure "apache2"-like access control lists. Values are read from file `/etc/default/pveproxy`. For example:

```
ALLOW_FROM="10.0.0.1-10.0.0.5,192.168.0.0/22"
DENY_FROM="all"
POLICY="allow"
```

IP addresses can be specified using any syntax understood by `Net::IP`. The name `all` is an alias for `0/0`.

The default policy is `allow`.

| Match | POLICY=deny | POLICY=allow |
|---|---|---|
| Match Allow only | allow | allow |
| Match Deny only | deny | deny |
| No match | deny | allow |
| Match Both Allow & Deny | deny | allow |

### 16.2.2 SSL Cipher Suite

You can define the cipher list in `/etc/default/pveproxy`, for example

`CIPHERS="HIGH:MEDIUM:!aNULL:!MD5"`

Above is the default. See the ciphers(1) man page from the openssl package for a list of all available options.

### 16.2.3 Diffie-Hellman Parameters

You can define the used Diffie-Hellman parameters in `/etc/default/pveproxy` by setting `DHPARAMS` to the path of a file containing DH parameters in PEM format, for example

`DHPARAMS="/path/to/dhparams.pem"`

If this option is not set, the built-in `skip2048` parameters will be used.

**Note**
DH parameters are only used if a cipher suite utilizing the DH key exchange algorithm is negotiated.

### 16.2.4 Alternative HTTPS certificate

By default, pveproxy uses the certificate `/etc/pve/local/pve-ssl.pem` (and private key `/etc/pve/local/pve-ssl.key`) for HTTPS connections. This certificate is signed by the cluster CA certificate, and therefor not trusted by browsers and operating systems by default.

In order to use a different certificate and private key for HTTPS, store the server certificate and any needed intermediate / CA certificates in PEM format in the file `/etc/pve/local/pveproxy-ssl.pem` and the associated private key in PEM format without a password in the file `/etc/pve/local/pveproxy-ssl.key`.

 **Warning**
Do not replace the automatically generated node certificate files in `/etc/pve/local/pve-ssl.pem` and `etc/pve/local/pve-ssl.key` or the cluster CA files in `/etc/pve/pve-root-ca.pem` and `/etc/pve/priv/pve-root-ca.key`.

**Note**
There is a detailed HOWTO for configuring commercial HTTPS certificates on the wiki, including setup instructions for obtaining certificates from the popular free Let's Encrypt certificate authority.

## 16.3   pvestatd - Proxmox VE Status Daemon

This daemon queries the status of VMs, storages and containers at regular intervals. The result is sent to all nodes in the cluster.

## 16.4   spiceproxy - SPICE Proxy Service

SPICE (the Simple Protocol for Independent Computing Environments) is an open remote computing solution, providing client access to remote displays and devices (e.g. keyboard, mouse, audio). The main use case is to get remote access to virtual machines and container.

This daemon listens on TCP port 3128, and implements an HTTP proxy to forward *CONNECT* request from the SPICE client to the correct Proxmox VE VM. It runs as user `www-data` and has very limited permissions.

### 16.4.1   Host based Access Control

It is possible to configure "apache2" like access control lists. Values are read from file `/etc/default/pveproxy`. See `pveproxy` documentation for details.

# Chapter 17

# Useful Command Line Tools

## 17.1   pvesubscription - Subscription Management

This tool is used to handle Proxmox VE subscriptions.

## 17.2   pveperf - Proxmox VE Benchmark Script

Tries to gather some CPU/hard disk performance data on the hard disk mounted at PATH (/ is used as default):

**CPU BOGOMIPS**
   bogomips sum of all CPUs

**REGEX/SECOND**
   regular expressions per second (perl performance test), should be above 300000

**HD SIZE**
   hard disk size

**BUFFERED READS**
   simple HD read test. Modern HDs should reach at least 40 MB/sec

**AVERAGE SEEK TIME**
   tests average seek time. Fast SCSI HDs reach values < 8 milliseconds. Common IDE/SATA disks get values from 15 to 20 ms.

**FSYNCS/SECOND**
   value should be greater than 200 (you should enable write back cache mode on you RAID controller - needs a battery backed cache (BBWC)).

**DNS EXT**
   average time to resolve an external DNS name

**DNS INT**

average time to resolve a local DNS name

# Chapter 18

# Frequently Asked Questions

---

**Note**

New FAQs are appended to the bottom of this section.

---

1. *What distribution is Proxmox VE based on?*

   Proxmox VE is based on Debian GNU/Linux

2. *What license does the Proxmox VE project use?*

   Proxmox VE code is licensed under the GNU Affero General Public License, version 3.

3. *Will Proxmox VE run on a 32bit processor?*

   Proxmox VE works only on 64-bit CPUs (AMD or Intel). There is no plan for 32-bit for the platform.

   ---

   **Note**

   VMs and Containers can be both 32-bit and/or 64-bit.

   ---

4. *Does my CPU support virtualization?*

   To check if your CPU is virtualization compatible, check for the vmx or svm tag in this command output:

   ```
   egrep '(vmx|svm)' /proc/cpuinfo
   ```

5. *Supported Intel CPUs*

   64-bit processors with Intel Virtualization Technology (Intel VT-x) support. (List of processors with Intel VT and 64-bit)

6. *Supported AMD CPUs*

   64-bit processors with AMD Virtualization Technology (AMD-V) support.

7. *What is a container, CT, VE, Virtual Private Server, VPS?*

   Operating-system-level virtualization is a server-virtualization method where the kernel of an operating system allows for multiple isolated user-space instances, instead of just one. We call such instances containers. As containers use the host's kernel they are limited to Linux guests.

8. *What is a QEMU/KVM guest (or VM)?*

   A QEMU/KVM guest (or VM) is a guest system running virtualized under Proxmox VE using QEMU and the Linux KVM kernel module.

9. *What is QEMU?*

   QEMU is a generic and open source machine emulator and virtualizer. QEMU uses the Linux KVM kernel module to achieve near native performance by executing the guest code directly on the host CPU. It is not limited to Linux guests but allows arbitrary operating systems to run.

10. *How long will my Proxmox VE version be supported?*

    Proxmox VE versions are supported at least as long as the corresponding Debian Version is oldstable. Proxmox VE uses a rolling release model and using the latest stable version is always recommended.

| Proxmox VE Version | Debian Version | First Release | Debian EOL | Proxmox EOL |
|---|---|---|---|---|
| Proxmox VE 5.x | Debian 9 (Stretch) | 2017-07 | tba | tba |
| Proxmox VE 4.x | Debian 8 (Jessie) | 2015-10 | 2018-06 | 2018-06 |
| Proxmox VE 3.x | Debian 7 (Wheezy) | 2013-05 | 2016-04 | 2017-02 |
| Proxmox VE 2.x | Debian 6 (Squeeze) | 2012-04 | 2014-05 | 2014-05 |
| Proxmox VE 1.x | Debian 5 (Lenny) | 2008-10 | 2012-03 | 2013-01 |

11. *LXC vs LXD vs Proxmox Containers vs Docker*

    LXC is a userspace interface for the Linux kernel containment features. Through a powerful API and simple tools, it lets Linux users easily create and manage system containers. LXC, as well as the former OpenVZ, aims at **system virtualization**, i.e. allows you to run a complete OS inside a container, where you log in as ssh, add users, run apache, etc...

    LXD is building on top of LXC to provide a new, better user experience. Under the hood, LXD uses LXC through `liblxc` and its Go binding to create and manage the containers. It's basically an alternative to LXC's tools and distribution template system with the added features that come from being controllable over the network.

    Proxmox Containers also aims at **system virtualization**, and thus uses LXC as the basis of its own container offer. The Proxmox Container Toolkit is called `pct`, and is tightly coupled with Proxmox VE. That means that it is aware of the cluster setup, and it can use the same network and storage resources as fully virtualized VMs. You can even use the Proxmox VE firewall, create and restore backups, or manage containers using the HA framework. Everything can be controlled over the network using the Proxmox VE API.

    Docker aims at running a **single** application running in a contained environment. Hence you're managing a docker instance from the host with the docker toolkit. It is not recommended to run docker directly on your Proxmox VE host.

    **Note**

    You can however perfectly install and use docker inside a Proxmox Qemu VM, and thus getting the benefit of software containerization with the very strong isolation that VMs provide.

# Chapter 19

# Bibliography

## 19.1  Books about Proxmox VE

[1] [Ahmed16] Wasim Ahmed. Mastering Proxmox - Second Edition. Packt Publishing, 2016. ISBN 978-1785888243

[2] [Ahmed15] Wasim Ahmed. Proxmox Cookbook. Packt Publishing, 2015. ISBN 978-1783980901

[3] [Cheng14] Simon M.C. Cheng. Proxmox High Availability. Packt Publishing, 2014. ISBN 978-1783980888

[4] [Goldman16] Rik Goldman. Learning Proxmox VE. Packt Publishing, 2016. ISBN 978-1783981786

[5] [Surber16]] Lee R. Surber. Virtualization Complete: Business Basic Edition. Linux Solutions (LRS-TEK), 2016. ASIN B01BBVQZT6

## 19.2  Books about related technology

[6] [Hertzog13] Raphaël Hertzog & Roland Mas. The Debian Administrator's Handbook: Debian Jessie from Discovery to Mastery, Freexian, 2013. ISBN 979-1091414050

[7] [Bir96] Kenneth P. Birman. Building Secure and Reliable Network Applications. Manning Publications Co, 1996. ISBN 978-1884777295

[8] [Walsh10] Norman Walsh. DocBook 5: The Definitive Guide. O'Reilly & Associates, 2010. ISBN 978-0596805029

[9] [Richardson07] Leonard Richardson & Sam Ruby. RESTful Web Services. O'Reilly Media, 2007. ISBN 978-0596529260

[10] [Singh15] Karan Singh. Learning Ceph. Packt Publishing, 2015. ISBN 978-1783985623

[11] [Singh16] Karan Signh. Ceph Cookbook Packt Publishing, 2016. ISBN 978-1784393502

[12] [Mauerer08] Wolfgang Mauerer. Professional Linux Kernel Architecture. John Wiley & Sons, 2008. ISBN 978-0470343432

[13] [Loshin03] Pete Loshin, IPv6: Theory, Protocol, and Practice, 2nd Edition. Morgan Kaufmann, 2003. ISBN 978-1558608108

[14] [Loeliger12] Jon Loeliger & Matthew McCullough. Version Control with Git: Powerful tools and techniques for collaborative software development. O'Reilly and Associates, 2012. ISBN 978-1449316389

[15] [Kreibich10] Jay A. Kreibich. Using SQLite, O'Reilly and Associates, 2010. ISBN 978-0596521189

## 19.3  Books about related topics

[16] [Bessen09] James Bessen & Michael J. Meurer, Patent Failure: How Judges, Bureaucrats, and Lawyers Put Innovators at Risk. Princeton Univ Press, 2009. ISBN 978-0691143217

# Appendix A

# Command Line Interface

## A.1   pvesm - Proxmox VE Storage Manager

**pvesm** <COMMAND> [ARGS] [OPTIONS]

**pvesm add** <type> <storage> [OPTIONS]

Create a new storage.


**<type>: <dir | drbd | glusterfs | iscsi | iscsidirect | lvm | lvmthin | nfs | rbd | sheepdog | zfs | zfspool>**
   Storage type.


**<storage>: <string>**
   The storage identifier.


**-authsupported <string>**
   Authsupported.


**-base <string>**
   Base volume. This volume is automatically activated.


**-blocksize <string>**
   block size


**-comstar_hg <string>**
   host group for comstar views


**-comstar_tg <string>**
   target group for comstar views


**-content <string>**
   Allowed content types.

> **Note**
>
> the value *rootdir* is used for Containers, and value *images* for VMs.

**-disable <boolean>**
    Flag to disable the storage.

**-export <string>**
    NFS export path.

**-format <string>**
    Default image format.

**-is_mountpoint <boolean>** (*default = no*)
    Assume the directory is an externally managed mountpoint. If nothing is mounted the storage will be considered offline.

**-iscsiprovider <string>**
    iscsi provider

**-krbd <boolean>**
    Access rbd through krbd kernel module.

**-maxfiles <integer> (0 - N)**
    Maximal number of backup files per VM. Use *0* for unlimted.

**-mkdir <boolean>** (*default = yes*)
    Create the directory if it doesn't exist.

**-monhost <string>**
    Monitors daemon ips.

**-nodes <string>**
    List of cluster node names.

**-nowritecache <boolean>**
    disable write caching on the target

**-options <string>**
    NFS mount options (see *man nfs*)

**-path <string>**
    File system path.

**-pool <string>**
    Pool.

**-portal <string>**
 iSCSI portal (IP or DNS name with optional port).

**-redundancy <integer>  (1 - 16) (*default = 2*)**
 The redundancy count specifies the number of nodes to which the resource should be deployed. It must be at least 1 and at most the number of nodes in the cluster.

**-saferemove <boolean>**
 Zero-out data when removing LVs.

**-saferemove_throughput <string>**
 Wipe throughput (cstream -t parameter value).

**-server <string>**
 Server IP or DNS name.

**-server2 <string>**
 Backup volfile server IP or DNS name.

---

**Note**

Requires option(s): `server`

---

**-shared <boolean>**
 Mark storage as shared.

**-sparse <boolean>**
 use sparse volumes

**-tagged_only <boolean>**
 Only use logical volumes tagged with *pve-vm-ID*.

**-target <string>**
 iSCSI target.

**-thinpool <string>**
 LVM thin pool LV name.

**-transport <rdma | tcp | unix>**
 Gluster transport: tcp or rdma

**-username <string>**
 RBD Id.

**-vgname <string>**
 Volume group name.

**-volume <string>**
> Glusterfs Volume.

**pvesm alloc** `<storage> <vmid> <filename> <size> [OPTIONS]`

Allocate disk images.

**<storage>: <string>**
> The storage identifier.

**<vmid>: <integer> (1 - N)**
> Specify owner VM

**<filename>: <string>**
> The name of the file to create.

**<size>: \d+[MG]?**
> Size in kilobyte (1024 bytes). Optional suffixes *M* (megabyte, 1024K) and *G* (gigabyte, 1024M)

**-format <qcow2 | raw | subvol>**
> no description available

---

**Note**
Requires option(s): `size`

---

**pvesm export** `<volume> <format> <filename> [OPTIONS]`

Export a volume.

**<volume>: <string>**
> Volume identifier

**<format>: <qcow2+size | raw+size | tar+size | vmdk+size | zfs>**
> Export stream format

**<filename>: <string>**
> Destination file name

**-base (?^:[a-z0-9_\-]{1,40})**
> Snapshot to start an incremental stream from

**-snapshot (?^:[a-z0-9_\-]{1,40})**
> Snapshot to export

**-with-snapshots <boolean> (*default* = 0)**
> Whether to include intermediate snapshots in the stream

**pvesm extractconfig** `<volume>`

Extract configuration from vzdump backup archive.

   **`<volume>`: `<string>`**
      Volume identifier

**pvesm free** `<volume>` `[OPTIONS]`

Delete volume

   **`<volume>`: `<string>`**
      Volume identifier

   **`-storage <string>`**
      The storage identifier.

**pvesm glusterfsscan** `<server>`

Scan remote GlusterFS server.

   **`<server>`: `<string>`**
      no description available

**pvesm help** `[<cmd>]` `[OPTIONS]`

Get help about specified command.

   **`<cmd>`: `<string>`**
      Command name

   **`-verbose <boolean>`**
      Verbose output format.

**pvesm import** `<volume>` `<format>` `<filename>` `[OPTIONS]`

Import a volume.

   **`<volume>`: `<string>`**
      Volume identifier

   **`<format>`: `<qcow2+size | raw+size | tar+size | vmdk+size | zfs>`**
      Import stream format

   **`<filename>`: `<string>`**
      Source file name

   **`-base (?^:[a-z0-9_\-]{1,40})`**
      Base snapshot of an incremental stream

**–delete–snapshot (?ˆ:[a–z0–9_\–]{1,80})**
    A snapshot to delete on success

**–with–snapshots <boolean>** (*default* = 0)
    Whether the stream includes intermediate snapshots

**pvesm iscsiscan** –portal <string> [OPTIONS]

Scan remote iSCSI server.

**–portal <string>**
    no description available

**pvesm list** <storage> [OPTIONS]

List storage content.

**<storage>: <string>**
    The storage identifier.

**–content <string>**
    Only list content of this type.

**–vmid <integer>  (1 – N)**
    Only list images for this VM

**pvesm lvmscan**

List local LVM volume groups.

**pvesm lvmthinscan** <vg>

List local LVM Thin Pools.

**<vg>: [a–zA–Z0–9\.\+\_][a–zA–Z0–9\.\+\_\–]+**
    no description available

**pvesm nfsscan** <server>

Scan remote NFS server.

**<server>: <string>**
    no description available

**pvesm path** <volume>

Get filesystem path for specified volume

**<volume>: <string>**
    Volume identifier

**pvesm remove** `<storage>`

Delete storage configuration.


`<storage>: <string>`
> The storage identifier.

**pvesm set** `<storage> [OPTIONS]`

Update storage configuration.


`<storage>: <string>`
> The storage identifier.

`-blocksize <string>`
> block size

`-comstar_hg <string>`
> host group for comstar views

`-comstar_tg <string>`
> target group for comstar views

`-content <string>`
> Allowed content types.

> ---
> **Note**
>
> the value *rootdir* is used for Containers, and value *images* for VMs.
> ---

`-delete <string>`
> A list of settings you want to delete.

`-digest <string>`
> Prevent changes if current configuration file has different SHA1 digest. This can be used to prevent concurrent modifications.

`-disable <boolean>`
> Flag to disable the storage.

`-format <string>`
> Default image format.

`-is_mountpoint <boolean> (default = no)`
> Assume the directory is an externally managed mountpoint. If nothing is mounted the storage will be considered offline.

**-krbd <boolean>**
Access rbd through krbd kernel module.

**-maxfiles <integer> (0 - N)**
Maximal number of backup files per VM. Use *0* for unlimted.

**-mkdir <boolean> (*default* = yes)**
Create the directory if it doesn't exist.

**-nodes <string>**
List of cluster node names.

**-nowritecache <boolean>**
disable write caching on the target

**-options <string>**
NFS mount options (see *man nfs*)

**-pool <string>**
Pool.

**-redundancy <integer> (1 - 16) (*default* = 2)**
The redundancy count specifies the number of nodes to which the resource should be deployed. It must be at least 1 and at most the number of nodes in the cluster.

**-saferemove <boolean>**
Zero-out data when removing LVs.

**-saferemove_throughput <string>**
Wipe throughput (cstream -t parameter value).

**-server <string>**
Server IP or DNS name.

**-server2 <string>**
Backup volfile server IP or DNS name.

---

**Note**
Requires option(s): `server`

---

**-shared <boolean>**
Mark storage as shared.

**-sparse <boolean>**
use sparse volumes

---

**-tagged_only <boolean>**
   Only use logical volumes tagged with *pve-vm-ID*.


**-transport <rdma | tcp | unix>**
   Gluster transport: tcp or rdma


**-username <string>**
   RBD Id.


**pvesm status** [OPTIONS]

Get status for all datastores.


**-content <string>**
   Only list stores which support this content type.


**-enabled <boolean>** (*default* = 0)
   Only list stores which are enabled (not disabled in config).


**-storage <string>**
   Only list status for specified storage


**-target <string>**
   If target is different to *node*, we only lists shared storages which content is accessible on this *node* and the specified *target* node.


**pvesm zfsscan**

Scan zfs pool list on local node.


## A.2  pvesubscription - Proxmox VE Subscription Manager

**pvesubscription** <COMMAND> [ARGS] [OPTIONS]

**pvesubscription get**

Read subscription info.

**pvesubscription help** [<cmd>] [OPTIONS]

Get help about specified command.


**<cmd>: <string>**
   Command name


**-verbose <boolean>**
   Verbose output format.

**pvesubscription set** `<key>`

Set subscription key.

**`<key>`: `<string>`**
>   Proxmox VE subscription key

**pvesubscription update** `[OPTIONS]`

Update subscription info.

**`-force <boolean>` (*default* = 0)**
>   Always connect to server, even if we have up to date info inside local cache.

# A.3   pveperf - Proxmox VE Benchmark Script

**pveperf** `[PATH]`

# A.4   pveceph - Manage CEPH Services on Proxmox VE Nodes

**pveceph** `<COMMAND>` `[ARGS]` `[OPTIONS]`

**pveceph createmon**

Create Ceph Monitor

**pveceph createosd** `<dev>` `[OPTIONS]`

Create OSD

**`<dev>`: `<string>`**
>   Block device name.

**`-bluestore <boolean>` (*default* = 0)**
>   Use bluestore instead of filestore.

**`-fstype <btrfs | ext4 | xfs>` (*default* = xfs)**
>   File system type (filestore only).

**`-journal_dev <string>`**
>   Block device name for journal.

**pveceph createpool** `<name>` `[OPTIONS]`

Create POOL

**`<name>`: `<string>`**
>   The name of the pool. It must be unique.

**-crush_ruleset <integer>** (0 - 32768) (*default = 0*)
  The ruleset to use for mapping object placement in the cluster.

**-min_size <integer>** (1 - 7) (*default = 1*)
  Minimum number of replicas per object

**-pg_num <integer>** (8 - 32768) (*default = 64*)
  Number of placement groups.

**-size <integer>** (1 - 7) (*default = 2*)
  Number of replicas per object

**pveceph destroymon** <monid>

Destroy Ceph monitor.

**<monid>: <integer>**
  Monitor ID

**pveceph destroyosd** <osdid> [OPTIONS]

Destroy OSD

**<osdid>: <integer>**
  OSD ID

**-cleanup <boolean>** (*default = 0*)
  If set, we remove partition table entries.

**pveceph destroypool** <name> [OPTIONS]

Destroy pool

**<name>: <string>**
  The name of the pool. It must be unique.

**-force <boolean>** (*default = 0*)
  If true, destroys pool even if in use

**pveceph help** [<cmd>] [OPTIONS]

Get help about specified command.

**<cmd>: <string>**
  Command name

**-verbose <boolean>**
  Verbose output format.

**pveceph init** [OPTIONS]

Create initial ceph default configuration and setup symlinks.

**-disable_cephx <boolean>** (*default* = 0)
    Disable cephx authentification.

**Warning**
cephx is a security feature protecting against man-in-the-middle attacks. Only consider disabling cephx if your network is private!

**-min_size <integer>** (1 - 7) (*default* = 2)
    Minimum number of available replicas per object to allow I/O

**-network <string>**
    Use specific network for all ceph related traffic

**-pg_bits <integer>** (6 - 14) (*default* = 6)
    Placement group bits, used to specify the default number of placement groups.

**Note**
*osd pool default pg num* does not work for default pools.

**-size <integer>** (1 - 7) (*default* = 3)
    Targeted number of replicas per object

**pveceph install** [OPTIONS]

Install ceph related packages.

**-version <luminous>**
    no description available

**pveceph lspools**

List all pools.

**pveceph purge**

Destroy ceph related data and configuration files.

**pveceph start** [<service>]

Start ceph services.

**<service>: (mon|mds|osd)\.[A-Za-z0-9]{1,32}**
    Ceph service name.

**pveceph status**

Get ceph status.

**pveceph stop** [<service>]

Stop ceph services.

```
<service>: (mon|mds|osd)\.[A-Za-z0-9]{1,32}
     Ceph service name.
```

## A.5   qm - Qemu/KVM Virtual Machine Manager

**qm** <COMMAND> [ARGS] [OPTIONS]

**qm agent** <vmid> <command>

Execute Qemu Guest Agent commands.

```
<vmid>: <integer> (1 - N)
     The (unique) ID of the VM.
```

```
<command>: <fsfreeze-freeze | fsfreeze-status | fsfreeze-thaw |
fstrim | get-fsinfo | get-memory-block-info | get-memory-blocks |
get-time | get-vcpus | info | network-get-interfaces | ping |
shutdown | suspend-disk | suspend-hybrid | suspend-ram>
     The QGA command.
```

**qm clone** <vmid> <newid> [OPTIONS]

Create a copy of virtual machine/template.

```
<vmid>: <integer> (1 - N)
     The (unique) ID of the VM.
```

```
<newid>: <integer> (1 - N)
     VMID for the clone.
```

```
-description <string>
     Description for the new VM.
```

```
-format <qcow2 | raw | vmdk>
     Target format for file storage.
```

**Note**
Requires option(s): full

**-full <boolean>** (*default* = 0)

    Create a full copy of all disk. This is always done when you clone a normal VM. For VM templates, we try to create a linked clone by default.

**-name <string>**

    Set a name for the new VM.

**-pool <string>**

    Add the new VM to the specified pool.

**-snapname <string>**

    The name of the snapshot.

**-storage <string>**

    Target storage for full clone.

---

**Note**

Requires option(s): `full`

---

**-target <string>**

    Target node. Only allowed if the original VM is on shared storage.

**qm config** <vmid> [OPTIONS]

Get current virtual machine configuration. This does not include pending configuration changes (see *pending* API).

**<vmid>: <integer>  (1 - N)**

    The (unique) ID of the VM.

**-current <boolean>** (*default* = 0)

    Get current values (instead of pending values).

**qm create** <vmid> [OPTIONS]

Create or restore a virtual machine.

**<vmid>: <integer>  (1 - N)**

    The (unique) ID of the VM.

**-acpi <boolean>** (*default* = 1)

    Enable/disable ACPI.

**-agent <boolean>** (*default* = 0)

    Enable/disable Qemu GuestAgent.

**-archive <string>**
　　The backup file.

**-args <string>**
　　Arbitrary arguments passed to kvm.

**-autostart <boolean>** (*default* = 0)
　　Automatic restart after crash (currently ignored).

**-balloon <integer> (0 - N)**
　　Amount of target RAM for the VM in MB. Using zero disables the ballon driver.

**-bios <ovmf | seabios>** (*default* = **seabios**)
　　Select BIOS implementation.

**-boot [acdn]{1,4}** (*default* = **cdn**)
　　Boot on floppy (a), hard disk (c), CD-ROM (d), or network (n).

**-bootdisk (ide|sata|scsi|virtio) \d+**
　　Enable booting from specified disk.

**-cdrom <volume>**
　　This is an alias for option -ide2

**-cores <integer> (1 - N)** (*default* = 1)
　　The number of cores per socket.

**-cpu [cputype=]<enum> [,hidden=<1|0>]**
　　Emulated CPU type.

**-cpulimit <number> (0 - 128)** (*default* = 0)
　　Limit of CPU usage.

**-cpuunits <integer> (0 - 500000)** (*default* = 1024)
　　CPU weight for a VM.

**-description <string>**
　　Description for the VM. Only used on the configuration web interface. This is saved as comment inside the configuration file.

**-efidisk0 [file=]<volume> [,format=<enum>] [,size=<DiskSize>]**
　　Configure a Disk for storing EFI vars

**-force <boolean>**
　　Allow to overwrite existing VM.

**Note**
Requires option(s): `archive`

---

**-freeze <boolean>**
    Freeze CPU at startup (use *c* monitor command to start execution).

**-hostpci[n] [host=]<HOSTPCIID[;HOSTPCIID2...]> [,pcie=<1|0>]**
**[,rombar=<1|0>] [,romfile=<string>] [,x-vga=<1|0>]**
    Map host PCI devices into guest.

**-hotplug <string> (*default* = network,disk,usb)**
    Selectively enable hotplug features. This is a comma separated list of hotplug features: *network*, *disk*, *cpu*, *memory* and *usb*. Use *0* to disable hotplug completely. Value *1* is an alias for the default *network,disk,usb*.

**-hugepages <1024 | 2 | any>**
    Enable/disable hugepages memory.

**-ide[n] [file=]<volume> [,aio=<native|threads>] [,backup=<1|0>]**
**[,bps=<bps>] [,bps_max_length=<seconds>] [,bps_rd=<bps>]**
**[,bps_rd_max_length=<seconds>] [,bps_wr=<bps>] [,bps_wr_max_length=**
**<seconds>] [,cache=<enum>] [,cyls=<integer>] [,detect_zeroes=<1|0>]**
**[,discard=<ignore|on>] [,format=<enum>] [,heads=<integer>] [,iops=**
**<iops>] [,iops_max=<iops>] [,iops_max_length=<seconds>] [,iops_rd=**
**<iops>] [,iops_rd_max=<iops>] [,iops_rd_max_length=<seconds>]**
**[,iops_wr=<iops>] [,iops_wr_max=<iops>] [,iops_wr_max_length=**
**<seconds>] [,mbps=<mbps>] [,mbps_max=<mbps>] [,mbps_rd=<mbps>]**
**[,mbps_rd_max=<mbps>] [,mbps_wr=<mbps>] [,mbps_wr_max=<mbps>]**
**[,media=<cdrom|disk>] [,model=<model>] [,replicate=<1|0>] [,rerror=**
**<ignore|report|stop>] [,secs=<integer>] [,serial=<serial>] [,size=**
**<DiskSize>] [,snapshot=<1|0>] [,trans=<none|lba|auto>] [,werror=**
**<enum>]**
    Use volume as IDE hard disk or CD-ROM (n is 0 to 3).

**-keyboard <da | de | de-ch | en-gb | en-us | es | fi | fr | fr-be |**
**fr-ca | fr-ch | hu | is | it | ja | lt | mk | nl | no | pl | pt |**
**pt-br | sl | sv | tr> (*default* = en-us)**
    Keybord layout for vnc server. Default is read from the */etc/pve/datacenter.conf* configuration file.

**-kvm <boolean> (*default* = 1)**
    Enable/disable KVM hardware virtualization.

**-localtime <boolean>**
    Set the real time clock to local time. This is enabled by default if ostype indicates a Microsoft OS.

**-lock <backup | migrate | rollback | snapshot>**
    Lock/unlock the VM.

**-machine (pc|pc(-i440fx)?-\d+\.\d+(\.pxe)?|q35|pc-q35-\d+\.\d+(\.pxe)?)**

> Specific the Qemu machine type.

**-memory <integer> (16 - N) (*default* = 512)**

> Amount of RAM for the VM in MB. This is the maximum available memory when you use the balloon device.

**-migrate_downtime <number> (0 - N) (*default* = 0.1)**

> Set maximum tolerated downtime (in seconds) for migrations.

**-migrate_speed <integer> (0 - N) (*default* = 0)**

> Set maximum speed (in MB/s) for migrations. Value 0 is no limit.

**-name <string>**

> Set a name for the VM. Only used on the configuration web interface.

**-net[n] [model=]<enum> [,bridge=<bridge>] [,firewall=<1|0>] [,link_down=<1|0>] [,macaddr=<XX:XX:XX:XX:XX:XX>] [,queues=<integer>] [,rate=<number>] [,tag=<integer>] [,trunks=<vlanid[;vlanid...]>] [,<model>=<macaddr>]**

> Specify network devices.

**-numa <boolean> (*default* = 0)**

> Enable/disable NUMA.

**-numa[n] cpus=<id[-id];...> [,hostnodes=<id[-id];...>] [,memory=<number>] [,policy=<preferred|bind|interleave>]**

> NUMA topology.

**-onboot <boolean> (*default* = 0)**

> Specifies whether a VM will be started during system bootup.

**-ostype <l24 | l26 | other | solaris | w2k | w2k3 | w2k8 | win10 | win7 | win8 | wvista | wxp>**

> Specify guest operating system.

**-parallel[n] /dev/parport\d+|/dev/usb/lp\d+**

> Map host parallel devices (n is 0 to 2).

**-pool <string>**

> Add the VM to the specified pool.

**-protection <boolean> (*default* = 0)**

> Sets the protection flag of the VM. This will disable the remove VM and remove disk operations.

-reboot <boolean> (*default* = 1)
    Allow reboot. If set to *0* the VM exit on reboot.


-sata[n] [file=]<volume> [,aio=<native|threads>] [,backup=<1|0>]
[,bps=<bps>] [,bps_max_length=<seconds>] [,bps_rd=<bps>]
[,bps_rd_max_length=<seconds>] [,bps_wr=<bps>] [,bps_wr_max_length=
<seconds>] [,cache=<enum>] [,cyls=<integer>] [,detect_zeroes=<1|0>]
[,discard=<ignore|on>] [,format=<enum>] [,heads=<integer>] [,iops=
<iops>] [,iops_max=<iops>] [,iops_max_length=<seconds>] [,iops_rd=
<iops>] [,iops_rd_max=<iops>] [,iops_rd_max_length=<seconds>]
[,iops_wr=<iops>] [,iops_wr_max=<iops>] [,iops_wr_max_length=
<seconds>] [,mbps=<mbps>] [,mbps_max=<mbps>] [,mbps_rd=<mbps>]
[,mbps_rd_max=<mbps>] [,mbps_wr=<mbps>] [,mbps_wr_max=<mbps>]
[,media=<cdrom|disk>] [,replicate=<1|0>] [,rerror=
<ignore|report|stop>] [,secs=<integer>] [,serial=<serial>] [,size=
<DiskSize>] [,snapshot=<1|0>] [,trans=<none|lba|auto>] [,werror=
<enum>]
    Use volume as SATA hard disk or CD-ROM (n is 0 to 5).


-scsi[n] [file=]<volume> [,aio=<native|threads>] [,backup=<1|0>]
[,bps=<bps>] [,bps_max_length=<seconds>] [,bps_rd=<bps>]
[,bps_rd_max_length=<seconds>] [,bps_wr=<bps>] [,bps_wr_max_length=
<seconds>] [,cache=<enum>] [,cyls=<integer>] [,detect_zeroes=<1|0>]
[,discard=<ignore|on>] [,format=<enum>] [,heads=<integer>] [,iops=
<iops>] [,iops_max=<iops>] [,iops_max_length=<seconds>] [,iops_rd=
<iops>] [,iops_rd_max=<iops>] [,iops_rd_max_length=<seconds>]
[,iops_wr=<iops>] [,iops_wr_max=<iops>] [,iops_wr_max_length=
<seconds>] [,iothread=<1|0>] [,mbps=<mbps>] [,mbps_max=<mbps>]
[,mbps_rd=<mbps>] [,mbps_rd_max=<mbps>] [,mbps_wr=<mbps>]
[,mbps_wr_max=<mbps>] [,media=<cdrom|disk>] [,queues=<integer>]
[,replicate=<1|0>] [,rerror=<ignore|report|stop>] [,scsiblock=
<1|0>] [,secs=<integer>] [,serial=<serial>] [,size=<DiskSize>]
[,snapshot=<1|0>] [,trans=<none|lba|auto>] [,werror=<enum>]
    Use volume as SCSI hard disk or CD-ROM (n is 0 to 13).


-scsihw <lsi | lsi53c810 | megasas | pvscsi | virtio-scsi-pci |
virtio-scsi-single> (*default* = lsi)
    SCSI controller model


-serial[n] (/dev/.+|socket)
    Create a serial device inside the VM (n is 0 to 3)


-shares <integer> (0 - 50000) (*default* = 1000)
    Amount of memory shares for auto-ballooning. The larger the number is, the more memory this VM
    gets. Number is relative to weights of all other running VMs. Using zero disables auto-ballooning

**-smbios1** **[family=<string>]** **[,manufacturer=<string>]** **[,product=** **<string>]** **[,serial=<string>]** **[,sku=<string>]** **[,uuid=<UUID>]** **[,version=<string>]**

> Specify SMBIOS type 1 fields.

**-smp <integer>** **(1 - N)** *(default = 1)*

> The number of CPUs. Please use option -sockets instead.

**-sockets <integer>** **(1 - N)** *(default = 1)*

> The number of CPU sockets.

**-startdate (now | YYYY-MM-DD | YYYY-MM-DDTHH:MM:SS)** *(default = now)*

> Set the initial date of the real time clock. Valid format for date are: *now* or *2006-06-17T16:01:21* or *2006-06-17*.

**-startup `[[order=]\d+] [,up=\d+] [,down=\d+]`**

> Startup and shutdown behavior. Order is a non-negative number defining the general startup order. Shutdown in done with reverse ordering. Additionally you can set the *up* or *down* delay in seconds, which specifies a delay to wait before the next VM is started or stopped.

**-storage <string>**

> Default storage.

**-tablet <boolean>** *(default = 1)*

> Enable/disable the USB tablet device.

**-tdf <boolean>** *(default = 0)*

> Enable/disable time drift fix.

**-template <boolean>** *(default = 0)*

> Enable/disable Template.

**-unique <boolean>**

> Assign a unique random ethernet address.

> ---
> **Note**
>
> Requires option(s): `archive`
>
> ---

**-unused[n] <string>**

> Reference to unused volumes. This is used internally, and should not be modified manually.

**-usb[n] [host=]<HOSTUSBDEVICE|spice>** **[,usb3=<1|0>]**

> Configure an USB device (n is 0 to 4).

-vcpus <integer>  (1 - N) (*default* = 0)
      Number of hotplugged vcpus.


-vga <cirrus | qxl | qxl2 | qxl3 | qxl4 | serial0 | serial1 |
serial2 | serial3 | std | vmware>
      Select the VGA type.


-virtio[n] [file=]<volume> [,aio=<native|threads>] [,backup=<1|0>]
[,bps=<bps>] [,bps_max_length=<seconds>] [,bps_rd=<bps>]
[,bps_rd_max_length=<seconds>] [,bps_wr=<bps>] [,bps_wr_max_length=
<seconds>] [,cache=<enum>] [,cyls=<integer>] [,detect_zeroes=<1|0>]
[,discard=<ignore|on>] [,format=<enum>] [,heads=<integer>] [,iops=
<iops>] [,iops_max=<iops>] [,iops_max_length=<seconds>] [,iops_rd=
<iops>] [,iops_rd_max=<iops>] [,iops_rd_max_length=<seconds>]
[,iops_wr=<iops>] [,iops_wr_max=<iops>] [,iops_wr_max_length=
<seconds>] [,iothread=<1|0>] [,mbps=<mbps>] [,mbps_max=<mbps>]
[,mbps_rd=<mbps>] [,mbps_rd_max=<mbps>] [,mbps_wr=<mbps>]
[,mbps_wr_max=<mbps>] [,media=<cdrom|disk>] [,replicate=<1|0>]
[,rerror=<ignore|report|stop>] [,secs=<integer>] [,serial=<serial>]
[,size=<DiskSize>] [,snapshot=<1|0>] [,trans=<none|lba|auto>]
[,werror=<enum>]
      Use volume as VIRTIO hard disk (n is 0 to 15).


-watchdog [[model=]<i6300esb|ib700>] [,action=<enum>]
      Create a virtual hardware watchdog device.

**qm delsnapshot** <vmid> <snapname> [OPTIONS]

Delete a VM snapshot.


  <vmid>: <integer>  (1 - N)
      The (unique) ID of the VM.


  <snapname>: <string>
      The name of the snapshot.


  -force <boolean>
      For removal from config file, even if removing disk snapshots fails.

**qm destroy** <vmid> [OPTIONS]

Destroy the vm (also delete all used/owned volumes).


  <vmid>: <integer>  (1 - N)
      The (unique) ID of the VM.


  -skiplock <boolean>
      Ignore locks - only root is allowed to use this option.

**qm help** [<cmd>] [OPTIONS]

Get help about specified command.

**<cmd>: <string>**
　　Command name

**-verbose <boolean>**
　　Verbose output format.

**qm importdisk** <vmid> <source> <storage> [OPTIONS]

Import an external disk image as an unused disk in a VM. The image format has to be supported by qemu-img(1).

**<vmid>: <integer> (1 - N)**
　　The (unique) ID of the VM.

**<source>: <string>**
　　Path to the disk image to import

**<storage>: <string>**
　　Target storage ID

**-format <qcow2 | raw | vmdk>**
　　Target format

**qm list** [OPTIONS]

Virtual machine index (per node).

**-full <boolean>**
　　Determine the full status of active VMs.

**qm listsnapshot** <vmid>

List all snapshots.

**<vmid>: <integer> (1 - N)**
　　The (unique) ID of the VM.

**qm migrate** <vmid> <target> [OPTIONS]

Migrate virtual machine. Creates a new migration task.

**<vmid>: <integer> (1 - N)**
　　The (unique) ID of the VM.

**<target>: <string>**
　　Target node.

**-force <boolean>**
> Allow to migrate VMs which use local devices. Only root may use this option.

**-migration_network <string>**
> CIDR of the (sub) network that is used for migration.

**-migration_type <insecure | secure>**
> Migration traffic is encrypted using an SSH tunnel by default. On secure, completely private networks this can be disabled to increase performance.

**-online <boolean>**
> Use online/live migration.

**-targetstorage <string>**
> Default target storage.

**-with-local-disks <boolean>**
> Enable live storage migration for local disk

**qm monitor** <vmid>

Enter Qemu Monitor interface.

**<vmid>: <integer> (1 - N)**
> The (unique) ID of the VM.

**qm move_disk** <vmid> <disk> <storage> [OPTIONS]

Move volume to different storage.

**<vmid>: <integer> (1 - N)**
> The (unique) ID of the VM.

**<disk>: <efidisk0 | ide0 | ide1 | ide2 | ide3 | sata0 | sata1 | sata2 | sata3 | sata4 | sata5 | scsi0 | scsi1 | scsi10 | scsi11 | scsi12 | scsi13 | scsi2 | scsi3 | scsi4 | scsi5 | scsi6 | scsi7 | scsi8 | scsi9 | virtio0 | virtio1 | virtio10 | virtio11 | virtio12 | virtio13 | virtio14 | virtio15 | virtio2 | virtio3 | virtio4 | virtio5 | virtio6 | virtio7 | virtio8 | virtio9>**
> The disk you want to move.

**<storage>: <string>**
> Target storage.

**-delete <boolean> (_default_ = 0)**
> Delete the original disk after successful copy. By default the original disk is kept as unused disk.

**-digest <string>**
　　Prevent changes if current configuration file has different SHA1 digest. This can be used to prevent
　　concurrent modifications.

**-format <qcow2 | raw | vmdk>**
　　Target Format.

## qm mtunnel

Used by qmigrate - do not use manually.

**qm nbdstop** <vmid>

Stop embedded nbd server.

**<vmid>: <integer> (1 - N)**
　　The (unique) ID of the VM.

**qm pending** <vmid>

Get virtual machine configuration, including pending changes.

**<vmid>: <integer> (1 - N)**
　　The (unique) ID of the VM.

**qm rescan** [OPTIONS]

Rescan all storages and update disk sizes and unused disk images.

**-vmid <integer> (1 - N)**
　　The (unique) ID of the VM.

**qm reset** <vmid> [OPTIONS]

Reset virtual machine.

**<vmid>: <integer> (1 - N)**
　　The (unique) ID of the VM.

**-skiplock <boolean>**
　　Ignore locks - only root is allowed to use this option.

**qm resize** <vmid> <disk> <size> [OPTIONS]

Extend volume size.

**<vmid>: <integer> (1 - N)**
　　The (unique) ID of the VM.

`<disk>: <efidisk0 | ide0 | ide1 | ide2 | ide3 | sata0 | sata1 | sata2 | sata3 | sata4 | sata5 | scsi0 | scsi1 | scsi10 | scsi11 | scsi12 | scsi13 | scsi2 | scsi3 | scsi4 | scsi5 | scsi6 | scsi7 | scsi8 | scsi9 | virtio0 | virtio1 | virtio10 | virtio11 | virtio12 | virtio13 | virtio14 | virtio15 | virtio2 | virtio3 | virtio4 | virtio5 | virtio6 | virtio7 | virtio8 | virtio9>`

> The disk you want to resize.

`<size>: \+?\d+(\.\d+)?[KMGT]?`

> The new size. With the + sign the value is added to the actual size of the volume and without it, the value is taken as an absolute one. Shrinking disk size is not supported.

`-digest <string>`

> Prevent changes if current configuration file has different SHA1 digest. This can be used to prevent concurrent modifications.

`-skiplock <boolean>`

> Ignore locks - only root is allowed to use this option.

**qm resume** `<vmid> [OPTIONS]`

Resume virtual machine.

`<vmid>: <integer> (1 - N)`

> The (unique) ID of the VM.

`-nocheck <boolean>`

> no description available

`-skiplock <boolean>`

> Ignore locks - only root is allowed to use this option.

**qm rollback** `<vmid> <snapname>`

Rollback VM state to specified snapshot.

`<vmid>: <integer> (1 - N)`

> The (unique) ID of the VM.

`<snapname>: <string>`

> The name of the snapshot.

**qm sendkey** `<vmid> <key> [OPTIONS]`

Send key event to virtual machine.

`<vmid>: <integer> (1 - N)`

> The (unique) ID of the VM.

**<key>: <string>**
   The key (qemu monitor encoding).

**-skiplock <boolean>**
   Ignore locks - only root is allowed to use this option.

**qm set** <vmid> [OPTIONS]

Set virtual machine options (synchrounous API) - You should consider using the POST method instead for any actions involving hotplug or storage allocation.

**<vmid>: <integer>  (1 - N)**
   The (unique) ID of the VM.

**-acpi <boolean> (*default* = 1)**
   Enable/disable ACPI.

**-agent <boolean> (*default* = 0)**
   Enable/disable Qemu GuestAgent.

**-args <string>**
   Arbitrary arguments passed to kvm.

**-autostart <boolean> (*default* = 0)**
   Automatic restart after crash (currently ignored).

**-balloon <integer>  (0 - N)**
   Amount of target RAM for the VM in MB. Using zero disables the ballon driver.

**-bios <ovmf | seabios> (*default* = seabios)**
   Select BIOS implementation.

**-boot [acdn]{1, 4} (*default* = cdn)**
   Boot on floppy (a), hard disk (c), CD-ROM (d), or network (n).

**-bootdisk (ide|sata|scsi|virtio)\d+**
   Enable booting from specified disk.

**-cdrom <volume>**
   This is an alias for option -ide2

**-cores <integer>  (1 - N) (*default* = 1)**
   The number of cores per socket.

**-cpu [cputype=]<enum>  [,hidden=<1|0>]**
   Emulated CPU type.

**-cpulimit <number>** (0 - 128) (*default = 0*)

 Limit of CPU usage.

**-cpuunits <integer>** (0 - 500000) (*default = 1024*)

 CPU weight for a VM.

**-delete <string>**

 A list of settings you want to delete.

**-description <string>**

 Description for the VM. Only used on the configuration web interface. This is saved as comment inside the configuration file.

**-digest <string>**

 Prevent changes if current configuration file has different SHA1 digest. This can be used to prevent concurrent modifications.

**-efidisk0 [file=]<volume> [,format=<enum>] [,size=<DiskSize>]**

 Configure a Disk for storing EFI vars

**-force <boolean>**

 Force physical removal. Without this, we simple remove the disk from the config file and create an additional configuration entry called *unused[n]*, which contains the volume ID. Unlink of unused[n] always cause physical removal.

---

**Note**

Requires option(s): delete

---

**-freeze <boolean>**

 Freeze CPU at startup (use *c* monitor command to start execution).

**-hostpci[n] [host=]<HOSTPCIID[;HOSTPCIID2...]> [,pcie=<1|0>]**
**[,rombar=<1|0>] [,romfile=<string>] [,x-vga=<1|0>]**

 Map host PCI devices into guest.

**-hotplug <string>** (*default = network,disk,usb*)

 Selectively enable hotplug features. This is a comma separated list of hotplug features: *network*, *disk, cpu, memory* and *usb*. Use *0* to disable hotplug completely. Value *1* is an alias for the default *network,disk,usb*.

**-hugepages <1024 | 2 | any>**

 Enable/disable hugepages memory.

```
-ide[n] [file=]<volume> [,aio=<native|threads>] [,backup=<1|0>]
[,bps=<bps>] [,bps_max_length=<seconds>] [,bps_rd=<bps>]
[,bps_rd_max_length=<seconds>] [,bps_wr=<bps>] [,bps_wr_max_length=
<seconds>] [,cache=<enum>] [,cyls=<integer>] [,detect_zeroes=<1|0>]
[,discard=<ignore|on>] [,format=<enum>] [,heads=<integer>] [,iops=
<iops>] [,iops_max=<iops>] [,iops_max_length=<seconds>] [,iops_rd=
<iops>] [,iops_rd_max=<iops>] [,iops_rd_max_length=<seconds>]
[,iops_wr=<iops>] [,iops_wr_max=<iops>] [,iops_wr_max_length=
<seconds>] [,mbps=<mbps>] [,mbps_max=<mbps>] [,mbps_rd=<mbps>]
[,mbps_rd_max=<mbps>] [,mbps_wr=<mbps>] [,mbps_wr_max=<mbps>]
[,media=<cdrom|disk>] [,model=<model>] [,replicate=<1|0>] [,rerror=
<ignore|report|stop>] [,secs=<integer>] [,serial=<serial>] [,size=
<DiskSize>] [,snapshot=<1|0>] [,trans=<none|lba|auto>] [,werror=
<enum>]
```
Use volume as IDE hard disk or CD-ROM (n is 0 to 3).

```
-keyboard <da | de | de-ch | en-gb | en-us | es | fi | fr | fr-be |
fr-ca | fr-ch | hu | is | it | ja | lt | mk | nl | no | pl | pt |
pt-br | sl | sv | tr> (default = en-us)
```
Keybord layout for vnc server. Default is read from the */etc/pve/datacenter.conf* configuration file.

```
-kvm <boolean> (default = 1)
```
Enable/disable KVM hardware virtualization.

```
-localtime <boolean>
```
Set the real time clock to local time. This is enabled by default if ostype indicates a Microsoft OS.

```
-lock <backup | migrate | rollback | snapshot>
```
Lock/unlock the VM.

```
-machine (pc|pc(-i440fx)?-\d+\.\d+(\.pxe)?|q35|pc-q35-\d+\.\d+(\.
pxe)?)
```
Specific the Qemu machine type.

```
-memory <integer>  (16 - N) (default = 512)
```
Amount of RAM for the VM in MB. This is the maximum available memory when you use the balloon device.

```
-migrate_downtime <number>  (0 - N) (default = 0.1)
```
Set maximum tolerated downtime (in seconds) for migrations.

```
-migrate_speed <integer>  (0 - N) (default = 0)
```
Set maximum speed (in MB/s) for migrations. Value 0 is no limit.

```
-name <string>
```
Set a name for the VM. Only used on the configuration web interface.

`-net[n] [model=]<enum> [,bridge=<bridge>] [,firewall=<1|0>]`
`[,link_down=<1|0>] [,macaddr=<XX:XX:XX:XX:XX:XX>] [,queues=`
`<integer>] [,rate=<number>] [,tag=<integer>] [,trunks=<vlanid[;`
`vlanid...]>] [,<model>=<macaddr>]`
Specify network devices.

`-numa <boolean> (default = 0)`
Enable/disable NUMA.

`-numa[n] cpus=<id[-id];...> [,hostnodes=<id[-id];...>] [,memory=`
`<number>] [,policy=<preferred|bind|interleave>]`
NUMA topology.

`-onboot <boolean> (default = 0)`
Specifies whether a VM will be started during system bootup.

`-ostype <124 | 126 | other | solaris | w2k | w2k3 | w2k8 | win10 |`
`win7 | win8 | wvista | wxp>`
Specify guest operating system.

`-parallel[n] /dev/parport\d+|/dev/usb/lp\d+`
Map host parallel devices (n is 0 to 2).

`-protection <boolean> (default = 0)`
Sets the protection flag of the VM. This will disable the remove VM and remove disk operations.

`-reboot <boolean> (default = 1)`
Allow reboot. If set to *0* the VM exit on reboot.

`-revert <string>`
Revert a pending change.

`-sata[n] [file=]<volume> [,aio=<native|threads>] [,backup=<1|0>]`
`[,bps=<bps>] [,bps_max_length=<seconds>] [,bps_rd=<bps>]`
`[,bps_rd_max_length=<seconds>] [,bps_wr=<bps>] [,bps_wr_max_length=`
`<seconds>] [,cache=<enum>] [,cyls=<integer>] [,detect_zeroes=<1|0>]`
`[,discard=<ignore|on>] [,format=<enum>] [,heads=<integer>] [,iops=`
`<iops>] [,iops_max=<iops>] [,iops_max_length=<seconds>] [,iops_rd=`
`<iops>] [,iops_rd_max=<iops>] [,iops_rd_max_length=<seconds>]`
`[,iops_wr=<iops>] [,iops_wr_max=<iops>] [,iops_wr_max_length=`
`<seconds>] [,mbps=<mbps>] [,mbps_max=<mbps>] [,mbps_rd=<mbps>]`
`[,mbps_rd_max=<mbps>] [,mbps_wr=<mbps>] [,mbps_wr_max=<mbps>]`
`[,media=<cdrom|disk>] [,replicate=<1|0>] [,rerror=`
`<ignore|report|stop>] [,secs=<integer>] [,serial=<serial>] [,size=`
`<DiskSize>] [,snapshot=<1|0>] [,trans=<none|lba|auto>] [,werror=`
`<enum>]`
Use volume as SATA hard disk or CD-ROM (n is 0 to 5).

```
-scsi[n] [file=]<volume> [,aio=<native|threads>] [,backup=<1|0>]
[,bps=<bps>] [,bps_max_length=<seconds>] [,bps_rd=<bps>]
[,bps_rd_max_length=<seconds>] [,bps_wr=<bps>] [,bps_wr_max_length=
<seconds>] [,cache=<enum>] [,cyls=<integer>] [,detect_zeroes=<1|0>]
[,discard=<ignore|on>] [,format=<enum>] [,heads=<integer>] [,iops=
<iops>] [,iops_max=<iops>] [,iops_max_length=<seconds>] [,iops_rd=
<iops>] [,iops_rd_max=<iops>] [,iops_rd_max_length=<seconds>]
[,iops_wr=<iops>] [,iops_wr_max=<iops>] [,iops_wr_max_length=
<seconds>] [,iothread=<1|0>] [,mbps=<mbps>] [,mbps_max=<mbps>]
[,mbps_rd=<mbps>] [,mbps_rd_max=<mbps>] [,mbps_wr=<mbps>]
[,mbps_wr_max=<mbps>] [,media=<cdrom|disk>] [,queues=<integer>]
[,replicate=<1|0>] [,rerror=<ignore|report|stop>] [,scsiblock=
<1|0>] [,secs=<integer>] [,serial=<serial>] [,size=<DiskSize>]
[,snapshot=<1|0>] [,trans=<none|lba|auto>] [,werror=<enum>]
```
Use volume as SCSI hard disk or CD-ROM (n is 0 to 13).

```
-scsihw <lsi | lsi53c810 | megasas | pvscsi | virtio-scsi-pci |
virtio-scsi-single> (default = lsi)
```
SCSI controller model

```
-serial[n] (/dev/.+|socket)
```
Create a serial device inside the VM (n is 0 to 3)

```
-shares <integer> (0 - 50000) (default = 1000)
```
Amount of memory shares for auto-ballooning. The larger the number is, the more memory this VM gets. Number is relative to weights of all other running VMs. Using zero disables auto-ballooning

```
-skiplock <boolean>
```
Ignore locks - only root is allowed to use this option.

```
-smbios1 [family=<string>] [,manufacturer=<string>] [,product=
<string>] [,serial=<string>] [,sku=<string>] [,uuid=<UUID>]
[,version=<string>]
```
Specify SMBIOS type 1 fields.

```
-smp <integer> (1 - N) (default = 1)
```
The number of CPUs. Please use option -sockets instead.

```
-sockets <integer> (1 - N) (default = 1)
```
The number of CPU sockets.

```
-startdate (now | YYYY-MM-DD | YYYY-MM-DDTHH:MM:SS) (default = now)
```
Set the initial date of the real time clock. Valid format for date are: *now* or *2006-06-17T16:01:21* or *2006-06-17*.

```
-startup `[[order=]\d+] [,up=\d+] [,down=\d+] `
```
Startup and shutdown behavior. Order is a non-negative number defining the general startup order.

Shutdown in done with reverse ordering. Additionally you can set the *up* or *down* delay in seconds, which specifies a delay to wait before the next VM is started or stopped.

**-tablet <boolean> (*default* = 1)**
> Enable/disable the USB tablet device.

**-tdf <boolean> (*default* = 0)**
> Enable/disable time drift fix.

**-template <boolean> (*default* = 0)**
> Enable/disable Template.

**-unused[n] <string>**
> Reference to unused volumes. This is used internally, and should not be modified manually.

**-usb[n] [host=]<HOSTUSBDEVICE|spice> [,usb3=<1|0>]**
> Configure an USB device (n is 0 to 4).

**-vcpus <integer> (1 - N) (*default* = 0)**
> Number of hotplugged vcpus.

**-vga <cirrus | qxl | qxl2 | qxl3 | qxl4 | serial0 | serial1 | serial2 | serial3 | std | vmware>**
> Select the VGA type.

**-virtio[n] [file=]<volume> [,aio=<native|threads>] [,backup=<1|0>] [,bps=<bps>] [,bps_max_length=<seconds>] [,bps_rd=<bps>] [,bps_rd_max_length=<seconds>] [,bps_wr=<bps>] [,bps_wr_max_length= <seconds>] [,cache=<enum>] [,cyls=<integer>] [,detect_zeroes=<1|0>] [,discard=<ignore|on>] [,format=<enum>] [,heads=<integer>] [,iops= <iops>] [,iops_max=<iops>] [,iops_max_length=<seconds>] [,iops_rd= <iops>] [,iops_rd_max=<iops>] [,iops_rd_max_length=<seconds>] [,iops_wr=<iops>] [,iops_wr_max=<iops>] [,iops_wr_max_length= <seconds>] [,iothread=<1|0>] [,mbps=<mbps>] [,mbps_max=<mbps>] [,mbps_rd=<mbps>] [,mbps_rd_max=<mbps>] [,mbps_wr=<mbps>] [,mbps_wr_max=<mbps>] [,media=<cdrom|disk>] [,replicate=<1|0>] [,rerror=<ignore|report|stop>] [,secs=<integer>] [,serial=<serial>] [,size=<DiskSize>] [,snapshot=<1|0>] [,trans=<none|lba|auto>] [,werror=<enum>]**
> Use volume as VIRTIO hard disk (n is 0 to 15).

**-watchdog [[model=]<i6300esb|ib700>] [,action=<enum>]**
> Create a virtual hardware watchdog device.

**qm showcmd** <vmid>

Show command line which is used to start the VM (debug info).

**`<vmid>`: `<integer>` (1 - N)**
> The (unique) ID of the VM.

**qm shutdown** `<vmid>` `[OPTIONS]`

Shutdown virtual machine. This is similar to pressing the power button on a physical machine.This will send an ACPI event for the guest OS, which should then proceed to a clean shutdown.

**`<vmid>`: `<integer>` (1 - N)**
> The (unique) ID of the VM.

**`-forceStop <boolean>` (*default* = 0)**
> Make sure the VM stops.

**`-keepActive <boolean>` (*default* = 0)**
> Do not deactivate storage volumes.

**`-skiplock <boolean>`**
> Ignore locks - only root is allowed to use this option.

**`-timeout <integer>` (0 - N)**
> Wait maximal timeout seconds.

**qm snapshot** `<vmid>` `<snapname>` `[OPTIONS]`

Snapshot a VM.

**`<vmid>`: `<integer>` (1 - N)**
> The (unique) ID of the VM.

**`<snapname>`: `<string>`**
> The name of the snapshot.

**`-description <string>`**
> A textual description or comment.

**`-vmstate <boolean>`**
> Save the vmstate

**qm start** `<vmid>` `[OPTIONS]`

Start virtual machine.

**`<vmid>`: `<integer>` (1 - N)**
> The (unique) ID of the VM.

**`-machine (pc|pc(-i440fx)?-\d+\.\d+(\.pxe)?|q35|pc-q35-\d+\.\d+(\.pxe)?)`**
> Specific the Qemu machine type.

**-migratedfrom <string>**
    The cluster node name.

**-migration_network <string>**
    CIDR of the (sub) network that is used for migration.

**-migration_type <insecure | secure>**
    Migration traffic is encrypted using an SSH tunnel by default. On secure, completely private networks this can be disabled to increase performance.

**-skiplock <boolean>**
    Ignore locks - only root is allowed to use this option.

**-stateuri <string>**
    Some command save/restore state from this location.

**-targetstorage <string>**
    Target storage for the migration. (Can be *1* to use the same storage id as on the source node.)

**qm status** <vmid> [OPTIONS]

Show VM status.

**<vmid>: <integer> (1 - N)**
    The (unique) ID of the VM.

**-verbose <boolean>**
    Verbose output format

**qm stop** <vmid> [OPTIONS]

Stop virtual machine. The qemu process will exit immediately. Thisis akin to pulling the power plug of a running computer and may damage the VM data

**<vmid>: <integer> (1 - N)**
    The (unique) ID of the VM.

**-keepActive <boolean> (*default* = 0)**
    Do not deactivate storage volumes.

**-migratedfrom <string>**
    The cluster node name.

**-skiplock <boolean>**
    Ignore locks - only root is allowed to use this option.

**-timeout <integer> (0 - N)**
    Wait maximal timeout seconds.

**qm suspend** <vmid> [OPTIONS]

Suspend virtual machine.

<vmid>: <integer> (1 - N)
    The (unique) ID of the VM.

-skiplock <boolean>
    Ignore locks - only root is allowed to use this option.

**qm template** <vmid> [OPTIONS]

Create a Template.

<vmid>: <integer> (1 - N)
    The (unique) ID of the VM.

-disk <efidisk0 | ide0 | ide1 | ide2 | ide3 | sata0 | sata1 | sata2
| sata3 | sata4 | sata5 | scsi0 | scsi1 | scsi10 | scsi11 | scsi12
| scsi13 | scsi2 | scsi3 | scsi4 | scsi5 | scsi6 | scsi7 | scsi8 |
scsi9 | virtio0 | virtio1 | virtio10 | virtio11 | virtio12 |
virtio13 | virtio14 | virtio15 | virtio2 | virtio3 | virtio4 |
virtio5 | virtio6 | virtio7 | virtio8 | virtio9>
    If you want to convert only 1 disk to base image.

**qm terminal** <vmid> [OPTIONS]

Open a terminal using a serial device (The VM need to have a serial device configured, for example *serial0: socket*)

<vmid>: <integer> (1 - N)
    The (unique) ID of the VM.

-iface <serial0 | serial1 | serial2 | serial3>
    Select the serial device. By default we simply use the first suitable device.

**qm unlink** <vmid> -idlist <string> [OPTIONS]

Unlink/delete disk images.

<vmid>: <integer> (1 - N)
    The (unique) ID of the VM.

-force <boolean>
    Force physical removal. Without this, we simple remove the disk from the config file and create an additional configuration entry called *unused[n]*, which contains the volume ID. Unlink of unused[n] always cause physical removal.

**-idlist <string>**
>    A list of disk IDs you want to delete.

**qm unlock** <vmid>

Unlock the VM.


**<vmid>: <integer> (1 - N)**
>    The (unique) ID of the VM.

**qm vncproxy** <vmid>

Proxy VM VNC traffic to stdin/stdout


**<vmid>: <integer> (1 - N)**
>    The (unique) ID of the VM.

**qm wait** <vmid> [OPTIONS]

Wait until the VM is stopped.


**<vmid>: <integer> (1 - N)**
>    The (unique) ID of the VM.


**-timeout <integer> (1 - N)**
>    Timeout in seconds. Default is to wait forever.


# A.6   qmrestore - Restore QemuServer vzdump Backups

**qmrestore** help

**qmrestore** <archive> <vmid> [OPTIONS]

Restore QemuServer vzdump backups.


**<archive>: <string>**
>    The backup file. You can pass - to read from standard input.


**<vmid>: <integer> (1 - N)**
>    The (unique) ID of the VM.


**-force <boolean>**
>    Allow to overwrite existing VM.


**-pool <string>**
>    Add the VM to the specified pool.


**-storage <string>**
>    Default storage.


**-unique <boolean>**
>    Assign a unique random ethernet address.

## A.7 pct - Proxmox Container Toolkit

**pct** <COMMAND> [ARGS] [OPTIONS]

**pct clone** <vmid> <newid> -experimental <boolean> [OPTIONS]

Create a container clone/copy

**<vmid>: <integer> (1 - N)**
    The (unique) ID of the VM.

**<newid>: <integer> (1 - N)**
    VMID for the clone.

**-description <string>**
    Description for the new CT.

**-experimental <boolean> (*default* = 0)**
    The clone feature is experimental, set this flag if you know what you are doing.

**-full <boolean> (*default* = 0)**
    Create a full copy of all disk. This is always done when you clone a normal CT. For CT templates, we try to create a linked clone by default.

**-hostname <string>**
    Set a hostname for the new CT.

**-pool <string>**
    Add the new CT to the specified pool.

**-snapname <string>**
    The name of the snapshot.

**-storage <string>**
    Target storage for full clone.

---

**Note**
Requires option(s): full

---

**pct config** <vmid>

Get container configuration.

**<vmid>: <integer> (1 - N)**
    The (unique) ID of the VM.

**pct console** <vmid>

Launch a console for the specified container.

**<vmid>: <integer> (1 - N)**
    The (unique) ID of the VM.

**pct cpusets**

Print the list of assigned CPU sets.

**pct create** <vmid> <ostemplate> [OPTIONS]

Create or restore a container.

**<vmid>: <integer> (1 - N)**
    The (unique) ID of the VM.

**<ostemplate>: <string>**
    The OS template or backup file.

**-arch <amd64 | i386>** (*default* = amd64)
    OS architecture type.

**-cmode <console | shell | tty>** (*default* = tty)
    Console mode. By default, the console command tries to open a connection to one of the available tty devices. By setting cmode to *console* it tries to attach to /dev/console instead. If you set cmode to *shell*, it simply invokes a shell inside the container (no login).

**-console <boolean>** (*default* = 1)
    Attach a console device (/dev/console) to the container.

**-cores <integer> (1 - 128)**
    The number of cores assigned to the container. A container can use all available cores by default.

**-cpulimit <number> (0 - 128)** (*default* = 0)
    Limit of CPU usage.

---

**Note**

If the computer has 2 CPUs, it has a total of *2* CPU time. Value *0* indicates no CPU limit.

---

**-cpuunits <integer> (0 - 500000)** (*default* = 1024)
    CPU weight for a VM. Argument is used in the kernel fair scheduler. The larger the number is, the more CPU time this VM gets. Number is relative to the weights of all the other running VMs.

---

**Note**

You can disable fair-scheduler configuration by setting this to 0.

---

**-description <string>**

    Container description. Only used on the configuration web interface.


**-force <boolean>**

    Allow to overwrite existing container.


**-hostname <string>**

    Set a host name for the container.


**-ignore-unpack-errors <boolean>**

    Ignore errors when extracting the template.


**-lock <backup | migrate | rollback | snapshot>**

    Lock/unlock the VM.


**-memory <integer> (16 — N) (*default* = 512)**

    Amount of RAM for the VM in MB.


**-mp[n] [volume=]<volume> ,mp=<Path> [,acl=<1|0>] [,backup=<1|0>] [,quota=<1|0>] [,replicate=<1|0>] [,ro=<1|0>] [,shared=<1|0>] [,size=<DiskSize>]**

    Use volume as container mount point.


**-nameserver <string>**

    Sets DNS server IP address for a container. Create will automatically use the setting from the host if you neither set searchdomain nor nameserver.


**-net[n] name=<string> [,bridge=<bridge>] [,firewall=<1|0>] [,gw= <GatewayIPv4>] [,gw6=<GatewayIPv6>] [,hwaddr=<XX:XX:XX:XX:XX:XX>] [,ip=<IPv4Format/CIDR>] [,ip6=<IPv6Format/CIDR>] [,mtu=<integer>] [,rate=<mbps>] [,tag=<integer>] [,trunks=<vlanid[;vlanid...]>] [,type=<veth>]**

    Specifies network interfaces for the container.


**-onboot <boolean> (*default* = 0)**

    Specifies whether a VM will be started during system bootup.


**-ostype <alpine | archlinux | centos | debian | fedora | gentoo | opensuse | ubuntu | unmanaged>**

    OS type. This is used to setup configuration inside the container, and corresponds to lxc setup scripts in /usr/share/lxc/config/<ostype>.common.conf. Value *unmanaged* can be used to skip and OS specific setup.


**-password**

    Sets root password inside container.

**-pool <string>**
> Add the VM to the specified pool.

**-protection <boolean> (*default* = 0)**
> Sets the protection flag of the container. This will prevent the CT or CT's disk remove/update operation.

**-restore <boolean>**
> Mark this as restore task.

**-rootfs [volume=]<volume> [,acl=<1|0>] [,quota=<1|0>] [,replicate= <1|0>] [,ro=<1|0>] [,shared=<1|0>] [,size=<DiskSize>]**
> Use volume as container root.

**-searchdomain <string>**
> Sets DNS search domains for a container. Create will automatically use the setting from the host if you neither set searchdomain nor nameserver.

**-ssh-public-keys <string>**
> Setup public SSH keys (one key per line, OpenSSH format).

**-startup `[[order=]\d+] [,up=\d+] [,down=\d+] `**
> Startup and shutdown behavior. Order is a non-negative number defining the general startup order. Shutdown in done with reverse ordering. Additionally you can set the *up* or *down* delay in seconds, which specifies a delay to wait before the next VM is started or stopped.

**-storage <string> (*default* = local)**
> Default Storage.

**-swap <integer> (0 - N) (*default* = 512)**
> Amount of SWAP for the VM in MB.

**-template <boolean> (*default* = 0)**
> Enable/disable Template.

**-tty <integer> (0 - 6) (*default* = 2)**
> Specify the number of tty available to the container

**-unprivileged <boolean> (*default* = 0)**
> Makes the container run as unprivileged user. (Should not be modified manually.)

**-unused[n] <string>**
> Reference to unused volumes. This is used internally, and should not be modified manually.

**pct delsnapshot** <vmid> <snapname> [OPTIONS]

Delete a LXC snapshot.

**<vmid>: <integer> (1 - N)**
    The (unique) ID of the VM.


**<snapname>: <string>**
    The name of the snapshot.


**-force <boolean>**
    For removal from config file, even if removing disk snapshots fails.

**pct destroy** <vmid>

Destroy the container (also delete all uses files).


**<vmid>: <integer> (1 - N)**
    The (unique) ID of the VM.

**pct df** <vmid>

Get the container's current disk usage.


**<vmid>: <integer> (1 - N)**
    The (unique) ID of the VM.

**pct enter** <vmid>

Launch a shell for the specified container.


**<vmid>: <integer> (1 - N)**
    The (unique) ID of the VM.

**pct exec** <vmid> [<extra-args>]

Launch a command inside the specified container.


**<vmid>: <integer> (1 - N)**
    The (unique) ID of the VM.


**<extra-args>: <array>**
    Extra arguments as array

**pct fsck** <vmid> [OPTIONS]

Run a filesystem check (fsck) on a container volume.


**<vmid>: <integer> (1 - N)**
    The (unique) ID of the VM.


**-device <mp0 | mp1 | mp2 | mp3 | mp4 | mp5 | mp6 | mp7 | mp8 | mp9 | rootfs>**
    A volume on which to run the filesystem check

**-force <boolean>** (*default = 0*)
> Force checking, even if the filesystem seems clean

**pct help** [<cmd>] [OPTIONS]

Get help about specified command.


**<cmd>: <string>**
> Command name


**-verbose <boolean>**
> Verbose output format.

**pct list**

LXC container index (per node).

**pct listsnapshot** <vmid>

List all snapshots.


**<vmid>: <integer> (1 - N)**
> The (unique) ID of the VM.

**pct migrate** <vmid> <target> [OPTIONS]

Migrate the container to another node. Creates a new migration task.


**<vmid>: <integer> (1 - N)**
> The (unique) ID of the VM.


**<target>: <string>**
> Target node.


**-force <boolean>**
> Force migration despite local bind / device mounts. NOTE: deprecated, use *shared* property of mount point instead.


**-online <boolean>**
> Use online/live migration.


**-restart <boolean>**
> Use restart migration


**-timeout <integer>** (*default = 180*)
> Timeout in seconds for shutdown for restart migration

**pct mount** <vmid>

Mount the container's filesystem on the host. This will hold a lock on the container and is meant for emergency maintenance only as it will prevent further operations on the container other than start and stop.

**<vmid>: <integer> (1 - N)**
    The (unique) ID of the VM.

**pct pull** <vmid> <path> <destination> [OPTIONS]

Copy a file from the container to the local system.

**<vmid>: <integer> (1 - N)**
    The (unique) ID of the VM.

**<path>: <string>**
    Path to a file inside the container to pull.

**<destination>: <string>**
    Destination

**-group <string>**
    Owner group name or id.

**-perms <string>**
    File permissions to use (octal by default, prefix with *0x* for hexadecimal).

**-user <string>**
    Owner user name or id.

**pct push** <vmid> <file> <destination> [OPTIONS]

Copy a local file to the container.

**<vmid>: <integer> (1 - N)**
    The (unique) ID of the VM.

**<file>: <string>**
    Path to a local file.

**<destination>: <string>**
    Destination inside the container to write to.

**-group <string>**
    Owner group name or id. When using a name it must exist inside the container.

**-perms <string>**
    File permissions to use (octal by default, prefix with *0x* for hexadecimal).

**-user <string>**
    Owner user name or id. When using a name it must exist inside the container.

**pct resize** <vmid> <disk> <size> [OPTIONS]

Resize a container mount point.

**<vmid>: <integer> (1 - N)**
    The (unique) ID of the VM.

**<disk>: <mp0 | mp1 | mp2 | mp3 | mp4 | mp5 | mp6 | mp7 | mp8 | mp9 | rootfs>**
    The disk you want to resize.

**<size>: \+?\d+(\.\d+)?[KMGT]?**
    The new size. With the + sign the value is added to the actual size of the volume and without it, the value is taken as an absolute one. Shrinking disk size is not supported.

**-digest <string>**
    Prevent changes if current configuration file has different SHA1 digest. This can be used to prevent concurrent modifications.

**pct restore** <vmid> <ostemplate> [OPTIONS]

Create or restore a container.

**<vmid>: <integer> (1 - N)**
    The (unique) ID of the VM.

**<ostemplate>: <string>**
    The OS template or backup file.

**-arch <amd64 | i386> (default = amd64)**
    OS architecture type.

**-cmode <console | shell | tty> (default = tty)**
    Console mode. By default, the console command tries to open a connection to one of the available tty devices. By setting cmode to *console* it tries to attach to /dev/console instead. If you set cmode to *shell*, it simply invokes a shell inside the container (no login).

**-console <boolean> (default = 1)**
    Attach a console device (/dev/console) to the container.

**-cores <integer> (1 - 128)**
    The number of cores assigned to the container. A container can use all available cores by default.

**-cpulimit <number> (0 - 128) (default = 0)**
    Limit of CPU usage.

---

**Note**
If the computer has 2 CPUs, it has a total of *2* CPU time. Value *0* indicates no CPU limit.

---

**-cpuunits <integer> (0 - 500000) (*default* = 1024)**

CPU weight for a VM. Argument is used in the kernel fair scheduler. The larger the number is, the more CPU time this VM gets. Number is relative to the weights of all the other running VMs.

---

**Note**

You can disable fair-scheduler configuration by setting this to 0.

---

**-description <string>**

Container description. Only used on the configuration web interface.

**-force <boolean>**

Allow to overwrite existing container.

**-hostname <string>**

Set a host name for the container.

**-ignore-unpack-errors <boolean>**

Ignore errors when extracting the template.

**-lock <backup | migrate | rollback | snapshot>**

Lock/unlock the VM.

**-memory <integer> (16 - N) (*default* = 512)**

Amount of RAM for the VM in MB.

**-mp[n] [volume=]<volume> ,mp=<Path> [,acl=<1|0>] [,backup=<1|0>] [,quota=<1|0>] [,replicate=<1|0>] [,ro=<1|0>] [,shared=<1|0>] [,size=<DiskSize>]**

Use volume as container mount point.

**-nameserver <string>**

Sets DNS server IP address for a container. Create will automatically use the setting from the host if you neither set searchdomain nor nameserver.

**-net[n] name=<string> [,bridge=<bridge>] [,firewall=<1|0>] [,gw=<GatewayIPv4>] [,gw6=<GatewayIPv6>] [,hwaddr=<XX:XX:XX:XX:XX:XX>] [,ip=<IPv4Format/CIDR>] [,ip6=<IPv6Format/CIDR>] [,mtu=<integer>] [,rate=<mbps>] [,tag=<integer>] [,trunks=<vlanid[;vlanid...]>] [,type=<veth>]**

Specifies network interfaces for the container.

**-onboot <boolean> (*default* = 0)**

Specifies whether a VM will be started during system bootup.

**-ostype <alpine | archlinux | centos | debian | fedora | gentoo | opensuse | ubuntu | unmanaged>**

> OS type. This is used to setup configuration inside the container, and corresponds to lxc setup scripts in /usr/share/lxc/config/<ostype>.common.conf. Value *unmanaged* can be used to skip and OS specific setup.

**-password**

> Sets root password inside container.

**-pool <string>**

> Add the VM to the specified pool.

**-protection <boolean>** (*default* = 0)

> Sets the protection flag of the container. This will prevent the CT or CT's disk remove/update operation.

**-rootfs [volume=]<volume> [,acl=<1|0>] [,quota=<1|0>] [,replicate= <1|0>] [,ro=<1|0>] [,shared=<1|0>] [,size=<DiskSize>]**

> Use volume as container root.

**-searchdomain <string>**

> Sets DNS search domains for a container. Create will automatically use the setting from the host if you neither set searchdomain nor nameserver.

**-ssh-public-keys <string>**

> Setup public SSH keys (one key per line, OpenSSH format).

**-startup `[[order=]\d+] [,up=\d+] [,down=\d+] `**

> Startup and shutdown behavior. Order is a non-negative number defining the general startup order. Shutdown in done with reverse ordering. Additionally you can set the *up* or *down* delay in seconds, which specifies a delay to wait before the next VM is started or stopped.

**-storage <string>** (*default* = local)

> Default Storage.

**-swap <integer>** (0 - N) (*default* = 512)

> Amount of SWAP for the VM in MB.

**-template <boolean>** (*default* = 0)

> Enable/disable Template.

**-tty <integer>** (0 - 6) (*default* = 2)

> Specify the number of tty available to the container

**-unprivileged <boolean>** (*default* = 0)

> Makes the container run as unprivileged user. (Should not be modified manually.)

**-unused[n] <string>**

    Reference to unused volumes. This is used internally, and should not be modified manually.

**pct resume** <vmid>

Resume the container.

**<vmid>: <integer> (1 - N)**

    The (unique) ID of the VM.

**pct rollback** <vmid> <snapname>

Rollback LXC state to specified snapshot.

**<vmid>: <integer> (1 - N)**

    The (unique) ID of the VM.

**<snapname>: <string>**

    The name of the snapshot.

**pct set** <vmid> [OPTIONS]

Set container options.

**<vmid>: <integer> (1 - N)**

    The (unique) ID of the VM.

**-arch <amd64 | i386>** *(default =* amd64*)*

    OS architecture type.

**-cmode <console | shell | tty>** *(default =* tty*)*

    Console mode. By default, the console command tries to open a connection to one of the available tty devices. By setting cmode to *console* it tries to attach to /dev/console instead. If you set cmode to *shell*, it simply invokes a shell inside the container (no login).

**-console <boolean>** *(default =* 1*)*

    Attach a console device (/dev/console) to the container.

**-cores <integer> (1 - 128)**

    The number of cores assigned to the container. A container can use all available cores by default.

**-cpulimit <number> (0 - 128)** *(default =* 0*)*

    Limit of CPU usage.

---

**Note**

If the computer has 2 CPUs, it has a total of *2* CPU time. Value *0* indicates no CPU limit.

---

**-cpuunits <integer> (0 - 500000) (*default* = 1024)**
> CPU weight for a VM. Argument is used in the kernel fair scheduler. The larger the number is, the more CPU time this VM gets. Number is relative to the weights of all the other running VMs.

---

> **Note**
> You can disable fair-scheduler configuration by setting this to 0.

---

**-delete <string>**
> A list of settings you want to delete.

**-description <string>**
> Container description. Only used on the configuration web interface.

**-digest <string>**
> Prevent changes if current configuration file has different SHA1 digest. This can be used to prevent concurrent modifications.

**-hostname <string>**
> Set a host name for the container.

**-lock <backup | migrate | rollback | snapshot>**
> Lock/unlock the VM.

**-memory <integer> (16 - N) (*default* = 512)**
> Amount of RAM for the VM in MB.

**-mp[n] [volume=]<volume> ,mp=<Path> [,acl=<1|0>] [,backup=<1|0>]**
**[,quota=<1|0>] [,replicate=<1|0>] [,ro=<1|0>] [,shared=<1|0>]**
**[,size=<DiskSize>]**
> Use volume as container mount point.

**-nameserver <string>**
> Sets DNS server IP address for a container. Create will automatically use the setting from the host if you neither set searchdomain nor nameserver.

**-net[n] name=<string> [,bridge=<bridge>] [,firewall=<1|0>] [,gw=**
**<GatewayIPv4>] [,gw6=<GatewayIPv6>] [,hwaddr=<XX:XX:XX:XX:XX:XX>]**
**[,ip=<IPv4Format/CIDR>] [,ip6=<IPv6Format/CIDR>] [,mtu=<integer>]**
**[,rate=<mbps>] [,tag=<integer>] [,trunks=<vlanid[;vlanid...]>]**
**[,type=<veth>]**
> Specifies network interfaces for the container.

**-onboot <boolean> (*default* = 0)**
> Specifies whether a VM will be started during system bootup.

**-ostype <alpine | archlinux | centos | debian | fedora | gentoo | opensuse | ubuntu | unmanaged>**

> OS type. This is used to setup configuration inside the container, and corresponds to lxc setup scripts in /usr/share/lxc/config/<ostype>.common.conf. Value *unmanaged* can be used to skip and OS specific setup.

**-protection <boolean> (*default* = 0)**

> Sets the protection flag of the container. This will prevent the CT or CT's disk remove/update operation.

**-rootfs [volume=]<volume> [,acl=<1|0>] [,quota=<1|0>] [,replicate= <1|0>] [,ro=<1|0>] [,shared=<1|0>] [,size=<DiskSize>]**

> Use volume as container root.

**-searchdomain <string>**

> Sets DNS search domains for a container. Create will automatically use the setting from the host if you neither set searchdomain nor nameserver.

**-startup `[[order=]\d+] [,up=\d+] [,down=\d+] `**

> Startup and shutdown behavior. Order is a non-negative number defining the general startup order. Shutdown in done with reverse ordering. Additionally you can set the *up* or *down* delay in seconds, which specifies a delay to wait before the next VM is started or stopped.

**-swap <integer> (0 - N) (*default* = 512)**

> Amount of SWAP for the VM in MB.

**-template <boolean> (*default* = 0)**

> Enable/disable Template.

**-tty <integer> (0 - 6) (*default* = 2)**

> Specify the number of tty available to the container

**-unprivileged <boolean> (*default* = 0)**

> Makes the container run as unprivileged user. (Should not be modified manually.)

**-unused[n] <string>**

> Reference to unused volumes. This is used internally, and should not be modified manually.

**pct shutdown** <vmid> [OPTIONS]

Shutdown the container. This will trigger a clean shutdown of the container, see lxc-stop(1) for details.

**<vmid>: <integer> (1 - N)**

> The (unique) ID of the VM.

**-forceStop <boolean> (*default* = 0)**

> Make sure the Container stops.

**-timeout <integer>  (0 - N)** (*default* = 60)
>    Wait maximal timeout seconds.

**pct snapshot** <vmid> <snapname> [OPTIONS]

Snapshot a container.


**<vmid>: <integer>  (1 - N)**
>    The (unique) ID of the VM.


**<snapname>: <string>**
>    The name of the snapshot.


**-description <string>**
>    A textual description or comment.

**pct start** <vmid> [OPTIONS]

Start the container.


**<vmid>: <integer>  (1 - N)**
>    The (unique) ID of the VM.


**-skiplock <boolean>**
>    Ignore locks - only root is allowed to use this option.

**pct status** <vmid> [OPTIONS]

Show CT status.


**<vmid>: <integer>  (1 - N)**
>    The (unique) ID of the VM.


**-verbose <boolean>**
>    Verbose output format

**pct stop** <vmid> [OPTIONS]

Stop the container. This will abruptly stop all processes running in the container.


**<vmid>: <integer>  (1 - N)**
>    The (unique) ID of the VM.


**-skiplock <boolean>**
>    Ignore locks - only root is allowed to use this option.

**pct suspend** <vmid>

Suspend the container.

**<vmid>: <integer> (1 - N)**
> The (unique) ID of the VM.

**pct template** <vmid> -experimental <boolean> [OPTIONS]

Create a Template.

**<vmid>: <integer> (1 - N)**
> The (unique) ID of the VM.

**-experimental <boolean> (*default* = 0)**
> The template feature is experimental, set this flag if you know what you are doing.

**pct unlock** <vmid>

Unlock the VM.

**<vmid>: <integer> (1 - N)**
> The (unique) ID of the VM.

**pct unmount** <vmid>

Unmount the container's filesystem.

**<vmid>: <integer> (1 - N)**
> The (unique) ID of the VM.

# A.8  pveam - Proxmox VE Appliance Manager

**pveam** <COMMAND> [ARGS] [OPTIONS]

**pveam available** [OPTIONS]

List available templates.

**-section <system | turnkeylinux>**
> Restrict list to specified section.

**pveam download** <storage> <template>

Download appliance templates.

**<storage>: <string>**
> The storage where the template will be stored

**<template>: <string>**
> The template wich will downloaded

**pveam help** [<cmd>] [OPTIONS]

Get help about specified command.


  **<cmd>: <string>**
      Command name


  **-verbose <boolean>**
      Verbose output format.

**pveam list** <storage>

Get list of all templates on storage


  **<storage>: <string>**
      Only list templates on specified storage


**pveam remove** <template_path>

Remove a template.


  **<template_path>: <string>**
      The template to remove.


**pveam update**

Update Container Template Database.


# A.9   pvecm - Proxmox VE Cluster Manager


**pvecm** <COMMAND> [ARGS] [OPTIONS]

**pvecm add** <hostname> [OPTIONS]

Adds the current node to an existing cluster.


  **<hostname>: <string>**
      Hostname (or IP) of an existing cluster member.


  **-force <boolean>**
      Do not throw error if node already exists.


  **-nodeid <integer> (1 - N)**
      Node id for this node.


  **-ring0_addr <string>**
      Hostname (or IP) of the corosync ring0 address of this node. Defaults to nodes hostname.

**-ring1_addr <string>**
> Hostname (or IP) of the corosync ring1 address, this needs an valid configured ring 1 interface in the cluster.

**-votes <integer> (0 - N)**
> Number of votes for this node

**pvecm addnode** <node> [OPTIONS]

Adds a node to the cluster configuration.

**<node>: <string>**
> The cluster node name.

**-force <boolean>**
> Do not throw error if node already exists.

**-nodeid <integer> (1 - N)**
> Node id for this node.

**-ring0_addr <string>**
> Hostname (or IP) of the corosync ring0 address of this node. Defaults to nodes hostname.

**-ring1_addr <string>**
> Hostname (or IP) of the corosync ring1 address, this needs an valid bindnet1_addr.

**-votes <integer> (0 - N)**
> Number of votes for this node

**pvecm create** <clustername> [OPTIONS]

Generate new cluster configuration.

**<clustername>: <string>**
> The name of the cluster.

**-bindnet0_addr <string>**
> This specifies the network address the corosync ring 0 executive should bind to and defaults to the local IP address of the node.

**-bindnet1_addr <string>**
> This specifies the network address the corosync ring 1 executive should bind to and is optional.

**-nodeid <integer> (1 - N)**
> Node id for this node.

**-ring0_addr <string>**
> Hostname (or IP) of the corosync ring0 address of this node. Defaults to the hostname of the node.

**-ring1_addr <string>**
  Hostname (or IP) of the corosync ring1 address, this needs an valid bindnet1_addr.

**-votes <integer> (1 - N)**
  Number of votes for this node.

**pvecm delnode** <node>

Removes a node to the cluster configuration.

**<node>: <string>**
  Hostname or IP of the corosync ring0 address of this node.

**pvecm expected** <expected>

Tells corosync a new value of expected votes.

**<expected>: <integer> (1 - N)**
  Expected votes

**pvecm help** [<cmd>] [OPTIONS]

Get help about specified command.

**<cmd>: <string>**
  Command name

**-verbose <boolean>**
  Verbose output format.

**pvecm keygen** <filename>

Generate new cryptographic key for corosync.

**<filename>: <string>**
  Output file name

**pvecm mtunnel** [<extra-args>] [OPTIONS]

Used by VM/CT migration - do not use manually.

**<extra-args>: <array>**
  Extra arguments as array

**-get_migration_ip <boolean> (_default_ = 0)**
  return the migration IP, if configured

**-migration_network <string>**
  the migration network used to detect the local migration IP

**-run-command <boolean>**
> Run a command with a tcp socket as standard input. The IP address and port are printed via this command's stdandard output first, each on a separate line.

**pvecm nodes**

Displays the local view of the cluster nodes.

**pvecm status**

Displays the local view of the cluster status.

**pvecm updatecerts** [OPTIONS]

Update node certificates (and generate all needed files/directories).

**-force <boolean>**
> Force generation of new SSL certifate.

**-silent <boolean>**
> Ignore errors (i.e. when cluster has no quorum).

# A.10   pveum - Proxmox VE User Manager

**pveum** <COMMAND> [ARGS] [OPTIONS]

**pveum acldel** <path> -roles <string> [OPTIONS]

Update Access Control List (add or remove permissions).

**<path>: <string>**
> Access control path

**-groups <string>**
> List of groups.

**-propagate <boolean>** (*default* = 1)
> Allow to propagate (inherit) permissions.

**-roles <string>**
> List of roles.

**-users <string>**
> List of users.

**pveum aclmod** <path> -roles <string> [OPTIONS]

Update Access Control List (add or remove permissions).

**<path>: <string>**
> Access control path

**-groups <string>**
  List of groups.

**-propagate <boolean> (*default* = 1)**
  Allow to propagate (inherit) permissions.

**-roles <string>**
  List of roles.

**-users <string>**
  List of users.

**pveum groupadd** <groupid> [OPTIONS]

Create new group.

**<groupid>: <string>**
  no description available

**-comment <string>**
  no description available

**pveum groupdel** <groupid>

Delete group.

**<groupid>: <string>**
  no description available

**pveum groupmod** <groupid> [OPTIONS]

Update group data.

**<groupid>: <string>**
  no description available

**-comment <string>**
  no description available

**pveum help** [<cmd>] [OPTIONS]

Get help about specified command.

**<cmd>: <string>**
  Command name

**-verbose <boolean>**
  Verbose output format.

**pveum passwd** `<userid>`

Change user password.

**`<userid>: <string>`**
    User ID

**pveum roleadd** `<roleid>` `[OPTIONS]`

Create new role.

**`<roleid>: <string>`**
    no description available

**`-privs <string>`**
    no description available

**pveum roledel** `<roleid>`

Delete role.

**`<roleid>: <string>`**
    no description available

**pveum rolemod** `<roleid>` `-privs <string>` `[OPTIONS]`

Create new role.

**`<roleid>: <string>`**
    no description available

**`-append <boolean>`**
    no description available

---

**Note**
Requires option(s): `privs`

---

**`-privs <string>`**
    no description available

**pveum ticket** `<username>` `[OPTIONS]`

Create or verify authentication ticket.

**`<username>: <string>`**
    User name

**-otp <string>**
>   One-time password for Two-factor authentication.

**-path <string>**
>   Verify ticket, and check if user have access *privs* on *path*

>   ---
>   **Note**
>   Requires option(s): `privs`
>   ---

**-privs <string>**
>   Verify ticket, and check if user have access *privs* on *path*

>   ---
>   **Note**
>   Requires option(s): `path`
>   ---

**-realm <string>**
>   You can optionally pass the realm using this parameter. Normally the realm is simply added to the username <username>@<relam>.

**pveum useradd** <userid> [OPTIONS]

Create new user.

**<userid>: <string>**
>   User ID

**-comment <string>**
>   no description available

**-email <string>**
>   no description available

**-enable <boolean>** (*default* = 1)
>   Enable the account (default). You can set this to *0* to disable the accout

**-expire <integer>  (0 - N)**
>   Account expiration date (seconds since epoch). *0* means no expiration date.

**-firstname <string>**
>   no description available

**-groups <string>**
>   no description available

**-keys <string>**
>   Keys for two factor auth (yubico).

**-lastname <string>**
>    no description available

**-password**
>    Initial password.

**pveum userdel** <userid>

Delete user.

**<userid>: <string>**
>    User ID

**pveum usermod** <userid> [OPTIONS]

Update user configuration.

**<userid>: <string>**
>    User ID

**-append <boolean>**
>    no description available

> ---
> **Note**
> Requires option(s): groups
> ---

**-comment <string>**
>    no description available

**-email <string>**
>    no description available

**-enable <boolean>**
>    Enable/disable the account.

**-expire <integer>  (0 - N)**
>    Account expiration date (seconds since epoch). *0* means no expiration date.

**-firstname <string>**
>    no description available

**-groups <string>**
>    no description available

**-keys <string>**
>    Keys for two factor auth (yubico).

**-lastname <string>**
>    no description available

# A.11   vzdump - Backup Utility for VMs and Containers

**vzdump** help

**vzdump** {<vmid>} [OPTIONS]

Create backup.


**<vmid>: <string>**
> The ID of the guest system you want to backup.


**-all <boolean> (*default* = 0)**
> Backup all known guest systems on this host.


**-bwlimit <integer>  (0 - N) (*default* = 0)**
> Limit I/O bandwidth (KBytes per second).


**-compress <0 | 1 | gzip | lzo> (*default* = 0)**
> Compress dump file.


**-dumpdir <string>**
> Store resulting files to specified directory.


**-exclude <string>**
> Exclude specified guest systems (assumes --all)


**-exclude-path <string>**
> Exclude certain files/directories (shell globs).


**-ionice <integer>  (0 - 8) (*default* = 7)**
> Set CFQ ionice priority.


**-lockwait <integer>  (0 - N) (*default* = 180)**
> Maximal time to wait for the global lock (minutes).


**-mailnotification <always | failure> (*default* = always)**
> Specify when to send an email


**-mailto <string>**
> Comma-separated list of email addresses that should receive email notifications.


**-maxfiles <integer>  (1 - N) (*default* = 1)**
> Maximal number of backup files per guest system.


**-mode <snapshot | stop | suspend> (*default* = snapshot)**
> Backup mode.

**-node <string>**
> Only run if executed on this node.

**-pigz <integer> (*default* = 0)**
> Use pigz instead of gzip when N>0. N=1 uses half of cores, N>1 uses N as thread count.

**-quiet <boolean> (*default* = 0)**
> Be quiet.

**-remove <boolean> (*default* = 1)**
> Remove old backup files if there are more than *maxfiles* backup files.

**-script <string>**
> Use specified hook script.

**-size <integer>  (500 - N) (*default* = 1024)**
> Unused, will be removed in a future release.

**-stdexcludes <boolean> (*default* = 1)**
> Exclude temporary files and logs.

**-stdout <boolean>**
> Write tar to stdout, not to a file.

**-stop <boolean> (*default* = 0)**
> Stop runnig backup jobs on this host.

**-stopwait <integer>  (0 - N) (*default* = 10)**
> Maximal time to wait until a guest system is stopped (minutes).

**-storage <string>**
> Store resulting file to this storage.

**-tmpdir <string>**
> Store temporary files to specified directory.

## A.12   ha-manager - Proxmox VE HA Manager

**ha-manager** <COMMAND> [ARGS] [OPTIONS]

**ha-manager add** <sid> [OPTIONS]

Create a new HA resource.

**<sid>: <type>:<name>**
> HA resource ID. This consists of a resource type followed by a resource specific name, separated with colon (example: vm:100 / ct:100). For virtual machines and containers, you can simply use the VM or CT id as a shortcut (example: 100).

-comment <string>
:   Description.


-group <string>
:   The HA group identifier.


-max_relocate <integer>  (0 - N) (*default = 1*)
:   Maximal number of service relocate tries when a service failes to start.


-max_restart <integer>  (0 - N) (*default = 1*)
:   Maximal number of tries to restart the service on a node after its start failed.


-state <disabled | enabled | started | stopped> (*default = started*)
:   Requested resource state.


-type <ct | vm>
:   Resource type.


**ha-manager config** [OPTIONS]

List HA resources.


-type <ct | vm>
:   Only list resources of specific type


**ha-manager groupadd** <group> -nodes <string> [OPTIONS]

Create a new HA group.


<group>: <string>
:   The HA group identifier.


-comment <string>
:   Description.


-nodes <node>[:<pri>]{,<node>[:<pri>]}*
:   List of cluster node names with optional priority.


-nofailback <boolean> (*default = 0*)
:   The CRM tries to run services on the node with the highest priority. If a node with higher priority comes online, the CRM migrates the service to that node. Enabling nofailback prevents that behavior.


-restricted <boolean> (*default = 0*)
:   Resources bound to restricted groups may only run on nodes defined by the group.


-type <group>
:   Group type.

**ha-manager groupconfig**

Get HA groups.

**ha-manager groupremove** `<group>`

Delete ha group configuration.

`<group>: <string>`
　　The HA group identifier.

**ha-manager groupset** `<group>` `[OPTIONS]`

Update ha group configuration.

`<group>: <string>`
　　The HA group identifier.

`-comment <string>`
　　Description.

`-delete <string>`
　　A list of settings you want to delete.

`-digest <string>`
　　Prevent changes if current configuration file has different SHA1 digest. This can be used to prevent concurrent modifications.

`-nodes <node>[:<pri>]{,<node>[:<pri>]}*`
　　List of cluster node names with optional priority.

`-nofailback <boolean>` (*default* = 0)
　　The CRM tries to run services on the node with the highest priority. If a node with higher priority comes online, the CRM migrates the service to that node. Enabling nofailback prevents that behavior.

`-restricted <boolean>` (*default* = 0)
　　Resources bound to restricted groups may only run on nodes defined by the group.

**ha-manager help** `[<cmd>]` `[OPTIONS]`

Get help about specified command.

`<cmd>: <string>`
　　Command name

`-verbose <boolean>`
　　Verbose output format.

**ha-manager migrate** `<sid>` `<node>`

Request resource migration (online) to another node.

**\<sid\>: \<type\>:\<name\>**
> HA resource ID. This consists of a resource type followed by a resource specific name, separated with colon (example: vm:100 / ct:100). For virtual machines and containers, you can simply use the VM or CT id as a shortcut (example: 100).

**\<node\>: \<string\>**
> The cluster node name.

**ha-manager relocate** \<sid\> \<node\>

Request resource relocatzion to another node. This stops the service on the old node, and restarts it on the target node.

**\<sid\>: \<type\>:\<name\>**
> HA resource ID. This consists of a resource type followed by a resource specific name, separated with colon (example: vm:100 / ct:100). For virtual machines and containers, you can simply use the VM or CT id as a shortcut (example: 100).

**\<node\>: \<string\>**
> The cluster node name.

**ha-manager remove** \<sid\>

Delete resource configuration.

**\<sid\>: \<type\>:\<name\>**
> HA resource ID. This consists of a resource type followed by a resource specific name, separated with colon (example: vm:100 / ct:100). For virtual machines and containers, you can simply use the VM or CT id as a shortcut (example: 100).

**ha-manager set** \<sid\> [OPTIONS]

Update resource configuration.

**\<sid\>: \<type\>:\<name\>**
> HA resource ID. This consists of a resource type followed by a resource specific name, separated with colon (example: vm:100 / ct:100). For virtual machines and containers, you can simply use the VM or CT id as a shortcut (example: 100).

**-comment \<string\>**
> Description.

**-delete \<string\>**
> A list of settings you want to delete.

**-digest \<string\>**
> Prevent changes if current configuration file has different SHA1 digest. This can be used to prevent concurrent modifications.

**-group <string>**
   The HA group identifier.


**-max_relocate <integer>** (0 - N) (*default* = 1)
   Maximal number of service relocate tries when a service failes to start.


**-max_restart <integer>** (0 - N) (*default* = 1)
   Maximal number of tries to restart the service on a node after its start failed.


**-state <disabled | enabled | started | stopped>** (*default* = started)
   Requested resource state.

**ha-manager status** [OPTIONS]

Display HA manger status.


**-verbose <boolean>** (*default* = 0)
   Verbose output. Include complete CRM and LRM status (JSON).

# Appendix B

# Service Daemons

## B.1  pve-firewall - Proxmox VE Firewall Daemon

**pve-firewall** `<COMMAND>` `[ARGS]` `[OPTIONS]`

**pve-firewall compile**

Compile and print firewall rules. This is useful for testing.

**pve-firewall help** `[<cmd>]` `[OPTIONS]`

Get help about specified command.

> **`<cmd>: <string>`**
> Command name

> **`-verbose <boolean>`**
> Verbose output format.

**pve-firewall localnet**

Print information about local network.

**pve-firewall restart**

Restart the Proxmox VE firewall service.

**pve-firewall simulate** `[OPTIONS]`

Simulate firewall rules. This does not simulate kernel *routing* table. Instead, this simply assumes that routing from source zone to destination zone is possible.

> **`-dest <string>`**
> Destination IP address.

> **`-dport <integer>`**
> Destination port.

> **`-from (host|outside|vm\d+|ct\d+|vmbr\d+/\S+)`** (*default* = `outside`)
> Source zone.

**-protocol (tcp|udp)** (*default =* `tcp`)
>   Protocol.


**-source <string>**
>   Source IP address.


**-sport <integer>**
>   Source port.


**-to (host|outside|vm\d+|ct\d+|vmbr\d+/\S+)** (*default =* `host`)
>   Destination zone.


**-verbose <boolean>** (*default =* 0)
>   Verbose output.

**pve-firewall start** [OPTIONS]

Start the Proxmox VE firewall service.


**-debug <boolean>** (*default =* 0)
>   Debug mode - stay in foreground

**pve-firewall status**

Get firewall status.

**pve-firewall stop**

Stop firewall. This removes all Proxmox VE related iptable rules. The host is unprotected afterwards.


# B.2   pvedaemon - Proxmox VE API Daemon

**pvedaemon** <COMMAND> [ARGS] [OPTIONS]

**pvedaemon help** [<cmd>] [OPTIONS]

Get help about specified command.


**<cmd>: <string>**
>   Command name


**-verbose <boolean>**
>   Verbose output format.

**pvedaemon restart**

Restart the daemon (or start if not running).

**pvedaemon start** [OPTIONS]

Start the daemon.

**-debug <boolean>** (*default* = 0)
> Debug mode - stay in foreground

**pvedaemon status**

Get daemon status.

**pvedaemon stop**

Stop the daemon.

## B.3   pveproxy - Proxmox VE API Proxy Daemon

**pveproxy** <COMMAND> [ARGS] [OPTIONS]

**pveproxy help** [<cmd>] [OPTIONS]

Get help about specified command.

**<cmd>: <string>**
> Command name

**-verbose <boolean>**
> Verbose output format.

**pveproxy restart**

Restart the daemon (or start if not running).

**pveproxy start** [OPTIONS]

Start the daemon.

**-debug <boolean>** (*default* = 0)
> Debug mode - stay in foreground

**pveproxy status**

Get daemon status.

**pveproxy stop**

Stop the daemon.

## B.4   pvestatd - Proxmox VE Status Daemon

**pvestatd** <COMMAND> [ARGS] [OPTIONS]

**pvestatd help** [<cmd>] [OPTIONS]

Get help about specified command.

**<cmd>: <string>**
    Command name

**-verbose <boolean>**
    Verbose output format.

**pvestatd restart**

Restart the daemon (or start if not running).

**pvestatd start** [OPTIONS]

Start the daemon.

**-debug <boolean>** (*default* = 0)
    Debug mode - stay in foreground

**pvestatd status**

Get daemon status.

**pvestatd stop**

Stop the daemon.

# B.5   spiceproxy - SPICE Proxy Service

**spiceproxy** <COMMAND> [ARGS] [OPTIONS]

**spiceproxy help** [<cmd>] [OPTIONS]

Get help about specified command.

**<cmd>: <string>**
    Command name

**-verbose <boolean>**
    Verbose output format.

**spiceproxy restart**

Restart the daemon (or start if not running).

**spiceproxy start** [OPTIONS]

Start the daemon.

**-debug <boolean>** (*default* = 0)
    Debug mode - stay in foreground

**spiceproxy status**

Get daemon status.

**spiceproxy stop**

Stop the daemon.

## B.6   pmxcfs - Proxmox Cluster File System

**pmxcfs** [OPTIONS]

Help Options:

**-h, --help**
   Show help options

Application Options:

**-d, --debug**
   Turn on debug messages

**-f, --foreground**
   Do not daemonize server

**-l, --local**
   Force local mode (ignore corosync.conf, force quorum)

This service is usually started and managed using systemd toolset. The service is called *pve-cluster*.

```
systemctl start pve-cluster

systemctl stop pve-cluster

systemctl status pve-cluster
```

## B.7   pve-ha-crm - Cluster Resource Manager Daemon

**pve-ha-crm** <COMMAND> [ARGS] [OPTIONS]

**pve-ha-crm help** [<cmd>] [OPTIONS]

Get help about specified command.

**<cmd>: <string>**
   Command name

**-verbose <boolean>**
   Verbose output format.

**pve-ha-crm start** [OPTIONS]

Start the daemon.

**-debug <boolean>** (*default* = 0)
   Debug mode - stay in foreground

**pve-ha-crm status**

Get daemon status.

**pve-ha-crm stop**

Stop the daemon.


# B.8 pve-ha-lrm - Local Resource Manager Daemon

**pve-ha-lrm** <COMMAND> [ARGS] [OPTIONS]

**pve-ha-lrm help** [<cmd>] [OPTIONS]

Get help about specified command.


  **<cmd>: <string>**
    Command name


  **-verbose <boolean>**
    Verbose output format.

**pve-ha-lrm start** [OPTIONS]

Start the daemon.


  **-debug <boolean>** (*default* = 0)
    Debug mode - stay in foreground

**pve-ha-lrm status**

Get daemon status.

**pve-ha-lrm stop**

Stop the daemon.

# Appendix C

# Configuration Files

## C.1  Datacenter Configuration

The file `/etc/pve/datacenter.cfg` is a configuration file for Proxmox VE. It contains cluster wide default values used by all nodes.

### C.1.1  File Format

The file uses a simple colon separated key/value format. Each line has the following format:

```
OPTION: value
```

Blank lines in the file are ignored, and lines starting with a # character are treated as comments and are also ignored.

### C.1.2  Options

**console: <applet | html5 | vv>**
    Select the default Console viewer. You can either use the builtin java applet (VNC), an external virt-viewer comtatible application (SPICE), or an HTML5 based viewer (noVNC).

**email_from: <string>**
    Specify email address to send notification from (default is root@$hostname)

**fencing: <both | hardware | watchdog>** (*default* = `watchdog`)
    Set the fencing mode of the HA cluster. Hardware mode needs a valid configuration of fence devices in /etc/pve/ha/fence.cfg. With both all two modes are used.

---

 **Warning**
*hardware* and *both* are EXPERIMENTAL & WIP

---

**http_proxy: http://.***

Specify external http proxy which is used for downloads (example: *http://username:password@host:port/*)

**keyboard: <da | de | de-ch | en-gb | en-us | es | fi | fr | fr-be | fr-ca | fr-ch | hu | is | it | ja | lt | mk | nl | no | pl | pt | pt-br | sl | sv | tr>**

Default keybord layout for vnc server.

**language: <de | en>**

Default GUI language.

**mac_prefix: (?^i:[a-f0-9]{2}(?::[a-f0-9]{2}){0,2}:?)**

Prefix for autogenerated MAC addresses.

**max_workers: <integer> (1 - N)**

Defines how many workers (per node) are maximal started on actions like *stopall VMs* or task from the ha-manager.

**migration: [type=]<secure|insecure> [,network=<CIDR>]**

For cluster wide migration settings.

    **network=<CIDR>**

    CIDR of the (sub) network that is used for migration.

    **type=<insecure | secure>** (*default* = secure)

    Migration traffic is encrypted using an SSH tunnel by default. On secure, completely private networks this can be disabled to increase performance.

**migration_unsecure: <boolean>**

Migration is secure using SSH tunnel by default. For secure private networks you can disable it to speed up migration. Deprecated, use the *migration* property instead!

# Appendix D

# Firewall Macro Definitions

*Amanda*        Amanda Backup

| Action | proto | dport | sport |
|--------|-------|-------|-------|
| PARAM  | udp   | 10080 |       |
| PARAM  | tcp   | 10080 |       |

*Auth*        Auth (identd) traffic

| Action | proto | dport | sport |
|--------|-------|-------|-------|
| PARAM  | tcp   | 113   |       |

*BGP*        Border Gateway Protocol traffic

| Action | proto | dport | sport |
|--------|-------|-------|-------|
| PARAM  | tcp   | 179   |       |

*BitTorrent*        BitTorrent traffic for BitTorrent 3.1 and earlier

| Action | proto | dport     | sport |
|--------|-------|-----------|-------|
| PARAM  | tcp   | 6881:6889 |       |
| PARAM  | udp   | 6881      |       |

*BitTorrent32*        BitTorrent traffic for BitTorrent 3.2 and later

| Action | proto | dport | sport |
|--------|-------|-------|-------|
| PARAM | tcp | 6881:6999 | |
| PARAM | udp | 6881 | |

*CVS*          Concurrent Versions System pserver traffic

| Action | proto | dport | sport |
|--------|-------|-------|-------|
| PARAM | tcp | 2401 | |

*Ceph*          Ceph Storage Cluster traffic (Ceph Monitors, OSD & MDS Deamons)

| Action | proto | dport | sport |
|--------|-------|-------|-------|
| PARAM | tcp | 6789 | |
| PARAM | tcp | 6800:7300 | |

*Citrix*          Citrix/ICA traffic (ICA, ICA Browser, CGP)

| Action | proto | dport | sport |
|--------|-------|-------|-------|
| PARAM | tcp | 1494 | |
| PARAM | udp | 1604 | |
| PARAM | tcp | 2598 | |

*DAAP*          Digital Audio Access Protocol traffic (iTunes, Rythmbox daemons)

| Action | proto | dport | sport |
|--------|-------|-------|-------|
| PARAM | tcp | 3689 | |
| PARAM | udp | 3689 | |

*DCC*          Distributed Checksum Clearinghouse spam filtering mechanism

| Action | proto | dport | sport |
|--------|-------|-------|-------|
| PARAM | tcp | 6277 | |

*DHCPfwd*          Forwarded DHCP traffic

| Action | proto | dport | sport |
|--------|-------|-------|-------|
| PARAM  | udp   | 67:68 | 67:68 |

*DHCPv6*        DHCPv6 traffic

| Action | proto | dport   | sport   |
|--------|-------|---------|---------|
| PARAM  | udp   | 546:547 | 546:547 |

*DNS*        Domain Name System traffic (upd and tcp)

| Action | proto | dport | sport |
|--------|-------|-------|-------|
| PARAM  | udp   | 53    |       |
| PARAM  | tcp   | 53    |       |

*Distcc*        Distributed Compiler service

| Action | proto | dport | sport |
|--------|-------|-------|-------|
| PARAM  | tcp   | 3632  |       |

*FTP*        File Transfer Protocol

| Action | proto | dport | sport |
|--------|-------|-------|-------|
| PARAM  | tcp   | 21    |       |

*Finger*        Finger protocol (RFC 742)

| Action | proto | dport | sport |
|--------|-------|-------|-------|
| PARAM  | tcp   | 79    |       |

*GNUnet*        GNUnet secure peer-to-peer networking traffic

| Action | proto | dport | sport |
|--------|-------|-------|-------|
| PARAM  | tcp   | 2086  |       |
| PARAM  | udp   | 2086  |       |
| PARAM  | tcp   | 1080  |       |

| Action | proto | dport | sport |
|--------|-------|-------|-------|
| PARAM | udp | 1080 | |

*GRE*            Generic Routing Encapsulation tunneling protocol

| Action | proto | dport | sport |
|--------|-------|-------|-------|
| PARAM | 47 | | |

*Git*            Git distributed revision control traffic

| Action | proto | dport | sport |
|--------|-------|-------|-------|
| PARAM | tcp | 9418 | |

*HKP*            OpenPGP HTTP keyserver protocol traffic

| Action | proto | dport | sport |
|--------|-------|-------|-------|
| PARAM | tcp | 11371 | |

*HTTP*            Hypertext Transfer Protocol (WWW)

| Action | proto | dport | sport |
|--------|-------|-------|-------|
| PARAM | tcp | 80 | |

*HTTPS*            Hypertext Transfer Protocol (WWW) over SSL

| Action | proto | dport | sport |
|--------|-------|-------|-------|
| PARAM | tcp | 443 | |

*ICPV2*            Internet Cache Protocol V2 (Squid) traffic

| Action | proto | dport | sport |
|--------|-------|-------|-------|
| PARAM | udp | 3130 | |

*ICQ*            AOL Instant Messenger traffic

| Action | proto | dport | sport |
|--------|-------|-------|-------|
| PARAM  | tcp   | 5190  |       |

*IMAP*            Internet Message Access Protocol

| Action | proto | dport | sport |
|--------|-------|-------|-------|
| PARAM  | tcp   | 143   |       |

*IMAPS*           Internet Message Access Protocol over SSL

| Action | proto | dport | sport |
|--------|-------|-------|-------|
| PARAM  | tcp   | 993   |       |

*IPIP*            IPIP capsulation traffic

| Action | proto | dport | sport |
|--------|-------|-------|-------|
| PARAM  | 94    |       |       |

*IPsec*           IPsec traffic

| Action | proto | dport | sport |
|--------|-------|-------|-------|
| PARAM  | udp   | 500   | 500   |
| PARAM  | 50    |       |       |

*IPsecah*         IPsec authentication (AH) traffic

| Action | proto | dport | sport |
|--------|-------|-------|-------|
| PARAM  | udp   | 500   | 500   |
| PARAM  | 51    |       |       |

*IPsecnat*        IPsec traffic and Nat-Traversal

| Action | proto | dport | sport |
|--------|-------|-------|-------|
| PARAM  | udp   | 500   |       |
| PARAM  | udp   | 4500  |       |

| Action | proto | dport | sport |
|--------|-------|-------|-------|
| PARAM | 50 | | |

*IRC*     Internet Relay Chat traffic

| Action | proto | dport | sport |
|--------|-------|-------|-------|
| PARAM | tcp | 6667 | |

*Jetdirect*     HP Jetdirect printing

| Action | proto | dport | sport |
|--------|-------|-------|-------|
| PARAM | tcp | 9100 | |

*L2TP*     Layer 2 Tunneling Protocol traffic

| Action | proto | dport | sport |
|--------|-------|-------|-------|
| PARAM | udp | 1701 | |

*LDAP*     Lightweight Directory Access Protocol traffic

| Action | proto | dport | sport |
|--------|-------|-------|-------|
| PARAM | tcp | 389 | |

*LDAPS*     Secure Lightweight Directory Access Protocol traffic

| Action | proto | dport | sport |
|--------|-------|-------|-------|
| PARAM | tcp | 636 | |

*MDNS*     Multicast DNS

| Action | proto | dport | sport |
|--------|-------|-------|-------|
| PARAM | udp | 5353 | |

*MSNP*     Microsoft Notification Protocol

| Action | proto | dport | sport |
|--------|-------|-------|-------|
| PARAM  | tcp   | 1863  |       |

*MSSQL*          Microsoft SQL Server

| Action | proto | dport | sport |
|--------|-------|-------|-------|
| PARAM  | tcp   | 1433  |       |

*Mail*          Mail traffic (SMTP, SMTPS, Submission)

| Action | proto | dport | sport |
|--------|-------|-------|-------|
| PARAM  | tcp   | 25    |       |
| PARAM  | tcp   | 465   |       |
| PARAM  | tcp   | 587   |       |

*Munin*          Munin networked resource monitoring traffic

| Action | proto | dport | sport |
|--------|-------|-------|-------|
| PARAM  | tcp   | 4949  |       |

*MySQL*          MySQL server

| Action | proto | dport | sport |
|--------|-------|-------|-------|
| PARAM  | tcp   | 3306  |       |

*NNTP*          NNTP traffic (Usenet).

| Action | proto | dport | sport |
|--------|-------|-------|-------|
| PARAM  | tcp   | 119   |       |

*NNTPS*          Encrypted NNTP traffic (Usenet)

| Action | proto | dport | sport |
|--------|-------|-------|-------|
| PARAM  | tcp   | 563   |       |

*NTP*            Network Time Protocol (ntpd)

| Action | proto | dport | sport |
|--------|-------|-------|-------|
| PARAM  | udp   | 123   |       |

*NeighborDiscovery*IPv6 neighbor solicitation, neighbor and router advertisement

| Action | proto  | dport                   | sport |
|--------|--------|-------------------------|-------|
| PARAM  | icmpv6 | router-solicitation     |       |
| PARAM  | icmpv6 | router-advertisement    |       |
| PARAM  | icmpv6 | neighbor-solicitation   |       |
| PARAM  | icmpv6 | neighbor-advertisement  |       |

*OSPF*           OSPF multicast traffic

| Action | proto | dport | sport |
|--------|-------|-------|-------|
| PARAM  | 89    |       |       |

*OpenVPN*        OpenVPN traffic

| Action | proto | dport | sport |
|--------|-------|-------|-------|
| PARAM  | udp   | 1194  |       |

*PCA*            Symantec PCAnywere (tm)

| Action | proto | dport | sport |
|--------|-------|-------|-------|
| PARAM  | udp   | 5632  |       |
| PARAM  | tcp   | 5631  |       |

*POP3*           POP3 traffic

| Action | proto | dport | sport |
|--------|-------|-------|-------|
| PARAM  | tcp   | 110   |       |

*POP3S*          Encrypted POP3 traffic

| Action | proto | dport | sport |
|--------|-------|-------|-------|
| PARAM  | tcp   | 995   |       |

*PPtP*          Point-to-Point Tunneling Protocol

| Action | proto | dport | sport |
|--------|-------|-------|-------|
| PARAM  | 47    |       |       |
| PARAM  | tcp   | 1723  |       |

*Ping*          ICMP echo request

| Action | proto | dport        | sport |
|--------|-------|--------------|-------|
| PARAM  | icmp  | echo-request |       |

*PostgreSQL*     PostgreSQL server

| Action | proto | dport | sport |
|--------|-------|-------|-------|
| PARAM  | tcp   | 5432  |       |

*Printer*          Line Printer protocol printing

| Action | proto | dport | sport |
|--------|-------|-------|-------|
| PARAM  | tcp   | 515   |       |

*RDP*          Microsoft Remote Desktop Protocol traffic

| Action | proto | dport | sport |
|--------|-------|-------|-------|
| PARAM  | tcp   | 3389  |       |

*RIP*          Routing Information Protocol (bidirectional)

| Action | proto | dport | sport |
|--------|-------|-------|-------|
| PARAM  | udp   | 520   |       |

*RNDC*          BIND remote management protocol

| Action | proto | dport | sport |
|--------|-------|-------|-------|
| PARAM  | tcp   | 953   |       |

*Razor*          Razor Antispam System

| Action | proto | dport | sport |
|--------|-------|-------|-------|
| ACCEPT | tcp   | 2703  |       |

*Rdate*          Remote time retrieval (rdate)

| Action | proto | dport | sport |
|--------|-------|-------|-------|
| PARAM  | tcp   | 37    |       |

*Rsync*          Rsync server

| Action | proto | dport | sport |
|--------|-------|-------|-------|
| PARAM  | tcp   | 873   |       |

*SANE*          SANE network scanning

| Action | proto | dport | sport |
|--------|-------|-------|-------|
| PARAM  | tcp   | 6566  |       |

*SMB*          Microsoft SMB traffic

| Action | proto | dport       | sport |
|--------|-------|-------------|-------|
| PARAM  | udp   | 135,445     |       |
| PARAM  | udp   | 137:139     |       |
| PARAM  | udp   | 1024:65535  | 137   |
| PARAM  | tcp   | 135,139,445 |       |

*SMBswat*     Samba Web Administration Tool

| Action | proto | dport | sport |
|--------|-------|-------|-------|
| PARAM | tcp | 901 | |

*SMTP*     Simple Mail Transfer Protocol

| Action | proto | dport | sport |
|--------|-------|-------|-------|
| PARAM | tcp | 25 | |

*SMTPS*     Encrypted Simple Mail Transfer Protocol

| Action | proto | dport | sport |
|--------|-------|-------|-------|
| PARAM | tcp | 465 | |

*SNMP*     Simple Network Management Protocol

| Action | proto | dport | sport |
|--------|-------|-------|-------|
| PARAM | udp | 161:162 | |
| PARAM | tcp | 161 | |

*SPAMD*     Spam Assassin SPAMD traffic

| Action | proto | dport | sport |
|--------|-------|-------|-------|
| PARAM | tcp | 783 | |

*SSH*     Secure shell traffic

| Action | proto | dport | sport |
|--------|-------|-------|-------|
| PARAM | tcp | 22 | |

*SVN*     Subversion server (svnserve)

| Action | proto | dport | sport |
|--------|-------|-------|-------|
| PARAM  | tcp   | 3690  |       |

*SixXS*          SixXS IPv6 Deployment and Tunnel Broker

| Action | proto | dport     | sport |
|--------|-------|-----------|-------|
| PARAM  | tcp   | 3874      |       |
| PARAM  | udp   | 3740      |       |
| PARAM  | 41    |           |       |
| PARAM  | udp   | 5072,8374 |       |

*Squid*          Squid web proxy traffic

| Action | proto | dport | sport |
|--------|-------|-------|-------|
| PARAM  | tcp   | 3128  |       |

*Submission*          Mail message submission traffic

| Action | proto | dport | sport |
|--------|-------|-------|-------|
| PARAM  | tcp   | 587   |       |

*Syslog*          Syslog protocol (RFC 5424) traffic

| Action | proto | dport | sport |
|--------|-------|-------|-------|
| PARAM  | udp   | 514   |       |
| PARAM  | tcp   | 514   |       |

*TFTP*          Trivial File Transfer Protocol traffic

| Action | proto | dport | sport |
|--------|-------|-------|-------|
| PARAM  | udp   | 69    |       |

*Telnet*          Telnet traffic

| Action | proto | dport | sport |
|--------|-------|-------|-------|
| PARAM  | tcp   | 23    |       |

*Telnets*        Telnet over SSL

| Action | proto | dport | sport |
|--------|-------|-------|-------|
| PARAM  | tcp   | 992   |       |

*Time*        RFC 868 Time protocol

| Action | proto | dport | sport |
|--------|-------|-------|-------|
| PARAM  | tcp   | 37    |       |

*Trcrt*        Traceroute (for up to 30 hops) traffic

| Action | proto | dport | sport |
|--------|-------|-------|-------|
| PARAM  | udp   | 33434:33524 |   |
| PARAM  | icmp  | echo-request |  |

*VNC*        VNC traffic for VNC display's 0 - 99

| Action | proto | dport | sport |
|--------|-------|-------|-------|
| PARAM  | tcp   | 5900:5999 |    |

*VNCL*        VNC traffic from Vncservers to Vncviewers in listen mode

| Action | proto | dport | sport |
|--------|-------|-------|-------|
| PARAM  | tcp   | 5500  |       |

*Web*        WWW traffic (HTTP and HTTPS)

| Action | proto | dport | sport |
|--------|-------|-------|-------|
| PARAM  | tcp   | 80    |       |
| PARAM  | tcp   | 443   |       |

*Webcache*        Web Cache/Proxy traffic (port 8080)

| Action | proto | dport | sport |
|--------|-------|-------|-------|
| PARAM  | tcp   | 8080  |       |

*Webmin*        Webmin traffic

| Action | proto | dport | sport |
|--------|-------|-------|-------|
| PARAM  | tcp   | 10000 |       |

*Whois*        Whois (nicname, RFC 3912) traffic

| Action | proto | dport | sport |
|--------|-------|-------|-------|
| PARAM  | tcp   | 43    |       |

# Appendix E

# GNU Free Documentation License

Version 1.3, 3 November 2008

Copyright © 2000, 2001, 2002, 2007, 2008 Free Software Foundation, Inc. http://fsf.org/

Everyone is permitted to copy and distribute verbatim copies of this license document, but changing it is not allowed.

### 0. PREAMBLE

The purpose of this License is to make a manual, textbook, or other functional and useful document "free" in the sense of freedom: to assure everyone the effective freedom to copy and redistribute it, with or without modifying it, either commercially or noncommercially. Secondarily, this License preserves for the author and publisher a way to get credit for their work, while not being considered responsible for modifications made by others.

This License is a kind of "copyleft", which means that derivative works of the document must themselves be free in the same sense. It complements the GNU General Public License, which is a copyleft license designed for free software.

We have designed this License in order to use it for manuals for free software, because free software needs free documentation: a free program should come with manuals providing the same freedoms that the software does. But this License is not limited to software manuals; it can be used for any textual work, regardless of subject matter or whether it is published as a printed book. We recommend this License principally for works whose purpose is instruction or reference.

### 1. APPLICABILITY AND DEFINITIONS

This License applies to any manual or other work, in any medium, that contains a notice placed by the copyright holder saying it can be distributed under the terms of this License. Such a notice grants a world-wide, royalty-free license, unlimited in duration, to use that work under the conditions stated herein. The "Document", below, refers to any such manual or work. Any member of the public is a licensee, and is addressed as "you". You accept the license if you copy, modify or distribute the work in a way requiring permission under copyright law.

A "Modified Version" of the Document means any work containing the Document or a portion of it, either copied verbatim, or with modifications and/or translated into another language.

A "Secondary Section" is a named appendix or a front-matter section of the Document that deals exclusively with the relationship of the publishers or authors of the Document to the Document's overall subject (or to related matters) and contains nothing that could fall directly within that overall subject. (Thus, if the Document is in part a textbook of mathematics, a Secondary Section may not explain any mathematics.) The relationship could be a matter of historical connection with the subject or with related matters, or of legal, commercial, philosophical, ethical or political position regarding them.

The "Invariant Sections" are certain Secondary Sections whose titles are designated, as being those of Invariant Sections, in the notice that says that the Document is released under this License. If a section does not fit the above definition of Secondary then it is not allowed to be designated as Invariant. The Document may contain zero Invariant Sections. If the Document does not identify any Invariant Sections then there are none.

The "Cover Texts" are certain short passages of text that are listed, as Front-Cover Texts or Back-Cover Texts, in the notice that says that the Document is released under this License. A Front-Cover Text may be at most 5 words, and a Back-Cover Text may be at most 25 words.

A "Transparent" copy of the Document means a machine-readable copy, represented in a format whose specification is available to the general public, that is suitable for revising the document straightforwardly with generic text editors or (for images composed of pixels) generic paint programs or (for drawings) some widely available drawing editor, and that is suitable for input to text formatters or for automatic translation to a variety of formats suitable for input to text formatters. A copy made in an otherwise Transparent file format whose markup, or absence of markup, has been arranged to thwart or discourage subsequent modification by readers is not Transparent. An image format is not Transparent if used for any substantial amount of text. A copy that is not "Transparent" is called "Opaque".

Examples of suitable formats for Transparent copies include plain ASCII without markup, Texinfo input format, LaTeX input format, SGML or XML using a publicly available DTD, and standard-conforming simple HTML, PostScript or PDF designed for human modification. Examples of transparent image formats include PNG, XCF and JPG. Opaque formats include proprietary formats that can be read and edited only by proprietary word processors, SGML or XML for which the DTD and/or processing tools are not generally available, and the machine-generated HTML, PostScript or PDF produced by some word processors for output purposes only.

The "Title Page" means, for a printed book, the title page itself, plus such following pages as are needed to hold, legibly, the material this License requires to appear in the title page. For works in formats which do not have any title page as such, "Title Page" means the text near the most prominent appearance of the work's title, preceding the beginning of the body of the text.

The "publisher" means any person or entity that distributes copies of the Document to the public.

A section "Entitled XYZ" means a named subunit of the Document whose title either is precisely XYZ or contains XYZ in parentheses following text that translates XYZ in another language. (Here XYZ stands for a specific section name mentioned below, such as "Acknowledgements", "Dedications", "Endorsements", or "History".) To "Preserve the Title" of such a section when you modify the Document means that it remains a section "Entitled XYZ" according to this definition.

The Document may include Warranty Disclaimers next to the notice which states that this License applies to the Document. These Warranty Disclaimers are considered to be included by reference in this License, but only as regards disclaiming warranties: any other implication that these Warranty Disclaimers may have is void and has no effect on the meaning of this License.

## 2. VERBATIM COPYING

You may copy and distribute the Document in any medium, either commercially or noncommercially, provided that this License, the copyright notices, and the license notice saying this License applies to the Document are reproduced in all copies, and that you add no other conditions whatsoever to those of this License. You may not use technical measures to obstruct or control the reading or further copying of the copies you make or distribute. However, you may accept compensation in exchange for copies. If you distribute a large enough number of copies you must also follow the conditions in section 3.

You may also lend copies, under the same conditions stated above, and you may publicly display copies.

## 3. COPYING IN QUANTITY

If you publish printed copies (or copies in media that commonly have printed covers) of the Document, numbering more than 100, and the Document's license notice requires Cover Texts, you must enclose the copies in covers that carry, clearly and legibly, all these Cover Texts: Front-Cover Texts on the front cover, and Back-Cover Texts on the back cover. Both covers must also clearly and legibly identify you as the publisher of these copies. The front cover must present the full title with all words of the title equally prominent and visible. You may add other material on the covers in addition. Copying with changes limited to the covers, as long as they preserve the title of the Document and satisfy these conditions, can be treated as verbatim copying in other respects.

If the required texts for either cover are too voluminous to fit legibly, you should put the first ones listed (as many as fit reasonably) on the actual cover, and continue the rest onto adjacent pages.

If you publish or distribute Opaque copies of the Document numbering more than 100, you must either include a machine-readable Transparent copy along with each Opaque copy, or state in or with each Opaque copy a computer-network location from which the general network-using public has access to download using public-standard network protocols a complete Transparent copy of the Document, free of added material. If you use the latter option, you must take reasonably prudent steps, when you begin distribution of Opaque copies in quantity, to ensure that this Transparent copy will remain thus accessible at the stated location until at least one year after the last time you distribute an Opaque copy (directly or through your agents or retailers) of that edition to the public.

It is requested, but not required, that you contact the authors of the Document well before redistributing any large number of copies, to give them a chance to provide you with an updated version of the Document.

## 4. MODIFICATIONS

You may copy and distribute a Modified Version of the Document under the conditions of sections 2 and 3 above, provided that you release the Modified Version under precisely this License, with the Modified Version filling the role of the Document, thus licensing distribution and modification of the Modified Version to whoever possesses a copy of it. In addition, you must do these things in the Modified Version:

- A. Use in the Title Page (and on the covers, if any) a title distinct from that of the Document, and from those of previous versions (which should, if there were any, be listed in the History section of the Document). You may use the same title as a previous version if the original publisher of that version gives permission.

- B. List on the Title Page, as authors, one or more persons or entities responsible for authorship of the modifications in the Modified Version, together with at least five of the principal authors of the Document (all of its principal authors, if it has fewer than five), unless they release you from this requirement.

- C. State on the Title page the name of the publisher of the Modified Version, as the publisher.

- D. Preserve all the copyright notices of the Document.

E. Add an appropriate copyright notice for your modifications adjacent to the other copyright notices.

F. Include, immediately after the copyright notices, a license notice giving the public permission to use the Modified Version under the terms of this License, in the form shown in the Addendum below.

G. Preserve in that license notice the full lists of Invariant Sections and required Cover Texts given in the Document's license notice.

H. Include an unaltered copy of this License.

I. Preserve the section Entitled "History", Preserve its Title, and add to it an item stating at least the title, year, new authors, and publisher of the Modified Version as given on the Title Page. If there is no section Entitled "History" in the Document, create one stating the title, year, authors, and publisher of the Document as given on its Title Page, then add an item describing the Modified Version as stated in the previous sentence.

J. Preserve the network location, if any, given in the Document for public access to a Transparent copy of the Document, and likewise the network locations given in the Document for previous versions it was based on. These may be placed in the "History" section. You may omit a network location for a work that was published at least four years before the Document itself, or if the original publisher of the version it refers to gives permission.

K. For any section Entitled "Acknowledgements" or "Dedications", Preserve the Title of the section, and preserve in the section all the substance and tone of each of the contributor acknowledgements and/or dedications given therein.

L. Preserve all the Invariant Sections of the Document, unaltered in their text and in their titles. Section numbers or the equivalent are not considered part of the section titles.

M. Delete any section Entitled "Endorsements". Such a section may not be included in the Modified Version.

N. Do not retitle any existing section to be Entitled "Endorsements" or to conflict in title with any Invariant Section.

O. Preserve any Warranty Disclaimers.

If the Modified Version includes new front-matter sections or appendices that qualify as Secondary Sections and contain no material copied from the Document, you may at your option designate some or all of these sections as invariant. To do this, add their titles to the list of Invariant Sections in the Modified Version's license notice. These titles must be distinct from any other section titles.

You may add a section Entitled "Endorsements", provided it contains nothing but endorsements of your Modified Version by various parties—for example, statements of peer review or that the text has been approved by an organization as the authoritative definition of a standard.

You may add a passage of up to five words as a Front-Cover Text, and a passage of up to 25 words as a Back-Cover Text, to the end of the list of Cover Texts in the Modified Version. Only one passage of Front-Cover Text and one of Back-Cover Text may be added by (or through arrangements made by) any one entity. If the Document already includes a cover text for the same cover, previously added by you or by arrangement made by the same entity you are acting on behalf of, you may not add another; but you may replace the old one, on explicit permission from the previous publisher that added the old one.

The author(s) and publisher(s) of the Document do not by this License give permission to use their names for publicity for or to assert or imply endorsement of any Modified Version.

## 5. COMBINING DOCUMENTS

You may combine the Document with other documents released under this License, under the terms defined in section 4 above for modified versions, provided that you include in the combination all of the Invariant Sections of all of the original documents, unmodified, and list them all as Invariant Sections of your combined work in its license notice, and that you preserve all their Warranty Disclaimers.

The combined work need only contain one copy of this License, and multiple identical Invariant Sections may be replaced with a single copy. If there are multiple Invariant Sections with the same name but different contents, make the title of each such section unique by adding at the end of it, in parentheses, the name of the original author or publisher of that section if known, or else a unique number. Make the same adjustment to the section titles in the list of Invariant Sections in the license notice of the combined work.

In the combination, you must combine any sections Entitled "History" in the various original documents, forming one section Entitled "History"; likewise combine any sections Entitled "Acknowledgements", and any sections Entitled "Dedications". You must delete all sections Entitled "Endorsements".

## 6. COLLECTIONS OF DOCUMENTS

You may make a collection consisting of the Document and other documents released under this License, and replace the individual copies of this License in the various documents with a single copy that is included in the collection, provided that you follow the rules of this License for verbatim copying of each of the documents in all other respects.

You may extract a single document from such a collection, and distribute it individually under this License, provided you insert a copy of this License into the extracted document, and follow this License in all other respects regarding verbatim copying of that document.

## 7. AGGREGATION WITH INDEPENDENT WORKS

A compilation of the Document or its derivatives with other separate and independent documents or works, in or on a volume of a storage or distribution medium, is called an "aggregate" if the copyright resulting from the compilation is not used to limit the legal rights of the compilation's users beyond what the individual works permit. When the Document is included in an aggregate, this License does not apply to the other works in the aggregate which are not themselves derivative works of the Document.

If the Cover Text requirement of section 3 is applicable to these copies of the Document, then if the Document is less than one half of the entire aggregate, the Document's Cover Texts may be placed on covers that bracket the Document within the aggregate, or the electronic equivalent of covers if the Document is in electronic form. Otherwise they must appear on printed covers that bracket the whole aggregate.

## 8. TRANSLATION

Translation is considered a kind of modification, so you may distribute translations of the Document under the terms of section 4. Replacing Invariant Sections with translations requires special permission from their copyright holders, but you may include translations of some or all Invariant Sections in addition to the original versions of these Invariant Sections. You may include a translation of this License, and all the license notices in the Document, and any Warranty Disclaimers, provided that you also include the original English version of this License and the original versions of those notices and disclaimers. In case of a disagreement between the translation and the original version of this License or a notice or disclaimer, the original version will prevail.

If a section in the Document is Entitled "Acknowledgements", "Dedications", or "History", the requirement (section 4) to Preserve its Title (section 1) will typically require changing the actual title.

## 9. TERMINATION

You may not copy, modify, sublicense, or distribute the Document except as expressly provided under this License. Any attempt otherwise to copy, modify, sublicense, or distribute it is void, and will automatically terminate your rights under this License.

However, if you cease all violation of this License, then your license from a particular copyright holder is reinstated (a) provisionally, unless and until the copyright holder explicitly and finally terminates your license, and (b) permanently, if the copyright holder fails to notify you of the violation by some reasonable means prior to 60 days after the cessation.

Moreover, your license from a particular copyright holder is reinstated permanently if the copyright holder notifies you of the violation by some reasonable means, this is the first time you have received notice of violation of this License (for any work) from that copyright holder, and you cure the violation prior to 30 days after your receipt of the notice.

Termination of your rights under this section does not terminate the licenses of parties who have received copies or rights from you under this License. If your rights have been terminated and not permanently reinstated, receipt of a copy of some or all of the same material does not give you any rights to use it.

## 10. FUTURE REVISIONS OF THIS LICENSE

The Free Software Foundation may publish new, revised versions of the GNU Free Documentation License from time to time. Such new versions will be similar in spirit to the present version, but may differ in detail to address new problems or concerns. See http://www.gnu.org/copyleft/.

Each version of the License is given a distinguishing version number. If the Document specifies that a particular numbered version of this License "or any later version" applies to it, you have the option of following the terms and conditions either of that specified version or of any later version that has been published (not as a draft) by the Free Software Foundation. If the Document does not specify a version number of this License, you may choose any version ever published (not as a draft) by the Free Software Foundation. If the Document specifies that a proxy can decide which future versions of this License can be used, that proxy's public statement of acceptance of a version permanently authorizes you to choose that version for the Document.

## 11. RELICENSING

"Massive Multiauthor Collaboration Site" (or "MMC Site") means any World Wide Web server that publishes copyrightable works and also provides prominent facilities for anybody to edit those works. A public wiki that anybody can edit is an example of such a server. A "Massive Multiauthor Collaboration" (or "MMC") contained in the site means any set of copyrightable works thus published on the MMC site.

"CC-BY-SA" means the Creative Commons Attribution-Share Alike 3.0 license published by Creative Commons Corporation, a not-for-profit corporation with a principal place of business in San Francisco, California, as well as future copyleft versions of that license published by that same organization.

"Incorporate" means to publish or republish a Document, in whole or in part, as part of another Document.

An MMC is "eligible for relicensing" if it is licensed under this License, and if all works that were first published under this License somewhere other than this MMC, and subsequently incorporated in whole or in part into the MMC, (1) had no cover texts or invariant sections, and (2) were thus incorporated prior to November 1, 2008.

The operator of an MMC Site may republish an MMC contained in the site under CC-BY-SA on the same site at any time before August 1, 2009, provided the MMC is eligible for relicensing.